Drive Around
Scotland

YOUR G RIVES

Titles in this series include:

- Andalucía and the Costa del Sol
- Australia
- Bavaria and the Austrian Tyrol
- Brittany and Normandy
- Burgundy and the Rhône Valley
- California
- Canadian Rockies
- Catalonia and the Spanish Pyrenees
- Dordogne and Western France
- England and Wales
- Florida
- Ireland
- Languedoc and Southwest France
- Loire Valley
- New England
- New Zealand
- Northern Italy and Italian Lakes
- Portugal
- Provence and the Côte d'Azur
- Scotland
- Tuscany and Umbria
- Vancouver and British Columbia
- Washington DC, Virginia, Maryland and Delaware

For further information about these and other Thomas Cook publications, write to Thomas Cook Publishing, PO Box 227, The Thomas Cook Business Park, 9 Coningsby Road, Peterborough PE3 8SB, United Kingdom.

Drive Around

Scotland

The best of Scotland, including
Edinburgh, Glasgow, Skye,
Mull, Iona and Orkney, plus
suggested driving tours for
Scotland's scenic mountains,
lochs, moors and glens

Donna Dailey

Thomas Cook
Publishing

www.thomascookpublishing.com

Written, researched and updated by Donna Dailey

Published by Thomas Cook Publishing
A division of Thomas Cook Tour Operations Limited.
Company registration no. 1450464 England
The Thomas Cook Business Park, Unit 9, Coningsby Road,
Peterborough PE3 8SB, United Kingdom
Email: books@thomascook.com, Tel: + 44 (0) 1733 416477
www.thomascookpublishing.com

Produced by Cambridge Publishing Management Limited
Burr Elm Court, Main Street, Caldecote CB23 7NU

ISBN: 978-1-84848-067-4

Series Editor: Adam Royal
Production/DTP: Steven Collins

Printed and bound in India by Replika Press PVT Ltd
Cover photography: Front: © Masterfile/Jochen Schlenker. Back: © Thomas Cook

About the author

Donna Dailey is an award-winning travel writer and photographer and writes for newspapers and magazines worldwide. She has written or contributed to more than 25 guidebooks covering destinations in Europe, Africa and North America, and is the author of Thomas Cook's Drive Around Ireland guide.

Above
Beech Row, near Selkirk

Acknowledgements

The author would like to thank the following people for their invaluable help in researching this guide: Gavin Forbes at Arnold Clark Car Rental; Don Roberts at ScotRail; Fred Fermor at John o' Groats Ferries; Graham Clark and Gillian Musk at the Scottish Tourist Board in London; Ian Gardner at The National Trust for Scotland; Jane Ferguson at Historic Scotland; Rona Wallace at the Scottish Tourist Board press office; Fiona Martin and Alan Graham at the Aberdeen and Grampian Tourist Board; Gillian Taylor at the Argyll, the Isles, Loch Lomond, Stirling and Trossachs Tourist Board; Karen Wilson at the Dumfries & Galloway Tourist Board; Jenni Steele and Lisa Truffelli at the Edinburgh and Lothians Tourist Board; Moira Dyer at the Greater Glasgow & Clyde Valley Tourist Board; Sally Monro at the Highlands of Scotland Tourist Board; Jo Melville at the Kingdom of Fife Tourist Board; Gillian Harrower and Gayle Wilson at the Perthshire Tourist Board; Claire Mathieson at the Scottish Borders Tourist Board; and Sheila Hamilton at Hamilton Associates.

The author would also like to thank all of her hosts at the following establishments who provided such a warm welcome and splendid hospitality, especially Shena McGhie for the wellies and Peter and Marina Braney for the music; Sherston House, Forres; The Lodge Guest House, Elgin; Fridayhill, Kinmuck, Inverurie; Merkland Guest House, Aberdeen; Castleton Guest House, Braemar; Barriemore Hotel, Oban; Highland Cottage Hotel, Tobermory; Taychreggan Hotel, Kilchrenan, Taynuilt; Roman Camp Country House Hotel, Callander; Castlecroft B&B, Stirling; Redbank House, Dumfries; High Park B&B, Balmaclellan, New Galloway; Channings Hotel, Edinburgh; Greywalls, Muirfield, Gullane; Ewington Hotel, Glasgow; Stakis Glasgow Grosvenor Hotel, Glasgow; Ardvreck Guest House, Ullapool; Moyness House Hotel, Inverness; Pool House Hotel, Poolewe; Dornoch Castle Hotel, Dornoch; Mackays Hotel, Wick; Inver Lodge Hotel, Lochinver; Sligachan Hotel, Sligachan; Ardlarig Guest House, Grantown-on-Spey; St Andrews West, Fort William; The Inn at Lathones, St Andrews; Stakis Perth City Mills Hotel, Perth; The Pend, Dunkeld; Easter Dunfallandy House, Pitlochry; Merlindale, Crieff; and Philipburn Country House Hotel, Selkirk.

Contents

About Drive Around Guides

Right
Glasgow cathedral
doorknocker

Thomas Cook's Drive Around Guides are designed to provide you with a comprehensive but flexible reference source to guide you as you tour a country or region by car. This guide divides Scotland into touring areas – one per chapter. Major cultural centres or cities form chapters in their own right. Each chapter contains enough attractions to provide at least a day's worth of activities – often more.

Ratings

To make it easier for you to plan your time and decide what to see, every area is rated according to its attractions in categories such as Architecture, Entertainment and Children.

Chapter contents

Every chapter has an introduction summing up the main attractions of the area, and a ratings box, which will highlight the area's strengths and weaknesses – some areas may be more attractive to families travelling with children, others to people interested in finding castles, churches, nature reserves or good beaches.

Each chapter is then divided into an alphabetical gazetteer, and a suggested tour. You can select whether you just want to visit a particular sight or attraction, choosing from those described in the gazetteer, or whether you want to tour the area comprehensively. If the latter, you can construct your own itinerary, or follow the author's suggested tour, which comes at the end of every area chapter.

The gazetteer

The gazetteer section describes all the major attractions in the area – the villages, towns, historic sites, nature reserves, parks or museums that you are most likely to want to see. Maps of the area highlight all the places mentioned in the text. Using this comprehensive overview of the area, you may choose just to visit one or two sights.

One way to use the guide is simply to find individual sights that interest you, using the index or overview map, and read what our authors have to say about them. This will help you decide whether to

Symbol Key

- ❶ Tourist Information Centre
- ⮂ Advice on arriving or departing
- 🅿 Parking locations
- ⊙ Advice on getting around
- ➲ Directions
- ⓝ Sights and attractions
- ◖ Accommodation
- ⑪ Eating
- ⬡ Shopping
- ⑨ Sport
- ◗ Entertainment

Practical information

The practical information in the page margins or sidebars will help you locate the services you need as an independent traveller – including the tourist information centre, car parks and public transport facilities. You will also find the opening times of sights, museums, churches and other attractions, as well as useful tips on shopping, market days, cultural events, entertainment, festivals and sports facilities.

visit the sight. If you do, you will find plenty of practical information, such as the street address, the telephone number for enquiries, websites and opening times.

Alternatively, you can choose a hotel, perhaps with the help of the accommodation recommendations contained in this guide. You can then turn to the overall map on pages 10–11 to help you work out which chapters in the book describe those cities and regions that lie closest to your chosen touring base.

Driving tours

The suggested tour is just that – a suggestion, with plenty of optional detours and one or two ideas for making your own discoveries, under the heading *Also worth exploring*. The routes are designed to link the attractions described in the gazetteer section, and to cover outstandingly scenic coastal, mountain and rural landscapes. The total distance is given for each tour, as is the time it will take you to drive the complete route, but bear in mind that this indication is just for the driving time: you will need to add on extra time for visiting attractions along the way.

Many of the routes are circular, so that you can join them at any point. Where the nature of the terrain dictates that the route has to be linear, the route can either be followed out and back, or you can use it as a link route, to get from one area in the book to another.

As you follow the route descriptions, you will find names picked out in bold capital letters – this means that the place is described fully in the gazetteer. Other names picked out in bold indicate additional villages or attractions worth a brief stop along the route.

Below
The elegant Greywalls Hotel

Accommodation and food

In every chapter you will find lodging and eating recommendations for individual towns, or for the area as a whole. These are designed to cover a range of price brackets and concentrate on more characterful small or individualistic hotels and restaurants. In addition, you will find information in the *Travel facts* chapter on chain hotels, with an address to which you can write for a guide, map or directory. The price indications used in the guide have the following meanings:

£	budget level
££	typical/average prices
£££	de luxe.

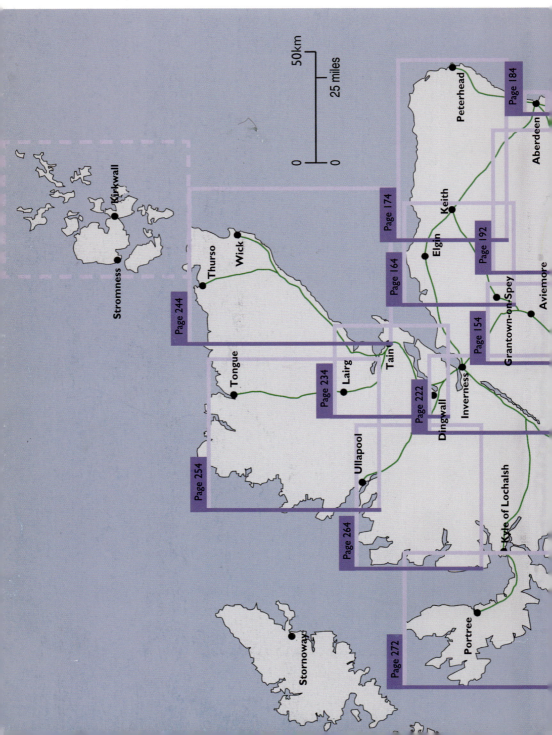

50km

25 miles

0

0

Page 184

Peterhead

Aberdeen

Kirkwall

Page 174

Keith

Stromness

Thurso

Wick

Elgin

Page 192

Aviemore

Page 164

Grantown-on-Spey

Page 244

Page 154

Page 234

Lairg

Tain

Inverness

Tongue

Page 222

Dingwall

Ullapool

Page 254

Kyle of Lochalsh

Page 264

Portree

Page 272

Stornoway

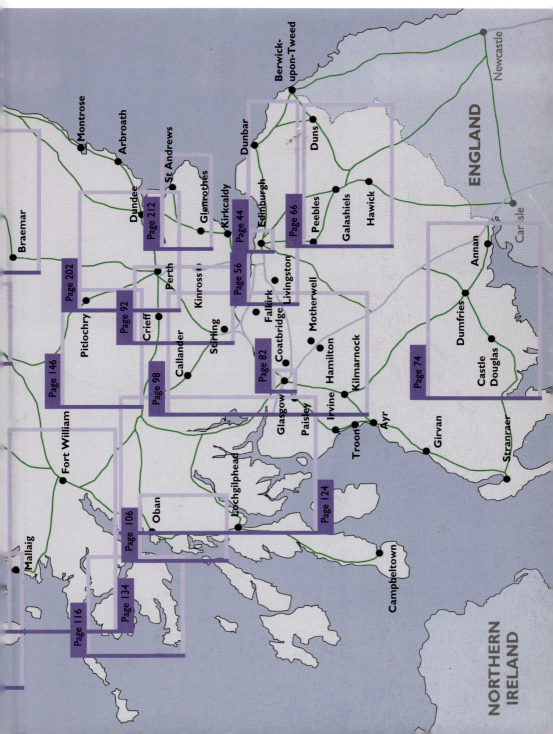

Above
Looking over the sea to Skye

Introduction

Scotland occupies only a third of Great Britain yet boasts a lion's share of the nation's most striking imagery. Dramatic mountains encircling windswept moors and shimmering lochs, ancient castles marooned on an islet or towering on cliffs above the sea, the swirl of a tartan kilt and the lonely lament of the bagpipes – such images draw visitors to Scotland year after year. They are rarely disappointed, for Scotland not only lives up to expectations but throws in a few surprises of its own.

The country is divided into distinct regions – the Highlands and the Lowlands – by the Highland Boundary Line. This massive geological fault runs from southwest to northeast, curving from the Clyde Estuary up to the Moray Firth. The Lowlands contain the most fertile agricultural lands and the most heavily populated areas of the country, including the capital, Edinburgh, and the largest city, Glasgow. Running south of these cities to the English border is the stretch of hills known as the Southern Uplands. The Highlands, with its mountains rising over 4,000ft (1,200m), contain some of Europe's oldest geological formations. As recently as the 18th century, this region of rugged mountains, bleak moorlands, deep peat bogs and rushing rivers remained largely isolated and forbidding.

Today the Highlands are sparsely populated, with vast tracts of treeless wilderness, and it is this lonely beauty and peaceful sense of space that attracts many visitors. Yet this land was once covered by the great Caledonian forest and, until the Clearances of the early 19th century, was home to a large Gaelic-speaking population. In some areas of the Highlands, particularly the islands and the northwest, a revival of Gaelic language, music and culture is under way, which reinforces, even to the casual visitor, a sense of the country's ancient roots and independent tradition.

One of the last great wildernesses in Europe

While the Highlands have suffered environmentally much more than at first meets the eye, many areas of pristine wilderness still exist, providing habitat for endangered species such as the golden eagle, the osprey and the Scottish wildcat. A more enlightened attitude to conservation now prevails, preserving areas of wild countryside where visitors can enjoy walking, climbing, fishing and other outdoor pursuits. The Lowlands, too, offer miles of bicycle trails, pony-trekking, long-distance footpaths, and watersports, as well as outstanding links courses for that most Scottish of sports, golf.

Then there is Scotland's coastline, deeply indented with sea lochs which ensure that no place in the country is very far from the sea. There are nearly 800 islands fringing the western and northern coasts, less than a quarter of which are inhabited, where the old Gaelic and Scandinavian influences hold sway. The western shores are warmed by the Gulf Stream, enabling palms to grow at latitudes more northerly than Moscow. Seals, dolphins and a variety of sea birds are common sights in the sounds and firths. And there are broad sweeps of largely deserted sandy beaches, dramatic rocky headlands, stark cliffs and some of the best surfing waters in Europe.

No overview of Scotland is complete without a mention of the weather. Capricious and unpredictable, it can wreak havoc with the best-laid plans but it can also inspire wonder at the dramatic forces of nature. Embracing it is part of the experience. And awed you will be as you watch the swirling skies or drive towards a pitch-dark horizon with a beam of sunlight over your shoulder and a rainbow plunging into the sea.

Forward-looking land of ancient traditions

Scotland has a vivid history, rich with painted tribes, warrior clans, a tragic queen, bold heroes and daring outlaws. But alongside its haunting beauty and romantic tales is a harsher reality of economic hardships, social ills and political struggles that also influence the country today. While the traditional occupations of fishing and agriculture still prevail in the Highlands and the northeast, the heavy industry of the Lowlands has given way to high-tech and service industries. Scotland's population of more than five million is modern and diverse, with cosmopolitan Edinburgh and design-conscious Glasgow as much a part of contemporary Scottish culture as the kilts and ceilidhs of the popular imagination.

Ironically, from 1822, the interest in all things Scottish was perpetuated by the English monarchy, who had usurped Scottish independence and suppressed Highland culture less than a century before. The canny Scots have turned any tartan clichés to their advantage and today tourism ranks as one of the country's main industries. With their legendary hospitality they may have had a head start in its success, but what also quickly becomes apparent is the superb quality of the food, accommodation, attractions and other services that exists at all levels. This stems largely from the Scots' strong national pride and their enjoyment in sharing their culture and history with visitors.

Scotland is a delight for touring by car, with good, fast main roads and minor roads that are both challenging and rewarding. The finest scenery is often accessible only via single-track roads in remote areas, although some of the most memorable vistas also occur on major highways. Because the country is small, it is tempting to try to cover as much ground as possible. But a more relaxing approach is to pick a base for several nights and do smaller tours from there, an alternative that may give you a more in-depth understanding and an equally rewarding experience of the true Scotland.

Travel facts

Publications

The Scottish Tourist Board has four accommodation guides for sale, listing a comprehensive range of accommodation throughout the country. These cover Hotels and Guesthouses, Bed and Breakfast, Caravan and Camping Parks and Self Catering. Guides can be purchased by post or from tourist information centres. *Tel: 0845 22 55 121* to order or use the website *www.visitscotland.com*

The free information brochures for individual regions also have lengthy accommodation sections.

Online booking

For general information, contact the Scottish Tourist Board's National Booking and Information Line, *tel: 0845 225 5121 (UK only) or +44 1506 832 121 (outside UK); fax: 01506 832 222; e-mail: info@visitscotland.com.* You can book accommodation online at *www.visitscotland.com*

The regional tourist boards also offer an online booking service. See pages 21–22 for a list of these offices and their websites.

Accommodation

The Scottish Tourist Board operates a quality grading system under which places of accommodation in all categories are awarded between one and five stars. The star awards are based on the quality of the hospitality, service, ambience, comfort, food and the condition of the property, rather than on its size or range of facilities. Trained inspectors visit the properties every year to ensure that ratings are up to date. Properties involved in the scheme display a blue plaque or sticker showing the number of stars and the type of accommodation and facilities offered. A higher star rating does not necessarily mean higher prices. The ratings are:

★★★★★   Exceptional
★★★★   Excellent
★★★   Very good
★★   Good
★   Acceptable

Note that all hotels and guesthouses are non-smoking.

Types of accommodation

● **International resort hotels** – At the top of the range, these hotels are of five-star quality and offer leisure and sporting facilities such as golf courses, leisure centres, swimming pools and country activities.

● **Hotels** – A wide-ranging category that includes some Scottish castles, hotels will have a minimum of six bedrooms, the majority of which must have en-suite or private bathroom facilities. They will usually have a drinks licence and will serve breakfast, dinner and normally lunch. Prices start from around £27 per person per night.

● **Guesthouses** – Guesthouses are commercial businesses and will have a minimum of four bedrooms to let, some of which have en-suite or private facilities. Breakfast is provided, and evening meals may also be served. Guesthouses can be slightly more expensive than B&Bs.

● **Bed-and-breakfasts** – B&B accommodation is generally offered in private homes, ranging from farmhouses to city-centre houses, and caters for up to six guests at a time. Hosts sometimes serve evening meals. Prices start from around £18 per person per night.

● **Inns** – Accommodation within a traditional inn or pub, with a restaurant and bar open to non-residents.

Booking

You ought to book accommodation in advance during the busy months of July and August, particularly if you will be visiting a destination during a major event such as the Edinburgh International Festival. To book from overseas, you can either contact the properties direct, book through a travel agent, or use a hotel chain's booking service or a self-catering agency. Some foreign tour operators offer bed-and-breakfast voucher schemes, which must be bought before you arrive in Scotland.

Within Scotland, the tourist information centres offer a local booking service; some are free of charge, others may require a small fee. Many operate the national Book-A-Bed-Ahead service, whereby they will book accommodation for you at your next destination, saving you time and anxiety at the end of the day. There is a small booking fee and you must also pay a 10 per cent deposit, which is deducted from your bill.

You can also book accommodation through the Scottish Tourist Board's London office and the area tourist boards (see pages 21–22).

- **Lodges** – This type of accommodation is often situated near a main road or in a city centre, with car parking space for each room. It may have associated restaurant facilities. Reception hours may be limited and payment may be required when checking in.
- **Self-catering** – Houses, cottages, apartments or other properties are normally let on a weekly basis, and are furnished and have cooking facilities. Prices vary depending on the season.
- **Serviced apartments** – These are self-catering units where cleaning and other services are available, and possibly meals and drinks as well.
- **Other** – Accommodation is also available in youth hostels, on college and university campuses at certain times of the year, and in restaurants with rooms to let.

Camping and caravanning

There is a good network of camping and caravanning sites throughout Scotland. Like other types of accommodation, these are graded by the Scottish Tourist Board for the quality of their facilities. Contact the tourist information centres for a list and map showing the location of sites throughout the country. You can also book accommodation in a Thistle Award caravan holiday home at more than 80 sites.

In Scotland, you can still pitch your tent in the wild, away from designated camping parks. However, it is best to first obtain permission from the owner of the land.

The Scottish Youth Hostel Association (SYHA) (*7 Glebe Crescent, Stirling FK8 2JA; tel: 01786 891 400 (enquiries); 0870 155 3255 (reservations); e-mail: info@syha.org.uk; www.syha.org.uk*) has special offers for budget travellers as well as information on over 80 youth hostels in Scotland.

Children

Scotland is an exciting holiday destination for children, with castles, beaches, parks, wildlife and lots of outdoor activities. There are several museums geared towards children in the cities, and others that provide special children's activities. The Scottish Tourist Board publishes a list of attractions by region that are of particular interest to children and families.

Climate

It is said that Scotland doesn't have a climate – it has *weather*. In what other country do weathercasters on the evening news give figures for the height of the cloud base as well as the temperature? (The importance of this will become all too apparent when your car is suddenly enveloped in fog, a phenomenon that can happen in the Borders as well as the Highlands!) Scottish weather can change

Conversion tables

Distances

Metric	Imperial
1m	3ft 3in
5m	16ft 6in
10m	33ft
50m	164ft
100m	330ft
1km	0.75 mile
2km	1.5 miles
5km	3 miles
10km	6 miles
20km	12.5 miles
50km	31 miles
100km	62 miles

Weight

Kg	Lbs
1	2.2
2	4.5
5	11
10	22
20	45
50	110
75	165
100	220

Fluid measures

Litres	Imperial gallon
5	1.1
10	2.2
20	4.4
50	11

Area

1 hectare = 2.471 acres
1 acre = 0.4 hectares

dramatically in an instant. Never let a rainy morning spoil your plans – or let a sunny one fool you into dropping your guard and hiking off into the hills leaving your jacket behind.

Scotland's northern location means that the north enjoys 18–20 hours of daylight in the summer. The east-coast resorts have the most sunshine, while the west is wetter, though very mild thanks to the Gulf Stream. The east is drier, chillier and has colder winds. The Cairngorms see the coldest weather and are often covered by snow in winter.

Currency

The currency in Scotland is the same as in England, but Scotland issues its own banknotes (£1, £5, £10, £20, £50 and £100). These are generally accepted in the rest of Britain, except for the £1 notes. English and Northern Ireland banknotes are legal tender in Scotland.

Banks usually give the best rate of exchange for foreign currency and traveller's cheques. You can also change money in airports, major rail stations, travel agents and larger hotels if you are a resident. Exchange bureaux usually charge a handling fee and commission.

Thomas Cook Traveller's Cheques free you from the hazards of carrying large amounts of cash. Thomas Cook Foreign Exchange Bureaux provide full foreign exchange facilities and will change currency and traveller's cheques (free of commission in the case of Thomas Cook Traveller's Cheques). They can also provide emergency assistance in the event of loss or theft of Thomas Cook Traveller's Cheques.

Cashpoint and credit cards

Cashpoint (ATM) machines are widely available. Between them, the five major banks – Bank of Scotland, Royal Bank of Scotland, Clydesdale Bank, TSB Scotland and Girobank – accept most cards and these are listed on the cashpoint.

Major credit cards are accepted at larger hotels, restaurants, petrol stations and stores. Smaller establishments, such as B&Bs, pubs, tearooms and small shops, are unlikely to take credit cards of any kind, so always have some cash on hand.

Customs regulations

Duty-free allowances for goods into Scotland from outside the EU are:
- 200 cigarettes, or 100 cigarillos, or 50 cigars, or 250g tobacco
- 2 litres still table wine
- 1 litre spirits, or 2 litres fortified or sparkling wine, or 2 litres additional still table wine
- 60cc/ml perfume

Left
A guard at Edinburgh Castle

Festivals

Scotland's most famous festival is the Edinburgh International Festival and its counterpart, the Festival Fringe, an arts extravaganza of music, theatre, dance, comedy and events held between mid-August and early September. Close on its heels is Hogmanay, the traditional Scottish New Year celebration, held in Edinburgh, Aberdeen and elsewhere. Highland Games or Gatherings – based on clan gatherings of old – involve sporting contests, pipe bands and other events. These are held around the country, generally in August; the Braemar Games are the best known because of the presence of the Royal Family, but those elsewhere in the Highlands are the more traditional.

Similar festivals, the Common Ridings or Marches, are held in the Borders. In January, celebrations are held throughout Scotland commemorating the national poet Robert Burns.

The main celebration of Gaelic culture is the Mod, held in autumn. A variety of other festivals and events ranging from traditional music to sport is held around the country. Contact the Scottish Tourist Board for a full list.

- 250cc/ml toilet water
- Other goods, gifts and souvenirs to a value of £145.

Drinking

The best drink in Scotland is water – the 'water of life', or whisky, that is. It would be a shame to visit the country and not try at least a 'wee dram' of the national drink. If you find the many different brands confusing, most hoteliers and bartenders are only too happy to recommend one. Even if you are not partial to whisky, you might find one of the smoky, peaty varieties, which are produced on the islands, a pleasant surprise. For those who like sweet liqueurs, try Drambuie, a whisky liqueur.

Fine wines are available at the better restaurants and hotels. If good coffee is an essential part of your day, you'll be happy to find that many restaurants, hotels and B&Bs serve the real thing in cafetières.

Eating out

You can find meals to suit all tastes and budgets in Scotland. In smaller towns and villages, your best bet is usually the pub of the local hotel, where you will find a good choice of meals at inexpensive prices. In larger towns there are pizza places, fish-and-chip shops and a wider range of fare. Not to be missed are the **Taste of Scotland** restaurants, with menus based on fresh local produce such as Aberdeen Angus beef, lamb, game or salmon. Many of these are a foodie's delight, with innovative menus and superb quality rivalling any of the top establishments in Britain. For a listing of these accredited restaurants visit the website *www.taste-of-scotland.com*

Electricity

The voltage in Scotland is 240V 50Hz. Plugs have three square pins. You will need an adaptor and a converter for appliances from abroad.

Entry formalities

Passport and visa requirements are the same as for the rest of the United Kingdom. US citizens need a valid passport, but visas are not required for stays of up to six months.

Ferries

Caledonian MacBrayne operates a passenger and car ferry service to the Scottish islands. Special discounted tickets such as Hopscotch and Rover tickets are available. Contact **Caledonian MacBrayne Ltd,**

Heritage organisations

The **National Trust for Scotland**, Scotland's largest conservation charity, manages stately homes, castles, gardens, countryside and nature reserves and other properties throughout the country. **Historic Scotland**, also a leading charity, manages castles, fortresses, tower houses, abbeys and prehistoric sites. If you are touring Scotland it is well worth joining either or both of these organisations. Members receive free admission to attractions under their care, and you will quickly recoup the membership fee in a few visits. There are additional membership benefits, as well as helping to rescue, restore and maintain Scotland's heritage.

For further information, contact the tourist information centres or **The National Trust for Scotland** (*Wemyss House, 28 Charlotte Square, Edinburgh EH2 4ET; tel: 0844 493 2100; fax: 0844 493 2102; e-mail: information@nts.org.uk; www.nts.org.uk*) and **Historic Scotland** (*Longmore House, Salisbury Place, Edinburgh EH9 1SH; tel: 0131 668 8600; e-mail: hs.friends@ scotland.gsi.gov.uk; www.historic-scotland.gov.uk*).

A Scottish Explorer Ticket, valid for three, seven or ten days, gives unlimited access to Historic Scotland sites and can be bought at any staffed property or online in advance.

The Ferry Terminal, Gourock, Renfrewshire PA19 1QP, tel: 01475 650 100; fax: 01475 637 607. Car ferry reservations, *tel: 08000 66 5000 (Freephone); fax: 01475 635 235; e-mail: reservations@calmac.co.uk; www.calmac.co.uk*

John o'Groats Ferry operates a passenger-only service in summer between John o'Groats and Burwick-on-Orkney. *Tel: 01955 611 353; e-mail: office@jogferry.co.uk; www.jogferry.co.uk*

NorthLink Ferries operate car ferry services to Orkney and Shetland. There are up to three sailings a day from Scrabster (near Thurso) to Stromness in Orkney, and nightly sailings from Aberdeen to Lerwick in Shetland, with four of these sailings via Kirkwall in Orkney. *Tel: 0845 6000 449 for bookings and enquiries; e-mail: info@northlinkferries.co.uk; www.northlinkferries.co.uk*

Food

As no place in Scotland is far from the sea, this is the place to indulge yourself in seafood. Rivers and inland lochs are abundant with salmon and trout. Fresh Scottish salmon is hard to beat, and is prepared in a variety of ways. Start at least one day with kippers or Arbroath smokies (smoked haddock cured using oak chips).

Even if you're not usually a carnivore, Aberdeen Angus beef is a treat. To try it at its best, perhaps with a light pepper sauce, have it prepared by a Taste of Scotland chef (*see page 18*). Game, too, is superb, from tasty, healthy venison to moorland grouse and pheasant. Venison sausages are a nice alternative with your Scottish breakfast.

Haggis is another national dish that should be tried, although it might sound revolting: it is made from the liver, heart and lungs of a sheep, mixed with oatmeal, onion and suet, seasoned and cooked in a sheep's stomach. Actually, it has the taste and consistency of a spicy mince and a good haggis is delicious. It is traditionally served with 'bashed neeps' (mashed turnips), although it often comes with mashed potatoes. Some hotel breakfast buffets serve haggis, but this is not the place to try it at its best.

Other things to try include Scottish cheeses, especially those made in the traditional manner without the use of artificial flavouring or colouring (Orkney cheeses are among the best); oatcakes, unsweetened biscuits eaten with cheese, marmalade or honey; and of course porridge – either salted (the Scottish way) or with cream and sugar. For those with a sweet tooth, shortbread, tablet (a kind of fudge) and other Scottish sweets are irresistible.

Health

There are no unusual health hazards in Scotland, except perhaps the midge, a vicious biting gnat that is prevalent in warm, humid conditions. While not disease-carrying, they can make you miserable

Entertainment

On Thursdays, the *Press and Journal* newspaper publishes a weekly guide to arts, events and entertainment in the Highlands and Islands, called *What's On?* (*www.pressandjournal.co.uk*). The tourist information centres also have publications listing events in the area.

National parks

Scotland is renowned for the natural beauty of its landscape, much of which is protected in national parks and nature reserves. These include Beinn Eighe – the oldest national nature reserve in Britain – in the Highlands, the Cairngorms National Park, the largest in the UK, Loch Lomond and The Trossachs National Park and Galloway Forest Park. For further information contact **Scottish Natural Heritage** *tel: 01463 725000; www.snh.org.uk*; the **Forestry Commission** *tel: 0845 367 3787; www.forestry.gov.uk*; **National Trust for Scotland** *tel: 0844 493 2100; www.nts.org.uk*; **Scottish Wildlife Trust** *tel: 0131 312 7765; www.swt.org.uk*; **Royal Society for the Protection of Birds** *tel: 0131 311 6500; www.rspb.org.uk*

Left
Glasgow's River Clyde

when camping or picnicking, so take plenty of strong insect repellent. Apart from the usual over-the-counter remedies, you will need a doctor's prescription to obtain medicines, so it is best to bring what you need from home. Chemists, or pharmacies, keep normal shop hours, though one in the area will generally be open for emergencies and a notice will be posted on the shop door.

Information

Most towns on the well-travelled tourist routes have a tourist information centre. Even small villages will have a seasonal kiosk or caravan. Those in large towns and major tourist centres are usually open all year, but smaller towns may be seasonal (*see page 23*). Information ranges from free leaflets and brochures to maps, books and other publications for sale. Many centres can also book tickets for entertainment and events, sightseeing tours or sporting activities such as golf and fishing.

The Scottish Tourist Board is helpful and efficient, with a series of informative publications on attractions, accommodation, activities, sports and equipment hire and other useful contacts. When planning your trip, the first point of information is Visit Scotland. Their website, *www.visitscotland.com*, has information on all regions of the country, and lists individual town visitor centres under their respective regions. However, note that in many cases phone calls are directed back to the central Visit Scotland information line, *tel: 0845 22 55 121*, rather than to locally based staff. Note, too, that numbers beginning with 0870, 0871, 0844 and 0845 will incur additional call charges and may not be accessible from abroad.

Some regions do continue to operate their own regional tourist boards which are listed here. Otherwise, contact the tourist information centres in the larger towns for general information on the entire region.

Regional tourist offices

● **Aberdeen and Grampian Tourist Board**, *Exchange House, 26–28 Exchange Street, Aberdeen AB11 6PH; tel: 01224 288 828; fax: 01224 288 838; e-mail: aberdeen.information@visitscotland.com; www.aberdeen-grampian.com*

● **Angus and Highlands Dundee Tourist Board**, *21 Castle Street, Dundee DD1 3AA; tel: 01382 527 527; fax: 01382 527 550; e-mail: dundee@visitscotland.com; www.angusanddundee.co.uk*

● **Argyll, The Isles, Loch Lomond, Stirling and Trossachs Tourist Board**, *e-mail: info@visitscotland.com; www.visitscottishheartlands.com*

● **Dumfries and Galloway Tourist Board**, *64 Whitesands, Dumfries DG1 2RS; tel: 01387 253 862; fax: 01387 245 555; e-mail: dumfriestic@visitscotland.com; www.visitdumfriesandgalloway.co.uk*

● **Edinburgh and Lothians Tourist Board**, *3 Princes Street, Edinburgh EH2 2QP; tel: 0845 22 55 121 or 01506 832 121; fax: 01506 832222; e-mail: info@visitscotland.com; www.edinburgh.org*

Shopping

From chunky knit sweaters to cashmere to tartan wraps and blankets, woollens are a good buy in Scotland. There are woollen shops in every main town, and you will even notice some woollen chain stores, but the best buys can often be found in small towns, particularly in the Borders. Local mills are getting fewer and farther between, but these offer a broader selection of colours and styles than you'll find in the chain stores. The main cities have shops specialising in tartans, where you can have a kilt or tartan garment made up in the tartan of your clan ancestors. Harris tweed, traditionally woven on handlooms on the Isle of Harris, is another Scottish speciality.

Caithness Glass, with factories in Wick, Perth and Oban where you can watch the process, makes a beautiful and unique gift or souvenir. Other regional specialities include beautiful jewellery fashioned with traditional Celtic designs and stones, and a variety of objects carved from deer horn.

Smoking

Smoking has been banned in all public places in Scotland since March 2006.

- **Greater Glasgow and Clyde Valley Tourist Board**, *11 George Square, Glasgow G2 1DY; tel: 0141 204 4400 or 566 0800; fax: 0141 566 0810; e-mail: glasgow@visitscotland.com; www.seeglasgow.com*
- **Highlands of Scotland Tourist Board**, *e-mail: info@visitscotland.com; www.visithighlands.com*
- **Kingdom of Fife Tourist Board**, *St Andrews Tourist Information Centre, 70 Market Street, St Andrews KY16 9NU; tel: 01334 472021; fax: 01334 478422; e-mail: standrews@visitscotland.com; www.visitfife.com*
- **Orkney Tourist Board**, *The Travel Centre, West Castle Street, Kirkwall, Orkney KW15 1NX; tel: 01856 872 856; fax: 01856 875 056; e-mail: info@visitorkney.com; www.visitorkney.com*
- **Perthshire Tourist Board**, *Lower City Mills, West Mill Street, Perth PH1 5QP; tel: 01738 450 600; fax: 01738 444 863; e-mail: info@visitscotland.com; www.perthshire.co.uk*
- **Scottish Borders Tourist Board**, *Jedburgh Information Centre, Murrays Green, Jedburgh TD8 6BE; tel: 01835 863 170; e-mail: bordersinfo@visitscotland.com; www.scot-borders.co.uk*

Overseas offices

For information about Scotland abroad, contact VisitBritain at:
- **Australia**: *Level 2, 15 Blue Street, North Sydney, NSW 2060; tel: (02) 9021 4400 or 1300 85 85 89; fax: (02) 9021 4499; e-mail: australia@visitbritain.org; www.visitbritain.com*
- **Canada**: *160 Bloor Street East, Suite 905, Toronto, Ontario M4W 1B9 (not open to the public); tel: 1 888 847 4885; fax: 905 405 8490; e-mail: britinfo@visitbritain.org; www.visitbritain.com*
- **New Zealand**: *For information tel: toll-free 0800 700 741 Mon–Fri 1030–1900; e-mail: newzealand@visitbritain.org; www.visitbritain.co.nz*
- **South Africa**: *www.visitbritain.co.za*
- **USA**: *551 5th Avenue at 45th Street, 7th Floor, #701, New York, NY 10176; tel: 1 800 462 2748; fax: (212) 986 1188; e-mail: travelinfo@visitbritain.org; www.visitbritain.com*

Other offices

- **Visit Britain**, *Britain and London Visitor Centre, 1 Regent Street, London SW1Y 4XT; open daily*, has information on all the Scottish regions and can also book accommodation.
- **The Scottish Tourist Board Central Information Department**, *PO Box 121, Livingston EH54 8AF; tel: 0845 2255 121; fax: 01506 832 222; www.visitscotland.com*

Insurance

Unless you are a UK or EU citizen, you are advised to take out medical insurance, as you will be expected to pay for treatment if you fall ill. Travel insurance covering theft or loss of luggage, travel delays, etc is always a good idea. Check your home contents policy to see if your property is covered while travelling.

Above
Rural post office on Black Isle

Public transport

Details of public transport within main cities are listed in the respective chapters. **ScotRail** provides a frequent and efficient train service between all mainland areas. A variety of discount tickets and passes is available. This can be a good alternative for travelling between regions or for touring areas where you don't need a car. You could, for example, tour Glasgow and Edinburgh before or after driving through other parts of the country; trains run hourly between the cities and the journey time is under an hour. For information, contact National Rail Enquiries, *tel: 0845 748 4950 (24 hours).*

Opening times

General opening times are as follows:
● **Banks:** Mon–Fri 0900 or 1000–1600 or 1700; some open later on Thursday and a few are open on Saturday morning.
● **Shops:** 0900–1730 or 1800. Some close on Saturday afternoons or one day a week in smaller communities. Others may stay open later in tourist areas or in summer. In cities, there is late-night shopping on Thursday until 1900 or 2000, and on Sunday.
● **Tourist offices:** 0900 or 1000–1700 or 1800 Mon–Fri. In popular areas they may be open later in summer and at weekends. Many are seasonal and close from October or November to March.
● **Restaurants:** Opening hours vary widely, but in general lunch is served from 1200–1330 or 1430 and dinner from 1800 to between 2100 and 2400. Last orders are often taken 45 minutes before closing.
● **Bars and pubs:** Standard opening times are 1100–1430 and 1700–2300 Mon–Sat; 1230–1430 and 1830–2300 on Sun. Many pubs stay open all afternoon and others have a late licence at weekends.
● **Museums:** Opening times vary considerably, so it is always best to check locally. In general, summer hours (Easter or Apr/May to Sep/Oct) are from 0930 or 1000 until 1700 or 1730, with longer hours in July and August. Some close one day a week, usually on Sunday or Monday. Winter hours are shorter and small museums may close altogether from November to March.
● **Historic sights:** Opening times at historic sights vary, but in general they are open daily in summer (Apr–Sep) from 0930 until 1730 or 1830 (some are open afternoons only on Sun). In winter (Oct–Mar) some properties close and others are open Mon–Sat 0930–1630 and Sun 1400–1630.

Packing

Scotland's weather is variable, so bring clothes for all conditions. It is best to bring layers that you can put on or shed as needed. Even in the warmer months you should bring a light waterproof jacket and a light jumper for cooler days and nights. From October to April you will want a heavier sweater and jacket or coat, especially in the mountain areas. For walking and climbing, it is best to bring sturdy leather hiking boots; many areas are wet and boggy and canvas boots and trainers quickly become soaked and uncomfortable. On rainy days, a pair of wellies will come in handy for tramping around the archaeological sites.

Postal services

Post offices are open during normal shopping hours, Mon–Fri 0900–1700 and on Saturday mornings. Many are located in

Travellers with disabilities

The Scottish Tourist Board publishes a brochure entitled *Accessible Scotland* to help direct people to visitor attractions, accommodation, banks and shops that are accessible to travellers with disabilities.

Capability Scotland
Advice Service Capability Scotland (ASCS), 11 Ellersly Road, Edinburgh EH12 6HY; tel: 0131 313 5510; fax: 0131 346 1681; e-mail: ascs@capability-scotland.org.uk; www.capability-scotland.org.uk

newsagents or other shops, but all are designated with the red-and-yellow Post Office signs. Many of the smaller branch offices close for an hour at lunchtime.

Public holidays

Unlike England and Wales, bank holidays in Scotland are generally just for banks and some commercial offices. However, there is a spring and autumn holiday, which varies from town to town but is usually on a Monday. Visitor attractions and restaurants remain open. Christmas Day, Boxing Day (26 Dec), New Year's Day and 2 Jan are general public holidays and most places are closed.

Safety and security

Crime is no worse in Scotland than anywhere else, and although you may feel safer in the Highlands and rural areas, the normal safety precautions should be taken. Leave valuable jewellery and other items at home. Don't leave cameras and bags unattended in public places or in cars. There is no need to carry large amounts of cash as cashpoints are widely available to replenish your supply. Your hotel may have safety-deposit box facilities for storing cash and valuables.

For lost property, enquire at the appropriate restaurant, attraction, train station or the police station, as there is a lost-and-found system. In case of theft, ask your hotel reception for advice and contact the police. If you lose your passport, the main foreign embassies are in London. A number of countries have consular offices in Scotland, which are listed in the Yellow Pages, including the **Australian Consulate**, Euro Business Centre, 21–23 Hill Street, Edinburgh EH2 3JP; *tel: 0131 226 8161* and the **American Consulate General**, 3 Regent Terrace, Edinburgh EH7 5BW; *tel: 0131 556 8315*.

Sport

Scotland is the birthplace of golf and top courses such as St Andrews, Gleneagles, Carnoustie and Dornoch are known round the world. There are hundreds of others, from links courses by the sea to lush parkland fairways. Golf passes offering extremely good value are available for courses in Aberdeen and Grampian, the Borders, Edinburgh and the Lothians, and Perthshire. Contact the area tourist boards. Many hotels offer golf packages and can arrange tee times for you. The *Golf in Scotland* brochure is available from the Scottish Tourist Board.

Fishing is another popular sport in Scotland. Permits are generally needed. Salmon fishing can be expensive in prime locations, but elsewhere fishing for trout, salmon and other species in many lochs and rivers is more affordable. You can buy permits from as little as £6.50 per day from hotels, tackle shops, post offices and local businesses. Many hotels offer fishing packages. The *Fishing in Scotland* brochure from the Scottish Tourist Board gives more details.

Scotland is a paradise for walking and there are trails to suit all abilities, from easy footpaths for strolling to long-distance trails including the West Highland Way, The Southern Upland Way and the Speyside Way. Although the mountains do not seem so very high or dangerous, the rapidly changing weather can present conditions that are challenging to experienced mountaineers and deadly to ill-equipped amateurs. Always seek local advice and never set out without proper clothing and supplies or without letting someone know where you are heading. The tourist board publishes a walking brochure, or visit *www.visitscotland.com/walking*

Cycling is also popular (ask for the tourist board's *Cycle Scotland* guide or visit *www.visitscotland.com/cycling*), with special trails such as the Four Abbeys Cycle Route in the Borders. Bicycle hire is widely available. There is a variety of watersports and pony-trekking and riding centres, as well as boating, canoeing, sailing, shooting and even surfing. Contact the tourist information centres.

Telephones

The international code for Scotland is the same as for the rest of the UK. To phone from abroad, dial +44 plus the area code minus the initial '0', then the number. You can make credit- and charge-card calls from most phone boxes, which also take coins or phone cards or both. Hotels will generally add a surcharge for calls made from your room. Charges will usually be listed in the room; otherwise, ask the hotel operator.

Time

The time in Scotland is the same as the rest of the UK.

Tipping

If you feel you have received good service you may wish to leave a tip. In restaurants, tips are normally 10 per cent of the total bill, unless a service charge has already been included. Bar staff do not expect a tip, although they are sometimes offered a drink which they take when off duty. Tipping in hotels is also discretionary. Taxi drivers are often tipped, especially on longer journeys – £1–£2 is normally sufficient.

Toilets

There are public toilets in every town and village, and most are well signposted. Many charge a small fee of 10p or 20p, which is a price well worth paying for clean and well-stocked facilities. If you use the facilities at a pub or restaurant, it is polite to buy a drink.

Driver's guide

Automobile clubs

It is a good idea to join an automobile association before your trip, as it can provide useful information and documents, as well as suggesting itineraries and routes. It may also have reciprocal agreements with local clubs in the event of a breakdown. Contact:

UK: Automobile Association (AA), *tel: 0870 600 0371 in the UK, (+44) 191 223 7071 from outside UK; www.theaa.com* Royal Automobile Club (RAC), *tel: 08705 722 722; www.rac.co.uk*

American Automobile Association (AAA), *tel: 1 800 922 8228; www.aaa.com*

Australian Automobile Association, *tel: 06 247 7311; www.aaa.asn.au*

Canadian Automobile Association, *tel: 613 247 0117; www.caa.ca*

New Zealand Automobile Association, *tel: 0800 500 444; www.nzaa.co.nz*

AA Republic of Ireland: *tel: 01 617 9999; www.aaireland.ie*

AA Northern Ireland: *tel: 0870 600 0371; www.theaa.com*

Accidents

If you have an accident, you are obliged by law to stop and give your name, address and car registration number to anyone involved. If anyone is injured, the police must be notified within 24 hours and a report filed. For fire, police or ambulance, dial 999. Exchange insurance details with other relevant drivers, and do not admit fault or liability, or give money to any person. If you can find any independent witnesses, ask for their details. Take photographs of the accident scene and vehicles. If you are involved in an accident with a rental car, you must notify the hire company immediately. Do not carry out any repairs without the company's permission.

To avoid having accidents in the first place, keep alert by taking sensible rest breaks and don't allow yourself to be distracted by the scenery. Most roads have places to pull off which are signposted. If you are unfamiliar with driving in Britain, take it steady, but be aware of other drivers and allow them to overtake (pass) you whenever possible. A line of frustrated motorists stuck behind a slow-moving vehicle is a recipe for disaster.

Breakdowns

Try to park as safely as possible; alert other drivers with hazard lights or a warning triangle if you have one. SOS telephones are located at regular intervals on the 'hard shoulder' (verge-side lane) of motorways. This is for emergency use only and you should never use it for a rest stop. (Remember, it can be very dangerous to walk on the hard shoulder of any motorway. Your passengers are probably safer out of the vehicle and well up the verge away from the traffic.)

Car hire companies will provide you with a contact number to ring if your rental car breaks down. Motoring organisations like the Automobile Association (AA) and the Royal Automobile Club (RAC) may have reciprocal arrangements with similar clubs overseas, and may provide a free rescue service or advice; check with your organisation before you leave home.

Emergency rescue services: AA: *0800 887766*; RAC: *0800 828282*.

Caravans and camper vans (trailers and RVs)

Most of Scotland's roads are suitable for caravans. However, some of the more remote roads are extremely narrow and winding, making

Documents

An overseas driving licence is valid for use in the UK for stays of up to a year, but only for the class of vehicle authorised on the licence. If you bring your own car, you'll need a green card (showing you have adequate insurance) as well as the registration documents for your car.

Before taking out additional insurance on your rental car, check to see what coverage you already have on your own car insurance policy or credit card, as this can sometimes include rental cars.

Drinking and driving

Penalties are severe for driving with more than the legal limit of blood alcohol, currently .80mg per cent (80mg/100ml), or driving while under the influence of any drugs. If you have an accident while in such a condition, you will automatically be considered at fault. Police have the right to administer a breathalyser test at any time, and if you refuse to take it you are likely to be prosecuted. The strong penalties apply to visitors as well as residents. The safest thing is not to drink and drive.

them unsuitable for caravans and large vehicles. Look for warning signs at the start of such roads and take them seriously.

Drivers with disabilities

The orange badge issued to drivers with disabilities in the United Kingdom should be displayed prominently when in use.

Driving in Scotland

Most cars in Britain have manual transmissions. A limited number of cars with automatic transmission is available, but you must specify this when reserving a rental car.

Roads are good and well maintained throughout the country. There are three main classes of road in Britain. Motorways are designated by the prefix 'M'. There is a motorway network in southern and central Scotland, and dual carriageways to cities such as Inverness and Aberdeen. Motorways in Scotland are toll-free, but tolls are charged on some bridges, such as the Tay, Erskine and the Forth road bridges. Primary roads, designated with the prefix 'A', may be either dual- or single-carriageway. 'B' roads are generally single-carriageway. In addition there are smaller, unclassified roads in rural areas.

In the more remote areas of the Highlands and Islands, you will often find yourself driving along single-track roads. Few of these are fenced, and they can present unexpected hazards to the urban motorist, though these can easily be avoided by following a few simple rules:

- Always pull in to the nearest passing place on your left when meeting oncoming traffic. Do not cross the road to use a passing place on the right even if it seems logical to do so. If you meet between passing places, reverse carefully into the nearest space available. Remember that it is easier for a car to reverse than a tractor and trailer.
- Always pull over to let cars behind you pass; they may be locals who know the road well and can travel a lot faster than you. Impeding following traffic is an offence.
- Approach sheep, cattle, deer and other animals with caution. They have no road sense and may unexpectedly dart in front of you.

Driving rules

In Britain, drive on the left and overtake (pass) on the right. A number of accidents is caused each year by visitors straying onto the wrong side of the road after a momentary lapse in concentration; arrows have been painted on the roads in some places as a reminder. Be

Essentials

It is recommended (but not required) to carry a red warning triangle in case of accident, a first-aid kit, spare bulbs, torch (flashlight) and petrol container.

Fines

Speed cameras are widely in use in Britain and fines are automatic. If you are caught speeding by a speed camera, a ticket will be sent to the address of the car registration. If you are driving a rental car, the ticket will be sent to the car hire company and they will pass it on to you, usually with an additional administration charge. Unpaid parking tickets will also be passed on to the car hire company and they will bill it to your credit card. If you are stopped by a police officer, he or she will take your licence and car registration details and any fine will be processed through the courts and sent to the address on the registration. If the address is overseas, it may not be enforced at present.

It is an offence to use a speed camera detector in Britain, and such equipment will be confiscated. It is illegal to use a hand-held mobile phone when driving, punishable by an on-the-spot fine.

particularly vigilant when starting off from the side of the road, when turning from one road to another and when driving on a road with little traffic.

Always go left at a roundabout. Cars on roundabouts have priority, and at unmarked road junctions the vehicle to the right has right of way. A continuous white line down the centre of the road means overtaking is prohibited. Crash helmets are a legal requirement for motorcyclists.

In Britain, flashed headlights are habitually used both as a warning (an alternative to the horn), and an invitation to take priority over another driver. You will simply have to use your judgement to decide what is meant – flashed headlights do not officially form part of the Highway Code. Elementary courtesy includes raising your hand to thank a driver who has given way to you.

The rules and regulations on driving in Britain (including Northern Ireland) can be found in the current edition of *The Highway Code*, available from bookshops, newsagents and motoring organisations such as the AA and RAC.

Fuel

Most modern vehicles in the UK run on unleaded petrol, available in virtually all petrol stations (look for the green hoses) along with diesel. Some petrol stations stay open 24 hours a day, but you will need to plan more carefully in rural areas. In remote areas of Scotland, the distance between stations is greater and the opening hours may be shorter; some may be closed on Sundays. Fuel costs in Britain are among the most expensive in the world. The most reasonable rates can be found at large supermarket petrol stations; motorway service areas tend to be more expensive.

Information

It is useful to have an up-to-date map. Free tourist maps are often available from the tourist offices, but you may want to buy a more detailed map or road atlas. These are available at bookshops and newsagents, as well as many of the larger tourist information centres.

There are several good road atlases for Britain, including the *AA Great Britain Road Atlas*.

Parking

Parking is a serious problem in many urban areas. Traffic wardens lie in wait with expensive tickets for illegally parked vehicles; worse, your vehicle may even be immobilised or towed away. If you are fined, you will generally get a discount for prompt settlement.

Lights

Dipped headlights should be used in rain or whenever weather conditions reduce light levels, as well as after the official 'lighting-up' time, when street lamps are switched on. Use fog lights when visibility falls below 328ft (100m). If you are driving a left-hand drive vehicle, don't forget that your headlights will need to be adjusted. Simple beam adjusters are available at ferry terminals, or from motoring organisations.

Mobile phones

The use of a hand-held phone or similar device while driving is prohibited and carries a penalty. Drivers can still be prosecuted for using a hands-free phone when driving, for failure to have proper control of the vehicle.

Seat belts

The use of seat belts is compulsory in the UK, including those in the rear seats if they are fitted. Babies and small children should not sit in the front seats, but should be properly restrained in a child seat or carrier in the back. Be sure to request a car seat for young children when making your car hire reservation.

Parking is always prohibited on double yellow lines, or on single lines during business hours (check the sign beside the road). Larger towns may have metered or pay-and-display zones, or parking bays which require you to display a time disc or purchase a voucher before parking. A ticket machine will be found along the street, or vouchers for on-street parking can be purchased from tourist offices, newsagents and other retailers. If in doubt, check locally. Keep some coins handy for parking meters.

Many urban areas contain zones restricted to residents' parking only. Signs specifying the parking restrictions on a particular street can generally be found nearby. The safest bet is to head for a designated parking area, usually marked by the letter 'P'. NCP car parks can be expensive, but you can stay as long as you like and you pay for your time when you leave. Park-and-ride facilities are useful on the outskirts of popular tourist cities, while National Trust members will find their parking spaces in rural areas invaluable.

In villages and rural areas parking space is limited and you may need to use a car park (generally free) at the edge of town. When visiting small archaeological sites in the countryside, there is often only parking space for one or two cars and you may have to park on the verge. Respect the needs of local farmers and do not block gates and private drives. Never, ever park in designated passing places – it is dangerous to obstruct traffic on single-track roads.

Whenever you leave your car, remove all valuables from sight or you may return to a smashed window and missing possessions.

Security

It seems the British are no longer the well-mannered drivers of the halcyon days of early motoring. 'Road rage' is an alarming phenomenon exacerbated by the stresses of congested roads. You'll see plenty of aggressive driving in Britain, especially on motorways. Don't react to it, and give yourself room to avoid the consequences.

Car theft is all too common, especially in the larger cities and at tourist attractions. Always lock your car if you leave it, even for a moment or two, and never leave cameras or other valuables on view inside, in the glove compartment or on a roof rack. Keep luggage in the boot (trunk) out of sight.

If you break down or need roadside assistance, take special care when getting out of your vehicle. To contact the police in an emergency, dial 999. Local police stations are listed in telephone directories or on the internet. Drivers unfortunate enough to find the police contacting them (via flashing blue lights or wailing sirens) should pull over as soon as it's safe to do so.

National Tourist Routes

Scotland has 12 National Tourist Routes that offer scenic routes through the countryside and smaller towns, as an alternative to the main trunk roads. Each route is signposted – a brown sign with white lettering and a blue thistle symbol – and there are leaflets available from the tourist information centres. The tours in this book incorporate many of these scenic routes.

Speed limits

Keep to the following speed limits in Britain unless otherwise posted:

Motorways and dual carriageways: 70mph (112kph)
Single carriageways: 60mph (96kph)
Towns and built-up areas: 30mph (48kph)

Speed limits are given in miles per hour in Britain. Camper vans or cars towing caravans are restricted to 50mph (80kph) on normal roads or 60mph (96kph) on motorways. On single-track roads you should drive with care according to road conditions. Always make allowances for adverse conditions (rain, fog, ice, etc.), when braking distances increase dramatically.

Road signs

Most regions of Britain conform to the standard style of road signage used in the rest of the European Union (EU). Generally, signing is clear, though city suburbs can be confusing. Distances are given in miles in England, Wales, Scotland and Northern Ireland.

Motorways are marked in blue, major trunk routes in green, minor routes in white. Advisory or warning signs are usually triangular, in red and white. Watch out for overhead electronic messages on motorways indicating road works, accidents, fog or other hazards, and the advised speed limit. Level crossings over railway lines have manually operated gates or more often automatic barriers. If the lights flash you must stop to let a train pass.

Visitor information is indicated on brown signs with white lettering. These signs indicate attractions, accommodation, tourist information centres, recreational facilities, natural attractions and picnic areas, as well as National Tourist Routes in Scotland. Archaeological sites are indicated by smaller white signs with blue lettering. Attractions approved by the Scottish Tourist Board are marked with a blue thistle.

Bilingual road signs in both English and Gaelic can be seen in the Western Highlands of Scotland, such as the A87 on Skye and the western section of the A830 Mallaig road.

Below
Highland traffic hazard

UK ROAD SIGNS

SIGNS GIVING ORDERS   Signs with red circles are mostly prohibitive

Maximum Speed Limit (mph)

No Right Turn (left if reversed)

No Entry for Vehicular Traffic

National Speed Limit

SIGNS GIVING SPECIFIC INSTRUCTIONS   Signs with a blue background mostly give positive instructions

Priority over approaching traffic

Bus and Cycle Lane

One Way Traffic

Turn Left Ahead (right if reversed)

WARNING SIGNS   Red triangles with a white background are warning signs

Roundabout

Dual Carriageway Ends

Railway Crossing with Gates

Give Way to Traffic on Major Road

DIRECTION SIGNS   Directional signs are mainly rectangular. On motorways they have a blue background

Route confirmatory sign approaching a junction (junction number may be shown on a black background)

On approaches to junctions

On approach to a junction in Wales (bilingual)

Thanks to the following websites for their kind permission to reproduce the above signs
www.europcar.co.uk
www.smartdriving.co.uk

Getting to Scotland

By air

There are international airports at Edinburgh, Glasgow, Aberdeen and Inverness. All handle direct flights from London, as well as from other cities and provincial airports in the United Kingdom. The main domestic operators are British Airways, bmi and easyJet. There are direct services from many European cities to Edinburgh, Glasgow and Aberdeen. Services at peak commuter times are heavily used and advance booking is essential.

Transatlantic flights generally land at Glasgow. Both scheduled airlines and charter tour operators offer fly-drive deals; ask your travel agent. If you are visiting Scotland as part of a wider tour of Britain, it is generally cheaper to fly to Scotland from the rest of the UK if you use an airpass. These are only valid with an international scheduled flight ticket and must be bought in your own country before you leave. British Airways and bmi both offer passes; check with your travel agent. There is also a rail service from Manchester Airport in England to Edinburgh four times daily. The journey time is about four hours.

There is a departure tax in Britain, currently levied at between £10 and £80 depending on destination and class of travel, included in the ticket price.

Airports

Edinburgh Airport (*tel: 0870 040 0007; www.baa.com/edinburgh*) is 8 miles (13km) from the city centre. Buses run every 10–15 minutes to the city centre. Taxis cost approximately £15.

Glasgow International Airport is located at Paisley, 8 miles (13km) from the city centre (*tel: 0870 040 0008; www.baa.com/glasgow*). An express connection runs every 15–30 minutes into the city and takes 30 minutes. Taxis cost approximately £19. There is also a service to Prestwick Airport (*tel: 0871 223 0700; www.gpia.co.uk*), 29 miles (46.5km) south of the city. Trains to Glasgow Central Station run from Prestwick every 30 minutes. A taxi into the city will cost approximately £45. Passengers travelling to or from Prestwick can buy AirTrain vouchers for return rail travel to any station in Scotland or on Glasgow Underground for 50 per cent off the standard rail fare. These can be purchased in the arrivals hall and at the information desk in the main concourse, from any rail booking office or from conductors on the trains. Glasgow Underground tickets can only be purchased from underground stations. Full details are listed on the Prestwick website.

For up-to-date details of long-distance bus, ferry and rail services, consult the *Thomas Cook Rail Timetable*.

Aberdeen Airport is located about 7 miles (11km) northwest of the city, at Dyce (*tel: 0870 040 0006; www.baa.com/aberdeen*). There is a bus service into the city at peak times. Taxis cost approximately £15.

Inverness Airport is 8 miles (13km) from the town centre (*tel: 01667 464 000; www.hial.co.uk/inverness-airport.html*). There is a regular bus service Mon–Sat, limited Sun. Taxis to the city centre cost around £12.

By rail

One of the best ways to get to Scotland from England is on the **Caledonian Sleeper** overnight service from London. Trains leave between 2100 and midnight and arrive early the following morning. There are five main destinations from London's King's Cross and Euston stations: Glasgow, Edinburgh, Aberdeen, Inverness and Fort William, with stops at smaller stations along the way. Single- and twin-berth cabins are available and fully equipped with everything you need for an overnight journey, including toiletries. This option not only saves time on a busy schedule, but also sets the stage for your visit to Scotland, starting with the pleasant camaraderie in the lounge car. If you choose Inverness or Fort William as your destination, you'll have a scenic breakfast with a view of the mountains and misty glens. For information and reservations *tel: 0845 755 0033*. Book at least five working days in advance of your journey. Further details can be found on First ScotRail's website: *www.firstscotrail.com*

Passengers on the Caledonian Sleeper can also receive a discount on car hire with Arnold Clark Car Rental, *tel: 0845 702 3946*, quoting the ScotRail discount.

There is a variety of regular rail services between Scotland and England. The journey from London to Edinburgh takes between four and six hours, depending on the route. Apex and SuperApex fares are very inexpensive, but these seats fill up quickly and must be booked up to two weeks in advance, and changes and refunds are not usually allowed. Call National Rail Enquiries, *tel: 0845 748 4950*. First ScotRail's internet address is *www.firstscotrail.com*, and the website provides full timetable and booking information, plus details of special offers.

By car

There are good motorway connections between Scotland and England via the A74(M) through Carlisle and the A7 through the Borders. The distance from London to Edinburgh is 412 miles (663km), and you will probably want to break your journey halfway. Driving up is fine if you want to use your own car and tour parts of England on the way, but if you are planning to hire a car it is quicker and more relaxing to fly or take the train and hire the car in Scotland.

Setting the scene

Above
Iona Abbey – the birthplace of Scottish Christianity

History

Scotland was settled in prehistoric times. The remains of shell middens and stone tools indicate that hunter-gatherers were living along the coast as early as 6000 BC, although the most visible examples of the first settlers are the mysterious burial cairns and *brochs* (stone towers) that appeared around 2000 years later. In the 8th century BC, the first Celtic tribes arrived from Europe with their metalworking skills, introducing the sword and shield. Their descendants were the fearsome northern race the Romans called *picti* (the painted ones), or the Picts. Unable to subdue these guerrilla warriors, the Romans withdrew around AD 212.

In addition to the Picts, three other groups now held sway on Scottish soil. The Celtic Britons occupied the lands southwest of the River Clyde. A new wave of Celtic settlers from Ireland arrived in the 3rd and 4th centuries, establishing the kingdom of Dalriada in Argyll. They were called the Scots, and eventually gave their name to all of Scotland. Finally, in the 5th century, the Germanic Angles established a base in Northumbria which included the Lothians.

The ensuing years were shaped by two powerful forces. In 397 St Ninian, a Briton from Galloway, established the first Christian centre at Whithorn. It was St Columba, however, arriving from Ireland to found a monastery on Iona, who sparked the rapid spread of Christianity to the Scots and Picts, forging a link among the Celtic groups. Around 800, Viking raiders threatened the lands of the north and west to such a degree that the kingdoms of the Scots and the Picts joined in a defensive alliance under Kenneth MacAlpin, who became the first Scottish king. This new kingdom was called Alba (hence Albion). It was the beginning of Scotland, but the demise of the Picts, whose once-dominant culture faded, unrecorded, into oblivion. In 1025, Malcolm II defeated the Angles and took over the Lothians. Nine years later he was succeeded by his grandson, Duncan I, ruler of the Britons, bringing the final piece of Scotland into place.

The real Macbeth

Although Shakespeare's story was not historically accurate, there was a real Macbeth, who killed Duncan in 1040 to become the last Celtic king. Scotland prospered under his reign. Macbeth was in turn killed by Duncan's son, Malcolm Canmore. The first links with England were formed when Malcolm married Margaret, daughter of the English King Edward the Confessor, who set up an English court. In the

Highlands and Islands the patriarchal clan system continued as it had always done, ruled by the Lords of the Isle, but in the Lowlands the old kingdoms were replaced by an English-style feudal system.

In the subsequent years, royal ties to England grew ever stronger. King David I's marriage to the daughter of an English earl brought him lands near Cambridge but also, under the feudal system, obligations to the English king. After a failed attempt to overthrow England's Henry II, King William was forced to sign a treaty of allegiance in 1174. Thus, when a dispute over the successor to the Scottish throne arose in the 13th century, Edward I of England exploited his self-proclaimed status as overlord and installed John Balliol as a puppet king. However, when Edward demanded that Scotland join with England in a war against the French, the Scots formed an alliance with the French instead; this Auld Alliance of 1295 was to last for centuries. The following year, after Scotland's defeat, the English occupied the country, forcing oaths of allegiance from the nobles and carrying off the Scottish symbol of sovereignty, the Stone of Destiny. But the Scots fought back, first with the victory of William Wallace at the Battle of Stirling Bridge in 1297. Then, after a seven-year military campaign known as the Wars of Independence, the English were defeated at Bannockburn under Robert the Bruce, who was crowned Scotland's king in 1307. Although peace was precarious, Scotland remained independent for nearly 400 years.

The road to union with England
The Stuarts ascended to the throne with the investiture of Bruce's grandson, Robert the Steward, as king in 1371. They retained sovereignty through troubled times until the birth of Scotland's most famous monarch, Mary Queen of Scots, in 1542. Her father, King James V, died a week later. The temptation to seize power was too great for England's Henry VIII, who launched destructive attacks known as the 'Rough Wooing' to try to force the marriage of the infant queen to his young son Edward. The Auld Alliance again came into play when France sent troops to Scotland's aid and Mary was whisked away across the Channel to safety – and a childhood marriage to the young French prince, the Dauphin. Mary returned, a 19-year-old widow, to take up her rule in 1561. She found Scotland gripped by the fires of the Reformation, led by the rabid reformer John Knox. The Scottish nobles, upset by the presence of French officials in the regent's court, had supported the Protestant religion, and in the vicious backlash against the church of Rome, cathedrals, abbeys and anything to do with Catholicism were reviled and destroyed. This revulsion extended to the young Catholic queen.

Mary wished no quarrel with the Protestants, but her reign seemed doomed from the start. After an ill-fated marriage to Lord Darnley, the treachery against her escalated. Darnley, who was implicated in the murder of her secretary, David Rizzio, was himself killed in suspicious circumstances. When Mary then married the Earl of Bothwell, the

Protestant nobility rose against her; she was imprisoned in Loch Leven Castle and her baby son, James VI, was installed on the throne. Mary escaped to England and the 'mercy' of her cousin, Queen Elizabeth I, who had her imprisoned for 20 years until her execution in 1587.

When Elizabeth died without an heir, James VI of Scotland also became James I of England, the Union of the Crowns, in 1603. But religion continued to shape Scotland's history. The Scottish Protestants were divided between those who wanted an austere Presbyterianism and the more elaborate, ritualistic Episcopacy of the English Church. This led to the signing of the National Covenant in 1638, an emotive yet conflict-ridden document in which Catholic practices were condemned and signatories agreed to uphold not only the 'true religion' but also the sovereignty of the king. This put them into conflict when Charles I, James's successor, tried to enforce an Anglican liturgy in the Scottish Kirk. Thus, the Covenanters supported Cromwell and the Parliamentarians during the English Civil War, which culminated in the execution of the king. The Scots welcomed the coronation of Charles II, who supported the Covenant, if in name only. But he was succeeded in 1685 by his brother James VII (James II of England), the first Catholic monarch in over 100 years. Four years later, James was forced into exile in France, replaced by his Protestant daughter Mary and her Dutch husband, William of Orange. This angered the supporters of James, mostly Highlanders, and the Jacobite rebellion was born (named from Jacobus, the Latin for James).

The first uprising came that same year, 1689, with a Jacobite victory at Killiecrankie. But their leader, John Graham of Claverhouse, the 'Bonnie Dundee', was killed and without his inspiration the movement was crushed at the next battle of Dunkeld. While the exiled Stuarts awaited their chance in France, Scotland was plunged into economic disaster – and political crisis – by an ill-fated scheme to establish a colony in Panama. The English forced their hand and the Scots aristocracy, eager to recoup their losses, agreed to the Union of Parliaments and signed away Scottish independence in 1707.

Bonnie Prince Charlie

England's old enemies, France and Spain, encouraged the Stuarts with promises (albeit empty ones, it transpired) of support, and further Jacobite uprisings took place in 1715 and 1719. The government responded by building military roads, bridges and forts, under General Wade, in the Highlands to try to subdue the clans. The final rebellion came in 1745 when the grandson of the exiled king, Prince Charles Edward Stuart, the dashing Bonnie Prince Charlie, landed on the northwest coast to win back the Stuart crown. The Hanoverians, who had succeeded to the crown, called him 'the Young Pretender', but in fact the Stuarts were the rightful bloodline. Although his support was less than he had hoped, on 19 August 1745 the prince raised his standard at Glenfinnan, rallying the clans for a year of battles with

Above
Kilts were once banned and
bagpipes were considered
to be weapons of war

English forces until, greatly outnumbered, the Jacobites were cut to pieces on the bloody battlefield of Culloden in April 1746. The prince escaped, hiding for the next five months in the Highlands with a price of £30,000 on his head, aided by brave supporters such as Flora MacDonald, until he sailed once again to exile in Europe.

The failure of the Jacobite rebellion changed the face of Scotland forever. The English and the Lowland Scots, who had never supported the Jacobites, were determined to crush the Highland clans. The Proscription Act of 1747–82 banned the wearing of tartan and kilts, the bearing of arms, and any symbol of Highland identity. By the turn of the century, the Clearances had begun. Crofters were evicted from their lands and homes and trees were burnt to create grazing land for sheep. Many were forced to emigrate abroad or to the cities, and by the end of the 19th century, the Highlands were nearly deserted.

Meanwhile in the Lowlands, trade and industry flourished. The prosperity of the textile mills and tobacco trade gave way to heavy industry. Glasgow became the world's largest shipbuilder, and elsewhere ironworks, coal mines, steel mills and factories proliferated. The economic boom dwindled with the Great Depression and, apart from the demand for arms and ships during World War II, slowly died out. In 1975 the North Sea oil industry brought a renewal to the east coast of Scotland, while elsewhere there was a turn to light industry.

The change in economic fortunes brought, in some quarters, a renewal of political discontent and a resurgence of Scottish nationalism in varying degrees. Those who favour autonomy maintain that rule by Westminster does not support Scotland's best interests. While the majority of Scots see themselves as an integral part of Britain, the need for recognition of Scottish issues and the power to act in its welfare was confirmed by the overwhelming vote in 1997 to establish a Scottish Parliament with tax-raising powers. That same year, the Stone of Destiny was returned from Westminster to its rightful place on Scottish soil.

Clans

The word 'clan' derives from the Gaelic word 'clanna', which means 'children'. Thus clansmen were descendants of a particular ancestor, and each was considered an equal member of the extended family. Many Scottish surnames bear the prefix 'Mac', which means 'son of'. All Highland clansmen claimed descent from the line of Fergus Mor McEarc. They took great pride in their lineage, and because of this blood kinship with the royal line, they displayed no awkwardness or servility to others, as is often the case with isolated rural communities. Clansmen bore allegiance to a chief, and in return for his protection he could call on them to fight for him at any time. Clan ties were strong, and there was much feuding and rivalry between them. After the battle of Culloden, the government was intent on breaking the clan system. Highland dress and other symbols of clan identity became illegal. With the death of the clan system, clan societies and associations arose to keep their heritage alive, and they remain active in maintaining clan seats and clan centres. Today Scots and expatriates alike take much pride in clan ancestry, but it holds no significance beyond a shared heritage and celebration.

Tartans

The wearing of checked and striped cloth, coloured with vegetable dyes, dates back to the 13th century, but it is not known whether the patterns, or 'setts', related to clans or territories. Plaids, up to 18ft (5.5m) long, were wrapped, belted and worn in different styles; they were even used as sleeping bags when sleeping rough on cold Highland nights. The kilt, the main article of Highland dress, developed from this. When proscription ended in the 18th century, the production of tartans along clan lines became much more rigid and standardised. When George IV visited Holyrood in 1822 dressed in a kilt, Highland dress became all the rage, a fashion perpetuated by Queen Victoria and Prince Albert. New tartans were designed for Lowlanders as well as people whose clan ties had long been in name only. With later synthetic dyes, tartans became brighter, leading to literally hundreds of colours termed 'modern', 'ancient', 'reproduction' and 'muted'. Today tartan is worn mainly for formal dress occasions, but there are also hunting tartans and tartans for everyday wear.

Tracing your ancestors

If you want to trace your Scottish ancestors, there are several organisations in Edinburgh that can help with your search. The **Scottish Roots Ancestral Research Service** (*16 Forth Street; tel: 0131 477 8214; e-mail: stuart@scottishroots.com; www.scottishroots.com; open Mon–Fri 0900–1700 by appointment*) employs professional genealogical researchers. They will give an initial free assessment without obligation. The **Scottish Genealogy Society Library and Family History Centre** (*15 Victoria Terrace; tel: 0131 220 3677; e-mail: enquiries@scotsgenealogy.com; www.scotsgenealogy.com*) is a library with books, microfilm and microfiche and copying facilities, as well as publications for sale. It is open to non-members at £5 per session, *Mon–Thu 1030–1730, Wed until 2030 and Sat 1000–1700*. Otherwise, a visit to the **Scottish Record Office** (*New Register House, 3 West Register Street; tel: 0131 334 0380; e-mail: records@gro-scotland.gov.uk; www.gro-scotland.gov.uk; open weekdays 0900–1630*) may prove productive.

Right
Grave detail from the churchyard of Greyfriars Kirk in Edinburgh

Music

Along with the rebirth of the Gaelic language has come a revival of Gaelic music. Ancient instruments such as the *clarsach* (harp) and Highland bagpipes can be heard at prestigious musical events and concerts, while the lowland pipes (smaller and blown with a bellows, using the elbow), fiddle and flute feature in the music of modern Gaelic bands such as Capercaillie. Ceilidhs (pronounced 'kay-lee') were traditionally informal gatherings in which neighbours would entertain each other with stories and song; today they are more often held as an entertainment event in a hotel or village hall and are an opportunity to get a taste of traditional music and dance.

Whisky

Uisge beatha, the 'water of life', is Scotland's most famous export. Like French champagne, it is defined by law and internationally recognised: a whisky that is not distilled and matured in Scotland cannot be called 'Scotch' (although this designation is never used in Scotland itself). A single malt whisky is a straight, unblended product distilled from barley and matured for varying lengths of time in oak casks. Blended whiskies contain a mixture of malt and a lighter grain. Factors which make one whisky different from the next include the barley used, the water, which may be filtered over peat or granite, the type of still and the skill of the producers. In the old days, the proof, or alcoholic strength, of the whisky was tested using gunpowder! Today there are some 116 single malts and many blends. More than 40 distilleries throughout Scotland are open to visitors, where you can observe this age-old process and sample a 'wee dram', or measure, of 'the real McCoy' (a phrase coined during Prohibition in the USA to denote the genuine product smuggled in by Captain Bill McCoy).

Architecture

Several remnants of Scotland's medieval architecture can be seen today. These include doocots, or dovecots, the round white buildings seen in rural areas in Fife, Angus, Moray and the Lothians. They were used to 'farm' pigeons for winter meat. Market crosses, called mercat crosses in Scotland, or their replicas still stand in many town squares, as do the tolbooths, attractive tower-like buildings that served as council chambers, courts, jails and tax collection points. Many old houses, particularly in Fife, sport crow-stepped gables, a feature that was influenced by trade with the Low Countries of Europe.

Scottish castles have particular styles related to their period in history. The fortified tower house was prevalent in the 14th century, when height and thick walls were important features for defence. In the 16th century, castle building expanded with the combination of

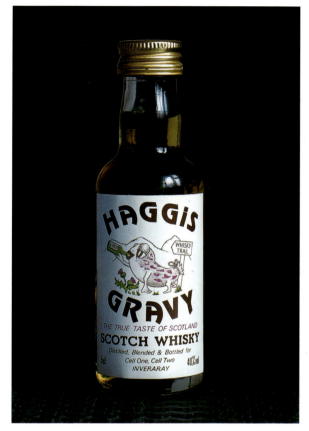

several towers into an L-plan or Z-plan. Corbelling – the addition of projecting round towers, turrets and stairwells – became a dominant feature, culminating in the splendid baronial castles of the late 16th and early 17th centuries, with their sheer lower walls and fairy-tale skylines.

Heraldry, once a means of identification in warfare, became popular as a decoration on buildings and furniture. In many Scottish castles and churches you will see heraldic ceilings with the coats of arms of nobles and clergymen, armorial panels carved into stone chimneypieces and above doorways, and armorials carved on church stalls and pulpits.

The elegance of Georgian architecture came to the fore in the 18th century, when James Smith, William Adam and his sons created magnificent stately homes for the aristocracy. The 19th century saw a Romantic revival of medieval styles. The 20th century's most famous architect was the innovative Charles Rennie Mackintosh, whose designs for buildings and furniture still seem contemporary today.

Above
Whisky with a sense of humour

The Scottish Enlightenment

The Scottish Enlightenment was an era of intellectual and artistic flowering that stretched roughly from the Union of 1707 until the mid-19th century. It produced some of Scotland's most famous figures, including the economist Adam Smith, who wrote *The Wealth of Nations*, and the philosopher David Hume. Above all it was noted for literary genius. Chief among these writers was Robert Burns (1759–96), the farmer-poet who captured the national spirit. His sharp observations on people and politics, his championing of haggis, whisky and the common man, his skill with rhyme and his own short love-torn life earned him an eternal place as the national bard. The second great writer of the time was Sir Walter Scott (1771–1832), a great lover of Scottish history, whose narrative poems and romantic novels did much to revive popular interest in the country.

Highlights

Best castles
- Edinburgh Castle – *Page 46*
- Stirling Castle – *Page 94*
- Blair Castle – *Page 146*
- Fyvie Castle – *Page 177*
- Crathes Castle – *Page 195*
- Drum Castle – *Page 196*
- Glamis Castle – *Page 204*
- Scone Palace – *Page 207*
- Falkland Palace – *Page 215*
- Dunrobin Castle – *Page 237*

Best stately homes
- Hopetoun House – *Page 58*
- House of the Binns – *Page 59*
- Abbotsford House – *Page 66*
- Duff House – *Page 175*
- Haddo House – *Page 178*
- Leith Hall – *Page 181*

Best cities
- Edinburgh – *Pages 44–55*
- Glasgow – *Pages 82–91*
- Stirling – *Page 94*
- Aberdeen – *Pages 184–191*
- St Andrews – *Pages 216–218*
- Inverness – *Page 226*

Best towns and villages
- Haddington – *Page 58*
- Kelso – *Page 69*
- Kirkcudbright – *Page 77*
- Fordyce – *Page 177*
- Dunkeld – *Page 204*
- Culross – *Page 212*
- East Neuk of Fife villages – *Page 214*
- Cromarty – *Page 237*
- Ullapool – *Page 259*

Best churches
- St Giles High Kirk – *Page 50*
- Rosslyn Chapel – *Page 60*
- Glasgow Cathedral – *Page 84*
- Church of the Holy Rude – *Page 94*
- Elgin Cathedral (ruins) – *Page 166*
- King's College Chapel – *Page 187*
- St John's Chapel, St Nicholas Kirk – *Page 189*
- Dunkeld Cathedral – *Page 204*

Best abbeys
- Jedburgh Abbey – *Page 69*
- Melrose Abbey – *Page 69*
- Dundrennan Abbey – *Page 79*
- Iona Abbey – *Page 118*
- Pluscarden Abbey – *Page 173*
- Dunfermline Abbey – *Page 213*

Best architecture
- Edinburgh New Town – *Page 47*
- Dryburgh Abbey – *Page 67*
- Sweetheart Abbey – *Page 77*
- Glasgow Merchant City – *Page 89*
- Charles Rennie Mackintosh House – *Page 91*
- Willow Tea Rooms – *Page 91*
- Glasgow School of Art – *Page 91*
- Marischal College – *Page 187*
- East Neuk villages – *Page 214*

Best art galleries
- National Gallery of Scotland – *Page 47*
- Scottish National Gallery
  of Modern Art – *Page 50*
- Scottish National Portrait Gallery – *Page 50*
- Tolbooth Art Centre, Kirkcudbright – *Page 77*
- The Burrell Collection – *Page 84*
- Gallery of Modern Art – *Page 84*
- Kelvingrove Art Gallery and Museum – *Page 85*
- Hunterian Art Gallery – *Page 85*
- Aberdeen Art Gallery – *Page 185*

Best museums
- Royal Museum of Scotland – *Page 49*
- National Museum of Scotland – *Page 49*
- Museum of Childhood – *Page 55*
- Kelvingrove Art Gallery and Museum – *Page 85*
- People's Palace – *Page 87*
- St Mungo Museum
  of Religious Life and Art – *Page 87*
- Pollok House – *Page 87*
- Crannog Centre – *Page 147*
- Elgin Museum – *Page 166*
- Maritime Museum – *Page 187*
- Grampian Transport Museum – *Page 192*
- Timespan Heritage Centre – *Page 238*
- Groam House Museum – *Page 241*
- Gairloch Heritage Museum – *Page 265*
- Skye Museum of Island Life – *Page 274*

Best gardens
- Royal Botanic Garden – *Page 49*
- Threave Garden – *Page 74*
- Glasgow Botanic Gardens – *Page 83*
- Arduaine Garden – *Page 112*
- Ardanaiseig Garden – *Page 113*
- Crarae Gardens – *Page 126*
- David Welch Winter Gardens – *Page 186*
- Cruickshank Botanic Garden – *Page 190*
- Branklyn Garden – *Page 206*
- Bell's Cherrybank Gardens – *Page 207*
- Achiltibuie Hydroponicum – *Page 254*

Best attractions for children
- Landmark Forest Theme Park – *Page 155*
- Highland Wildlife Park – *Page 156*
- Working Sheepdogs – *Page 156*
- Cairngorm Reindeer Centre – *Page 160*
- Inverness Aquadome – *Page 231*
- Smoo Cave – *Page 256*

Historic sights
- Bannockburn – *Page 92*
- National Wallace Monument – *Page 95*
- Glencoe – *Page 135*
- Glenfinnan – *Page 137*
- Killiecrankie – *Page 149*
- Culloden – *Page 224*

Best prehistoric sites
- Cairn Holy – *Page 80*
- Dunadd Fort – *Page 108*
- Kilmartin Glen, Linear Cemetery – *Page 110*
- Dunfallandy Stone – *Page 149*
- Sueno's Stone – *Page 167*
- Easter Aquhorthies – *Page 176*
- Loanhead of Daviot – *Page 178*
- Cairn Liath – *Page 237*
- Skara Brae – *Page 248*
- Ring of Brodgar – *Page 248*

Best walks
- Loch Katrine – *Page 101*
- Glen Nevis – *Page 137*
- Black Wood of Rannoch – *Page 153*
- The Angus Glens – *Page 202*
- Fife Coastal Path – *Page 219*
- Glen Affric – *Page 231*
- The Quirang – Skye – *Page 276*

Best scenic drives
- Detour from Aberfoyle to Inversnaid – *Page 103*
- Gruline to Calgary – *Page 123*
- Drive to Ardnamurchan Point – *Page 144*
- Drive through Glen Lyon – *Page 152*
- Drive to Rannoch Station – *Page 153*
- The drive to Fort William from Pitlochry via Dalwhinny – *Page 153*
- Northwest Highlands main route – *Page 260*
- Strathnaver detour – *Page 260*
- Assynt peninsula – *Page 261*
- Achiltibuie and Coigach peninsula – *Page 262*
- Bealach na Bà pass – *Page 269*
- Shieldaig to Gairloch past the Torridons and Loch Maree – *Page 270*
- Isle of Skye – *Page 279*

Best beauty spots
- Loch Awe – *Page 110*
- Loch Lomond – *Page 126*
- Falls of Dochart – *Page 149*
- Queen's View – *Page 153*
- Cairngorms – *Page 155*
- Linn of Dee – *Page 194*
- Loch Ness – *Page 229*
- Stacks of Duncansby – *Page 246*
- Dunnet Head – *Page 251*
- Kyle of Tongue – *Page 257*
- Loch Eriboll – *Page 261*
- Loch Maree – *Page 266*
- Torridon – *Page 267*
- Corrieshalloch Gorge and Falls of Measach – *Page 271*
- Cuillin Hills – *Page 272*

Best distilleries
- Glenturret – *Page 93*
- Tobermory – *Page 120*
- Glenfiddich – *Page 165*
- Strathisla – *Page 167*
- Glen Grant – *Page 168*
- Dallas Dhu – *Page 171*
- Cardhu – *Page 171*
- Glenlivet – *Page 172*
- Glenfarclas – *Page 172*

Edinburgh

Ratings

Architecture	●●●●●
Art	●●●●●
Food and drink	●●●●●
Historical sights	●●●●●
Museums	●●●●●
Shopping	●●●●●
Children	●●●○○
Wildlife	●○○○○

No tour of Scotland is complete without a visit to Edinburgh, and for many visitors this showcase city is the gateway to the rest of the country. Aesthetically and culturally, it is one of the most appealing cities in all of Europe. Beneath its distinctive skyline, Edinburgh wears its history in grand swathes that fall in long, neat folds like a tartan cape. From the medieval wynds of the Royal Mile to the Georgian elegance of the New Town, it is always delightful, hiding any grim corners neatly out of sight. Although smaller than Glasgow, Edinburgh has been Scotland's capital for nearly 500 years, and the Scottish Parliament convenes here again for the first time since 1707. Literature and the arts have long flourished in Edinburgh, and it is home to three national art collections and a number of galleries. Celebrations abound, especially in late summer, when the upper crust colludes with the decadent fringe to produce one of the greatest arts festivals in the world.

Getting there and getting around

ⓘ Edinburgh and Scotland Information Centre
Waverley Market, 3 Princes Street, Edinburgh EH2 2QP; tel: 0845 22 55 121 or 01506 832 121; e-mail: info@visitscotland.com is the main tourist information office. There is also a tourist information desk at Edinburgh Airport. Or visit the Edinburgh and Lothians website at *www.edinburgh.org*

Airport: Edinburgh Airport, *tel: 0870 040 0007*, is 8 miles (13km) from the city centre. Buses run every 10–15 minutes to Waverley Bridge during peak hours.

Rail: Waverley Station handles trains to all parts of the country and is located right in the city centre.

Parking: On-street parking is expensive in the city centre. Parking uses the 'pay-and-display' system, or parking meters. Parking is not allowed on the main roads into the city between 0800 and 1800 Mon–Sat. Other areas have parking restrictions. Look for signs detailing hours and length of stay. Many spaces are reserved for resident permit holders and visitors cannot park there. It is easier and usually less expensive to use the off-street car parks. Those outside the city centre are cheaper and have more space. The tourist office

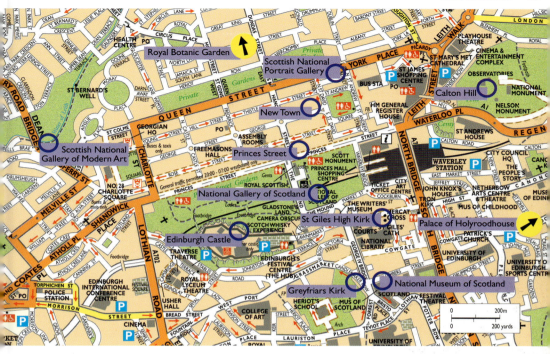

publishes a guide to 20 car parks, with notes on the parking guidance system and other useful information. There is a tow-away scheme for those who flout the regulations. Should you be so unfortunate, *tel: 0131 555 1742 (Tower Street Car Pound)/or the police tel: 0131 311 3131* to retrieve your vehicle.

Driving: All the main sights are centrally located and easily reached on foot or by bus, so driving is not necessary in the city centre.

Public transport: Edinburgh has an extensive bus system serving all parts of the city and enabling easy access to the centre from outlying areas. Fares are inexpensive, especially with a daily, weekly or multi-journey ticket. Some operators have an exact fare policy, so keep a supply of coins handy. All buses are non-smoking. For help in planning your journey, call National Traveline Service, *tel: 0871 200 22 33; www.traveline.org.uk*, or contact Lothian Buses (*Hanover Street; tel: 0131 555 6363; www.lothianbuses.co.uk*). For a good overview of the city, take an open-top sightseeing bus tour.

Sights

Calton Hill

If Edinburgh is the 'Athens of the North', Calton Hill, with its classical buildings, is its acropolis. This volcanic outcrop affords a splendid

Nelson Monument
£ *Calton Hill, tel: 0131
556 2716; www.cac.org.uk.
Open Apr–Sep Mon–Sat
1000–1800; Oct–Mar
Mon–Sat 1000–1500.*

Edinburgh Castle £££
*Castlehill; tel: 0131 225
9846;
www.edinburghcastle.gov.uk.
Open daily Apr–Sep
0930–1800; Oct–Mar
0930–1700. Last admission
45 minutes before closing
time.*

view of the city from the east end of Princes Street taking in
Edinburgh Castle, Arthur's Seat and the Firth of Forth. Climb the
staircase to the top from Waterloo Place, or drive up via a small road
off Regent Road, opposite St Andrew's House. Monuments include the
Old City Observatory, which is still used by students; the unfinished
National Monument, modelled on the Parthenon; the temple-like
Dugald Stewart Memorial, and the 106-ft (32-m) tall Nelson
Monument, topped with a viewing gallery. There is also a memorial to
Abraham Lincoln and the Scottish-Americans who died in the
American Civil War.

Edinburgh Castle

The impressive fortress that dominates the city from atop Castle Rock
has harboured royalty since the 11th century, although few of the
original structures remain. Tiny St Margaret's Chapel (12th century),
dedicated to Malcolm III's queen, is thought to be the oldest
building in the city. Once inside the Portcullis Gate, the northern
batteries provide superb views over Princes Street and the New Town.
A field gun salute is fired here daily at 1300. Surrounding Crown
Square at the heart of the castle are a military museum, the war
memorial, and the Great Hall with its restored hammerbeam roof.
Below ground are the sinister Vaults, formerly used as a prison and
now housing the great 15th-century siege cannon, Mons Meg. In the
east wing of the Palace Block is the chamber where Mary Queen of
Scots gave birth to James VI, and an exhibition on Scottish kings and
coronations that helps pass the time while queuing to see the Honours

Below
Edinburgh Castle

ⓘ Greyfriars Kirk
Greyfriars Place,
tel: 0131 226 5429;
www.greyfriarskirk.com.
Open Apr–Oct Mon–Fri
1030–1630, Sat
1030–1430; Nov–Mar Thu
1330–1530 or by
arrangement.

**National Gallery
of Scotland**
The Mound;
tel: 0131 624 6200;
www.nationalgalleries.org.
Open daily 1000–1700, Thu
until 1900. Admission charge
for special exhibitions.

of Scotland. These splendid crown jewels, the oldest in Britain, are reverently displayed alongside the Stone of Destiny upon which the Celtic kings were crowned (*see page 208*). As you wander around the grounds, make use of the free audiotape tours to take in the fascinating history of the castle and its inhabitants.

Greyfriars Kirk

Greyfriars Kirk (1620) was the first church to be built in the city after the Reformation. Its grounds formerly belonged to the friars of St Francis, or Greyfriars, from which it takes its name. Mary Queen of Scots gave the land to the town council to use as the city's burial ground, and the old tombstones and memorials dating from this time make for an interesting stroll. While the church itself is not particularly impressive, having suffered over the years from fire, a gunpowder explosion and Cromwell's army, it has two claims to fame. The National Covenant (*see page 78*) was adopted here in 1638, sparking off the bloody religious battles of the 17th century, and in 1679 more than 1000 Covenanters were imprisoned in the churchyard. An exhibit in the church tells the grim story.

The most famous figure, however, is Greyfriars Bobby. When his master was laid to rest in the churchyard in 1858, the little Skye terrier loyally guarded the grave until his own death 14 years later. The locals became so fond of the dog that they erected a memorial fountain nearby in Candlemaker Row.

National Gallery of Scotland

Housed in a fine neoclassical building designed by William Playfair in 1850–57, this gallery is a joy to visit. The collection, which features works from the Renaissance to Post-Impressionism, is neither too large or overwhelming, but contains enough outstanding masterpieces to leave viewers feeling happily satisfied. The interconnecting octagonal rooms and claret-coloured walls add a sense of elegance and intimacy. Pride of place goes to Canova's exquisite statue group, *The Three Graces*, while Rembrandt's *Self-Portrait At Age 51* (Gallery VI) and Julien Bastien-Lepage's expressive painting of a barge boy, *Pas Mèche* (Room A5), are also worth seeking out. The New Wing in the basement contains an extensive collection of Scottish paintings. Next door, the recently restored Royal Scottish Academy, also designed by Playfair, is a world-class space for showing major international exhibitions. It is joined to the National Gallery by an underground link.

New Town

By the turn of the 18th century, Edinburgh's Old Town was bursting at the seams and wealthier residents were desperate to escape the unhealthy squalor. James Craig, a young unknown architect, won the competition to design a new residential area with his simple symmetrical grid of streets linked by public squares. This comprised

**ⓗ The Georgian
House (National
Trust for Scotland) ££**
*7 Charlotte Square;
tel: 0131 226 3318;
www.nts.org.uk. Open
Apr–Oct daily 1000–1700;
Jul–Aug 1000–1800; Nov
and Mar 1100–1600.*

**Palace of
Holyroodhouse ££**
*Canongate, Royal Mile;
tel: 0131 556 5100;
www.royal.gov.uk. Open daily
Apr–Oct 0930–1800;
Nov–Mar 0930–1630 (last
admission 45 mins before
closing). May be closed
occasionally.*

the area between Queen Street and Princes Street, each of these facing gardens. Running parallel between them, connecting Charlotte and St Andrew squares at either end, is the 0.5-mile (0.8-km) long George Street, built wide enough to enable a coach and six horses to turn full circle. Its intersections, graced by statues, allow views down to the Forth and up to the castle and Old Town.

Charlotte Square, designed by Robert Adam in 1791, features elegant Georgian homes surrounding the green with its equestrian statue of Prince Albert. At No 7 the National Trust for Scotland has restored the **Georgian House** to its 18th-century splendour. Three floors reflect the lifestyle of the New Town well-to-do, from the airy green drawing room to the curious kitchen gadgets.

On the western side, the old St George's church, now West Register House, was intended to be balanced by a sister church in St Andrew Square. However, Sir Laurence Dundas finagled the land to build his private mansion, **Dundas House**, now the Royal Bank of Scotland headquarters. It's worth popping in for a peek at the opulent entrance hall, with gold leaf on the capitals and roof bosses, and the star-domed banking hall. The church, now called **St Andrew's and St George's**, built nearby on George Street, is worth a visit.

The streets of the New Town repay exploration for architecture buffs, primarily in spotting the decorative elements such as fanlights, cast ironwork, foot scrapers and lamp holders. For refreshment, Rose Street is lined with jolly pubs serving cheap meals.

Palace of Holyroodhouse

The Queen's official residence in Scotland lies at the end of the Royal Mile. The Abbey of Holy Rood was founded here by David I in 1128, and when the 15th-century monarchs preferred the abbey guesthouse to the castle as a place of residence, James IV began converting it into a palace and built the northwest tower. The abbey was burnt in 1650 during Cromwell's occupation, and its ruins are an odd anticlimax to a palace visit.

The Queen's standard flies when she is in residence, in which case the palace is closed. As it is used primarily for state functions, its atmosphere, although elegant, is rather cold. Highlights include the Throne Room and the Morning Drawing Room with its intricate, decorative ceiling and 17th-century French tapestries. Of most interest are the rooms in the round tower used by Mary Queen of Scots, including the room adjoining her bedchamber where her secretary David Rizzio was murdered.

The Queen's Gallery, which features rotating exhibits of fine art, opened in the palace as part of Her Majesty's Golden Jubilee celebrations in 2002. The adjacent Holyrood Park, marked by the volcanic Salisbury Crags, is Edinburgh's largest green space. From the car park on Queen's Road you can climb up to Arthur's Seat, at 823ft (244m), for a bird's-eye view.

Opposite
The view of Edinburgh from
Calton Hill

ⓘ The Scottish Tartans Museum £
39–41 Princes Street; tel: 0131 556 1252. Open Mon–Sat 0900–1730.

Royal Botanic Garden
20A Inverleith Row; tel: 0131 552 7171. Open daily Nov–Feb 1000–1600; Mar–Oct 1000–1800; Apr–Sep 1000–1900 Free. Charge for glasshouses.

National Museum of Scotland *Chambers Street; tel: 0131 225 7534; www.nms.ac.uk. Open Mon–Sat 1000–1700, Sun 1200–1700, Tue 1000–2000. Free.*

Princes Street

Edinburgh's main thoroughfare, part of the New Town development, had turned commercial by the middle of the 19th century. Today it is the city's primary shopping district. **Princes Street Gardens** run along the valley of the old Nor'Loch, drained in the 17th century, which once formed part of the castle defences. They contain the Scottish-American War Memorial and the Floral Clock, composed of around 2000 plants. Some two million cartloads of landfill from the New Town foundations were used to create **The Mound**, the sweeping link between Princes Street and the Old Town. The **Scott Monument**, rising 200ft (61m) to the tip of its Gothic spire, is an Edinburgh landmark; the viewing platforms provide good views over the town centre. Nearby, inside the Scotch House, the **Scottish Tartans Museum** displays some 700 tartans, including rare pieces dating back to the 4th century.

Royal Botanic Garden

With over 70 landscaped acres (28ha), the botanic garden, established in 1670, is among the country's most popular attractions. Highlights

include the Rock Garden, the Arboretum, the Pringle Chinese Collection and the masses of rhododendrons. The Glasshouse Experience leads you along a floral trail through several continents.

National Museum of Scotland

The story of Scotland and its people is told in a fascinating collection of exhibits spread over seven levels. The roof terrace affords splendid views over the city. Adjacent to the museum, the magnificent Victorian building that houses the **Royal Museum of Scotland** is undergoing a renovation (due for completion 2012) that will enhance the exhibition space and better integrate the two museums. Its world-class collections include natural history, archaeology, geology, costume and decorative art. More than half the building will stay open during the renovation.

St Giles' Cathedral
*Royal Mile; tel: 0131
225 9442; Open May–Sep
Mon–Fri 0900–1900, Sat
0900–1700, Sun
1300–1700; Oct–Apr
Mon–Sat 0900–1700, Sun
1300–1700.*

**Scottish National
Gallery of Modern Art**
*75 Belford Road;
tel: 0131 624 6200;
www.nationalgalleries.org.
Open daily 1000–1700.
Admission charge for special
exhibitions.*

**Scottish National
Portrait Gallery**
*1 Queen Street;
tel: 0131 624 6200;
www.nationalgalleries.org.
Open daily 1000–1700,
Thu 1000–1900. Admission
charge for special exhibitions.*

City Art Centre
*2 Market Street; tel: 0131
529 3993; www.cac.org.uk.
Open Mon–Sat 1000–1700,
Sun 1200–1700.*

**The Fruitmarket
Gallery** *45 Market Street;
tel: 0131 225 2383;
www.fruitmarket.co.uk.
Open Mon–Sat 1100–1800,
Sun 1200–1700.*

Stills Gallery
*23 Cockburn Street;
tel: 0131 622 6200;
www.stills.org. Open daily
1100–1800.*

Talbot Rice Gallery
*Old College, South Bridge;
tel: 0131 650 2210;
www.trg.ed.ac.uk. Open
Tue–Sat 1000–1700.*

The Dean Gallery
*73 Belford Road;
tel: 0131 624 6200;
www.nationalgalleries.org.
Open daily 1000–1700.*

St Giles, High Kirk of Edinburgh

For centuries St Giles was the only church in the Old Town. It is often called the Cathedral, although it only achieved this status briefly in the 17th century. The fiery reformer John Knox served as minister here. Its impressive crown spire, an Edinburgh landmark, is one of the few surviving features of the original 15th-century building. The 19th-century refacing of the exterior destroyed much of its character, and the interior also suffered during the Reformation, when the statue of the patron saint was cast into the Nor'Loch. Even so, its sheer size and details such as the fine windows and the chancel vaulting are impressive. The highlight is the ornately carved **Thistle Chapel** (20th century). Look for the wooden angel playing the bagpipes!

Scottish National Gallery of Modern Art

Just outside the town centre to the west of the New Town, this collection of 20th-century art is housed in a neoclassical former school building. The comprehensive collection of Scottish works is particularly strong on the Scottish Colourists – Fergusson, Peploe, Hunter and Cadell – while the international collection features a sampling of the major names and movements, with the surrealist collection a highlight. The spacious wooded grounds make a fine backdrop for the works of Hepworth, Moore and others in the sculpture garden. The cafeteria is a local favourite.

Scottish National Portrait Gallery

Put faces to the names of Scotland's kings, queens, heroes and literary giants. This celebration of Scottishness is housed in a Gothic Revival building of 1889 and includes many fine portraits of famous characters right up to the present day. There are also changing exhibitions and photography displays.

Galleries

In addition to the national art collections, Edinburgh has several noteworthy galleries. The **City Art Centre** houses Edinburgh's own collection of Scottish paintings in a former warehouse on Market Street and also stages top-quality international exhibitions. Across the road, the **Fruitmarket Gallery** is a showcase for national and international contemporary art and design. Nearby on Cockburn Street, the **Stills Gallery** is Scotland's premier photographic gallery specialising in international contemporary work. Edinburgh University's Old Masters collection is on display at the **Talbot Rice Gallery**, which also sponsors seven temporary exhibitions each year.

The former Dean Orphanage, a Victorian building designed by William Playfair, is the home of a more recent addition to Edinburgh's

Most shops are *open from 0900 to 1730,* with late-night shopping on *Thursday until 1930 or 2000.* Many of the larger stores are *open on Sunday,* as are those catering for tourists.

All the familiar high-street chains, such as Next and Marks & Spencer, have shops on Princes Street or Frederick and Hanover streets. Jenners, at 48 Princes Street, is to Edinburgh what Harrods is to London. Its newest rival is Harvey Nichols, the first branch of the popular Knightsbridge London store to open in Scotland, with designer labels, a food hall, restaurant and even an Oxygen Bar.

The Royal Mile has several shops selling Scottish woollens, clothing and traditional Highland dress. Towards the bottom end are speciality shops such as R Somerville (*82 Canongate*) with over 2000 different packs of playing cards.

Victoria Street and the Grassmarket is another area for original boutiques and giftshops. Mr Wood's Fossils (*5 Cowgatehead*) is famous in its field. Byzantium (*9a Victoria Street*) is a small market in a converted church where you'll find everything from jewellery and crafts to maps and antique lace. The New Town has a wealth of antiques shops.

art scene, the **Dean Gallery**. Along with changing exhibitions of modern art, it features the Paolozzi sculpture and graphic art collection.

Entertainment

In August, Edinburgh becomes the Festival City. The **Edinburgh International Festival** offers music, theatre and dance from top performers around the world. Close on its heels, the **Festival Fringe** is an avant-garde gathering of artists, musicians, actors and comedians, and throughout the month the city pulsates non-stop with both official and impromptu performances and events. The

Above right
Balanchine's *Don Quixote* at the Edinburgh International Festival

Above
John Knox House, Royal Mile home of the 16th-century religious reformer

🚫 Note that many attractions are also open on Sundays during the **Edinburgh Festival**, and some may have longer hours in high summer.

According to legend, the thistle became the floral emblem of Scotland after Viking invaders trod on this humble weed and their cries warned the Scots of imminent attack. James III first used the thistle as a royal emblem in the 15th century. James VII of Scotland (James II of England) established the Order of the Thistle in 1687, and it was revived by Queen Anne in 1703.

Edinburgh Military Tattoo takes place in the same month on the Castle Esplanade, and if that weren't enough, the Film, Book and Jazz festivals are also held at this time.

Edinburgh's second great festival is **Hogmanay**, the Scottish New Year celebration, with a spectacular Fire Procession and fireworks, a carnival and open-air concerts running for several days. Other events throughout the year include the International Science Festival in April, and festivals devoted to storytelling, puppetry and animation.

King's Theatre (*2 Leven Street; tel: 0131 529 6000; www.eft.co.uk*) presents drama, musicals, dance and pantomime in an Edwardian setting, while the **Edinburgh Playhouse** (*18–21 Greenside Place; tel: 0870 606 3424*) hosts West End musicals. The **Royal Lyceum Theatre Company** (*Grindlay Street; tel: 0131 248 4848; www.lyceum.org.uk*) is Edinburgh's leading drama company and performs in a beautiful Victorian theatre. **Traverse Theatre** (*10 Cambridge Street; tel: 0131 228 1404; www.traverse.co.uk*) puts on original and experimental productions in a modern venue. The **Edinburgh Festival Theatre** (*13–29 Nicolson Street; tel: 0131 529 6000; www.eft.co.uk*) offers an international programme of opera, ballet, drama and dance. Concert halls include **Usher Hall** (*Lothian Road; tel: 0131 228 1155; www.usherhall.co.uk*) and the **Queen's Hall** (*Clerk Street; tel: 0131 668 2019; www.thequeenshall.net*).

If you fancy an evening of Scottish dancing and entertainment, there are several dinner shows around town. Check with the tourist information office. For listings of clubs, music and events, try the Saturday edition of *The Scotsman*, or *The List*.

Accommodation and food

Edinburgh is such a popular destination that it's busy all year round, and it is always advisable to book ahead. There are all the luxurious and comfortable city-centre hotels one would expect, as well as plenty of lower-priced guesthouses and B&Bs within easy reach of the core attractions. If you want to come at Festival time, however, it is essential to book far in advance. Prices are also highest at this time, and finding suitable last-minute accommodation is very difficult.

For help with reserving accommodation, contact the Edinburgh and Scotland Information Centre (*Waverley Market; 3 Princes Street; Edinburgh EH2 2QP*). Or call the Edinburgh and Lothians Tourist Board (*tel: 0845 22 55 121 or 01506 832 121; e-mail: info@visitscotland.com*)

The Athens of the North

The many writers and visionaries who made their base in Edinburgh gave the city its sobriquet 'the Athens of the North'. Sir Arthur Conan Doyle, creator of Sherlock Holmes, was born in Picardy Place and is commemorated there with a statue of the great detective. Robert Louis Stevenson, another native, wrote a poem about the local lamplighter he watched from his window at 17 Heriot Row in the New Town, and Sir Walter Scott penned many poems and novels from his home on Castle Street. He met his idol Robbie Burns at a literary soirée, as indeed Burns met his 'Clarinda', the subject of his greatest love poem, here. The city can also claim the first publication of *Encyclopaedia Britannica*, the first circulating library, and the first British university to admit women (in 1884). Today Edinburgh boasts more booksellers per head of population than any other city in Britain.

who can make the booking for you. You can also view and book accommodation online, at *www.edinburgh.org*

Edinburgh has a cosmopolitan range of restaurants and you can find Southeast Asian, Indian, Mexican and European cuisines alongside top-quality Scottish fare. A trendy area for wining and dining with numerous good restaurants is Leith, the city's seaport. Many wine bars and pubs also serve inexpensive meals, especially at lunchtime.

Allison House Hotel £ *17 Mayfield Gardens; tel: 0800 328 9003 or 0131 667 8049; fax: 0131 667 5001; e-mail: enquiry@allisonhousehotel.com; www.allisonhousehotel.com.* On the south side of the city, this lovely family-run hotel is convenient for both the city centre and surrounding regions. Several of the large, comfortable rooms look out over delightful gardens to Arthur's Seat. Complimentary sherry and whisky decanters when you arrive, and free wifi internet access. Off-street parking and regular bus service to the city centre.

Whighams Wine Cellars ££ *13 Hope Street; tel: 0131 225 8674; www.whighams.com.* Boisterous basement wine bar full of character, and if you can grab a table you'll get friendly service and delicious food, including the perfect risotto.

The Witchery ££ *Castlehill, Royal Mile; tel: 0131 225 5613; www.thewitchery.com.* By the gates of Edinburgh Castle, this highly acclaimed restaurant serves classic cuisine with inspired accompaniments, such as seared scallops served with lobster risotto. Classy dining room. Outstanding wine cellar. Book well ahead.

Channings £££ *15 South Learmonth Gardens; tel: 0131 315 2226; reservations: 0131 274 7405; fax: 0131 332 9631; e-mail: reserve@ channings.co.uk; www.channings.co.uk.* Lovely, quiet hotel with 46 rooms set in five joined Edwardian townhouses in a cobbled street. Attentive service, comfortable lounge rooms with fireplaces, terraced garden, fine dining in **Channings Restaurant**, or a light meal in the wine bar with its extensive bar menu. Fifteen minutes' walk from the city centre.

Suggested tour

⓫ Edinburgh Old Town Weaving Company £ 555 Castlehill; tel: 0131 226 1555; www.geoffreykilts.co.uk. Open Mon–Sat 0900–1730, Sun 1000–1730; Apr–Oct Mon–Sat 0900–1830, Sun 1000–1830.

Camera Obscura ££ Castlehill; tel: 0131 226 3709. Open daily Apr–Oct 0930–1800; Jul–Aug 0930–1930; Nov–Mar 1000–1700.

Scotch Whisky Experience ££ 354 Castlehill; tel: 0131 220 0441. Open daily 1000–1800; May–Sep 0930–1830.

Gladstone's Land (National Trust for Scotland) ££ 477b Lawnmarket; tel: 0131 226 5856; www.nts.org.uk. Open Apr–Oct daily 1000–1700; Jul–Aug 1000–1900.

Writers' Museum Lady Stair's Close; tel: 0131 529 4901; www.cac.org.uk. Open Mon–Sat 1000–1700, Sun 1200–1700. Free.

Museum of Childhood 42 High Street; tel: 0131 529 4142; www.cac.org.uk. Open Mon–Sat 1000–1700, Sun 1200–1700. Free.

Brass Rubbing Centre Trinity Apse, Chalmers Close; tel: 0131 556 4364; www.cac.org.uk. Open Apr–Sep Mon–Sat 1000–1630. Free.

John Knox House £ 43–45 High Street; tel: 0131 556 9579. Open Mon–Sat 1000–1800, also Sun 1200–1800 in Jul–Sep.

Edinburgh's famous Royal Mile runs from the 'crag' of Castle Rock down the 'tail' to the Palace of Holyroodhouse. It is actually a succession of four streets – Castlehill, Lawnmarket, High Street and Canongate – lined with visitor attractions, eateries, pubs and, of course, shops. You can walk the Royal Mile in 30 minutes, although if you take in the sights you will have a full day. The detour to Grassmarket and Greyfriars Kirk will add another 30 minutes, and you can extend the walk by an hour by returning along Princes Street. Those with limited time should concentrate on the Castle and the walk along the Royal Mile.

Your starting point for this route depends to a large degree on your stamina. If you're fit and enthusiastic, approach the castle on the steep path through Princes Street Gardens to get a sense of the fortress's impregnable strength. If you're driving, you can park at the castle esplanade for a moderate fee and walk the Royal Mile, although you may want to save the Mound and Princes Street for a separate tour to avoid the uphill walk back to your car. The gardens close early in autumn and winter, so note the signs if you plan to return this way.

Begin your tour at **EDINBURGH CASTLE ❶**, allowing up to an hour and a half for a visit. As you start down Castlehill, attractions beckon. The **Edinburgh Old Town Weaving Company ❷** tells the story of tartan production, the **Camera Obscura ❸** presents a view of the city through a giant Victorian camera, while tours at the **Scotch Whisky Experience ❹** show the whisky-making process. As you wander along the Royal Mile, venture into the atmospheric wynds (narrow passages) leading off the main street and imagine the sights, sounds and smells of the teeming medieval city. At Lawnmarket, look for the small street called Upper Bow to the right of the roundabout. Peer over the railings at its end for a charming view of Victoria Street below. Lawnmarket has two sights of interest, the restored 17th-century merchant's house, **Gladstone's Land ❺**, and the **Writers' Museum ❻** situated down the close in Lady Stair's House, with memorabilia of Robert Burns, Sir Walter Scott and Robert Louis Stevenson.

Turn right at the main street called George IV Bridge for a detour along **Victoria Street ❼**. This picturesque little street, lined with interesting boutiques and good restaurants, curves down to the **Grassmarket ❽**, the medieval marketplace. St Andrew's Cross, surrounded by railings, marks the hanging place where criminals and the Covenant martyrs were executed. From here it's a short stroll up Candlemaker's Row to **GREYFRIARS KIRK ❾**. Return to the Royal Mile via George IV Bridge.

After a visit to **ST GILES ❿**, notice the other landmarks on Parliament Square: the Mercat Cross, Parliament Hall (now the law courts) and the Heart of Midlothian, a heart shape set into the cobbles which marks the location of the old tolbooth.

The Museum of Edinburgh *142*
Canongate; tel: 0131 529 4143. Open Mon–Sat 1000–1700, also Sun 1200–1700 in Aug.

The People's Story
Tolbooth, Canongate; tel: 0131 529 4057; www.cac.org.uk. Open Mon–Sat 1000–1700, also Sun 1200–1700 in Aug.

Craigmillar Castle £
Tel: 0131 661 4445; www.historic-scotland.gov.uk. Open daily Apr–Sep 0930–1730; Oct–Mar Sat–Wed 0930–1630.

Royal Yacht Britannia ££
Ocean Terminal, Leith; tel: 0131 555 5566; www. royalyachtbritannia.co.uk. Open Apr–Oct 1000–1630; Nov–Mar 1000–1530.

Scottish Parliament Building *Horse Wynd; tel: 0131 348 5000; www.scottish.parliament.uk. Open daily, tours ££.*

High Street attractions include the **Museum of Childhood ⑪**, the **Brass Rubbing Centre ⑫** in Chalmers Close and the **John Knox House ⑬**, although the reformer's presumed residence here is dubious. Further along, **The Museum of Edinburgh ⑭** is filled with historic shop signs, pottery, glass and artefacts, while **The People's Story ⑮** presents an insightful view of everyday life in the Royal Mile.

End your tour with a visit (allow an hour) to the abbey and **PALACE OF HOLYROODHOUSE ⑯**. Opposite the palace is the striking new Scottish Parliament Building, designed by the late Catalan architect Enric Miralles with materials and motifs that represent Scotland's landscape and heritage. You can see the interior on a guided tour. Return along the Royal Mile, or extend the walk by following Calton Road to Waterloo Place. From here you can climb Calton Hill, or head west along Princes Street to the Mound and Princes Street Gardens.

Also worth seeing

Craigmillar Castle, 3 miles (5km) southeast, is an impressive fortress where Mary Queen of Scots fled after the murder of her secretary, David Rizzio, and where her enemies plotted the murder of her husband. The **Royal Yacht Britannia** sailed over 1 million miles (1.6 million km) before making her final home in the historic port of Leith. You'll see the Royal Apartments, Sun Lounge, State Dining Room and the working ship on a tour of her five decks.

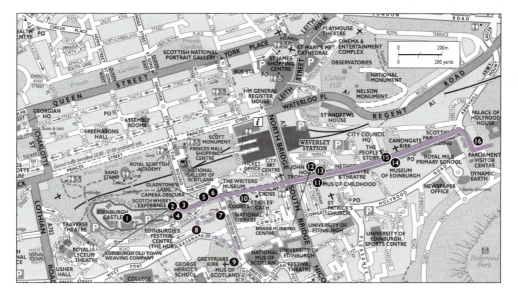

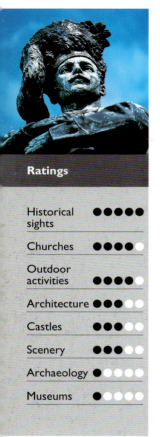

The Lothians

Ratings

Historical sights	●●●●●
Churches	●●●●○
Outdoor activities	●●●●○
Architecture	●●●○○
Castles	●●●○○
Scenery	●●●○○
Archaeology	●○○○○
Museums	●○○○○

Edinburgh sits at the heart of the Lothians, a region rich in history and attractions. It is well worth enduring the tangle of traffic and roadways on the outskirts of the city for a foray into the countryside, and the Lothians offer many day-trip possibilities that provide an enjoyable sampler of Scotland for those who haven't the time to explore farther afield. The West Lothians, lying in the central belt between Edinburgh, Glasgow and Stirling, are crossed by busy motorways whose slip-roads lead to great stately homes, country parks and even a Neolithic sanctuary. The East Lothians are blessed with Scotland's sunniest and driest weather. This region is a golfer's heaven, with over 20 excellent courses running parallel to the magnificent coastal scenery. Here, and in Midlothian, there are atmospheric castles and churches to explore, pretty villages and a host of sightseeing and recreational pursuits that provide ample interest for a longer holiday.

CRICHTON CASTLE

Crichton Castle £
Near Pathead, Midlothian; tel: 01875 320 017; www.historic-scotland.gov.uk. Open Easter–Sep daily 0930–1730.

Set in beautiful countryside, Crichton Castle is unique for its Italian-style diamond-faceted stonework. It was built between the late 14th and late 16th centuries; the outstanding north façade, added by the fifth Earl of Bothwell, dates from 1591. Although in ruins, the rooms of the castle contain fine architectural details. Crichton Parish Church (15th century) is also worth a look.

DIRLETON

Charming cottages surround a pretty village green, overlooked by the ruins of Dirleton Castle. The fortress's two circular towers were built in the early 13th century by the De Vaux family. In 1298 it fell to the

Dirleton Castle and Gardens £

Dirleton, near North Berwick; tel: 01620 850 330; www.historic-scotland.gov.uk. Open daily Easter–Sep 0930–1730; Oct–Mar 0930–1630.

English king, Edward I, and was strategically significant until destroyed by Cromwell's troops in 1650. Among the ruins are apartments, vaults, a chapel and a dungeon dug out of solid rock. There are also beautiful gardens and a 17th-century bowling green lined with yew trees. East of the castle, an access road leads to a scenic sandy beach at Yellowcraigs; the island of Fidra lies offshore.

DUNBAR

Dunbar Tourist Information Centre *143 High Street; tel: 01368 863 353. Open Apr–Sep.*

John Muir Birthplace *126 High Street, Dunbar; tel: 01368 865 899; www.jmbt.org.uk. Open Apr–Oct Mon–Sat 1000–1700, Sun 1300–1700; Nov–Mar closed Mon and Tue.*

Once a thriving fishing port, Dunbar is one of the sunniest spots in Scotland. The elegant sandstone buildings lining the High Street were built in the 18th century. The façade of **Lauderdale House**, at the north end, has many features by Robert Adam. Breweries have been sited here since the Middle Ages, and traditional real ales are still produced. The town's two harbours are overlooked by the ruins of **Dunbar Castle**, where Mary Queen of Scots stayed prior to her marriage to the Earl of Bothwell in 1567. It was one of the most important Scottish strongholds of the Middle Ages, as it commanded the coastal route used by English invaders. The Scots were defeated here in 1296 by Edward I, and by Cromwell in 1650. John Muir, the 19th-century conservationist who founded America's national park system, was born here; you can visit his **birthplace** and the **John Muir Country Park**, which encompasses 175 acres (71ha) of coastal scenery.

The Falkirk Wheel

At the heart of a millennium project to rejuvenate the Forth & Clyde and Union canals was the Falkirk Wheel. This 115-ft (35-m) revolving boat lift replaced the flight of 11 locks that originally connected the two canals. Made of glistening steel, it has two giant, water-filled caissons capable of carrying four boats at a time. Boats are transported between the canals in one smooth seven-minute movement. Visitors can ride the wheel on a boat trip, starting from the Falkirk Wheel Visitor Centre. *www.thefalkirkwheel.co.uk*

HADDINGTON

St Mary's Collegiate Church
Sidegate, Haddington;
tel: 01620 823 109.
Open May–Sep Mon–Sat
1100–1600, Sun
1400–1630.

Lennoxlove House £
Haddington; tel: 01620 823
720; www.lennoxlove.com.
Open Apr–Oct Wed, Thu
and Sun 1330–1700.

Haddington, set on the banks of the River Tyne, was founded in the 12th century and at one time was the country's fourth-largest town. It was the birthplace of the Reformation leader John Knox, and was a popular place of residence for Scottish royalty. Although it was ransacked and burned several times in its tumultuous history, some 284 listed buildings have survived and today it is one of the best-preserved 18th-century towns in Scotland. The High Street, with its market cross and the handsome townhouse built by William Adam in 1748, is lined with prosperous Georgian façades. Lodge Street, Market Street and Hardgate, with the harled and gabled Kinloch House, are all worth exploring. Look for the wealth of decorative detail on chimneys, dormer windows, balconies and cornices. **St Mary's Church** is the country's largest parish church, dating back to the 14th century. **Lennoxlove House**, seat of the Duke of Hamilton, has fine furnishings and artefacts connected with Mary Queen of Scots.

HOPETOUN HOUSE

Hopetoun House ££
South Queensferry;
tel: 0131 331 2451;
www.hopetounhouse.com.
Open Easter–Sep daily
1030–1700.

This opulent pile is situated in 100 acres (40.5ha) of parkland along the shores of the Firth of Forth at South Queensferry. Hopetoun House is the work of two outstanding Scottish architects. The original building, designed by Sir William Bruce in the classical style and constructed between 1699 and 1707, is adorned with superb carving, wainscoting and ceiling painting. In 1721 the house was enlarged by the architect William Adam, who added the handsome façade, colonnades, ballroom and state apartments. Hopetoun House is stuffed with treasures and fine furnishings that reflect the elegant lifestyle of the 18th-century Scottish aristocracy. George IV's visit to Hopetoun House in 1822 prompted the revival of Highland dress and an interest in Scottish traditions. There are fine views from the rooftop terrace, while the grounds contain a Spring Garden, Red Deer Park, picnic spots and woodland walks.

LINLITHGOW

ⓘ Burgh Halls *High Street, tel: 01506 844 600. Open Apr–Sep.*

ⓘ Linlithgow Palace £ *Tel: 01506 842 896; www.historic-scotland.gov.uk. Open daily Easter–Sep 1030–1700; Oct–Mar 0930–1630.*

The Linlithgow Story £ *Annet House, 143 High Street; tel: 01506 670 677; www.linlithgowstory.org.uk. Open Apr–Oct Mon–Sat 1100–1700, Sun 1300–1600.*

St Michael's Kirk *Tel: 01506 842 188. Open Apr–Sep daily 1030–1600; Oct–Mar Mon–Fri 1030–1530.*

House of the Binns ££ *Near Linlithgow; tel: 01506 834 255; www.nts.org.uk. Open Jun–Sep Sat–Wed 1400–1700.*

Below
Lochside Linlithgow Palace

Once an important royal burgh, Linlithgow grew up beside the loch, around the **palace** which was founded in the 13th century. It became the favourite royal residence of the Stuart kings, James IV and James V, who enlarged it and made it a grand place of merrymaking. Mary Queen of Scots was born here in 1542. Cromwell and his troops occupied the palace from 1650 to 1659. Following a brief visit by Bonnie Prince Charlie in 1745, the Duke of Cumberland's men accidentally set the palace on fire, leaving it a roofless shell. Its sheer size, however, is impressive and the architectural details in many of the rooms make it worth exploring.

In the High Street, which retains its medieval features, **The Linlithgow Story** at **Annet House** recounts the history of the prosperous town. In 1822, the **Union Canal** opened, linking Edinburgh to the Forth & Clyde canal, near Falkirk. The Canal Museum has displays about the waterway, and there are half-hour boat trips as well as longer cruises to the Avon aqueduct. **St Michael's Kirk**, rebuilt in the 15th century after its predecessor was destroyed by fire, is one of the largest pre-Reformation churches in Scotland. The windows are particularly fine, with their decorative tracery and stained glass. The highlight is the window in the south transept chapel; it was here that James IV reportedly saw a ghost who warned him not to fight at Flodden in 1513 (he ignored it and was killed in the battle).

Near Linlithgow, the **House of the Binns** has been the home of the Dalyell family since the 17th century. It contains portraits, period furniture and a collection of porcelain. There are good views over the Forth from the extensive grounds.

MUSSELBURGH

The largest town in East Lothian, Musselburgh is situated on the River Esk and gained its present appellation from the bountiful mussel beds in the estuary. The tollbooth was built in 1590 from the ruins of a chapel that had been destroyed by the English. The townsfolk were apparently unaware that it was a sacrilege to use the sacred stones and the whole town was excommunicated for more than 200 years. Tradition has it that James IV played on the ancient golf course here in 1504. The local fishwives took to the sport in the 18th century, with the golf club putting up a special prize for the best player. The town also boasts Scotland's oldest racecourse, founded in 1816, and its oldest sporting trophy, the Silver Arrow, contested by the Royal Company of Archers each year.

NORTH BERWICK

North Berwick Tourist Information Centre
Quality Street;
tel: 01620 892 197;
e-mail:
info@visitscotland.com.
Open Jan–Oct.

Formerly a prosperous grain and fishing port, North Berwick is a popular holiday resort with large sandy beaches, golf courses and a host of shops and galleries. The conical volcanic hill called North Berwick Law rises 613ft (187m) behind the town, giving splendid views of the sea and countryside. Three miles (5km) offshore, Bass Rock harbours gannets, puffins, guillemots and razorbills in its sheer cliffs, making it one of Europe's most important seabird colonies. You can see them on a summer ferryboat trip which circles the rock, and learn about them at the new National Seabird Centre in town.

ROSSLYN CHAPEL

Rosslyn Chapel ££
Roslin; tel: 0131 440 2159; www.rosslyn-chapel.com. Open Apr–Sep Mon–Sat 0930–1800, rest of year 1700, Sun 1200–1645.

Just outside the village of Roslin, this Gothic chapel has arguably the best medieval stone carving in the country. It was founded by Sir William St Clair, Third Earl of Orkney, who intended to build a much larger monument that was never completed. Work began in 1446, but ceased 40 years later, following the earl's death. The rich decorative detail covering every interior surface is awesome. The magnificent carvings are full of biblical and masonic symbolism, as well as pagan figures such as the 'green man'. The Apprentice Pillar is outstanding, while carvings of New World plants predate the voyage of Columbus. The chapel is situated above the wooded Rosslyn Glen, where there are good walks and views of Rosslyn Castle (private). Rosslyn Chapel features prominently in *The Da Vinci Code*, the best-selling novel by Dan Brown.

South Queensferry

South Queensferry takes its name from the first ferry across the Firth of Forth, which was established here in the 11th century by Queen Margaret to aid pilgrims travelling to Dunfermline. The service continued until 1964, when the New Road Bridge opened. The town's esplanade is the place to view the great Forth bridges – road and rail – that link Edinburgh and the south with Fife. The cantilevered **Forth Rail Bridge**, which opened in 1890, was an engineering feat in its day and remains a magnificent, 1.5-mile (2.4-km) long landmark of steel. A visitor centre on the north bank (follow signs to the tourist information centre off the approach to the road bridge) tells the fascinating story of its construction.

To the west of town is **Hopetoun House** (*see page 58*). **Dalmeny House**, to the east, is filled with French furniture, beautiful paintings, tapestries, porcelain and a Napoleonic collection. There are pleasant walks through the lovely grounds and along the shore of the Forth.

Dalmeny House ££
South Queensferry;
tel: 0131 331 1888;
www.dalmeny.co.uk.
*Reopening during 2009
with new opening times;
call for times.*

Tantallon Castle

Tantallon Castle £
Near North Berwick;
tel: 01620 892 727;
www.historic-scotland.gov.uk.
*Open Apr–Sep daily
0930–1730; Oct–Mar
Sat–Wed 0930–1630.*

Sir Walter Scott described Tantallon in his poem *Marmion* as 'broad, massive, high and stretching far'. Built in the late 14th century, it was the stronghold of the powerful earls of Douglas until it was captured by General Monck in 1651. Now in ruins, it is darkly impressive, with its formidable clifftop position surrounded on three sides by the sea. The landward side is protected by massive curtain walls 50ft (15m) high and more than 12ft (3.6m) thick which connect the red sandstone towers. You can explore the towers, apartments, pit prison and wall-walk. Bass Rock lies offshore.

Accommodation and food

Greywalls £££ *Muirfield, Gullane, tel: 01620 842 144; fax: 01620 842 241; e-mail: enquiries@greywalls.co.uk; www.greywalls.co.uk.* Designed by the famous Edwardian architect Sir Edwin Lutyens, this grand family

Above
The Forth Rail Bridge

➔ The outskirts of Edinburgh can be quite congested with numerous roads converging in a series of roundabouts, but roads are generally well signposted.

➋ Many towns can be easily reached by train, but you will need a car to visit the stately homes unless you take an organised coach tour.

⛳ Along with numerous golf clubs, the Lothians offer a range of sporting activities including sailing, fly-fishing, riding and horseracing. The tourist office has a list of venues.

🅹 **Prestongrange Industrial Heritage Museum**
Morison's Haven, Prestonpans; tel: 0131 653 2904; www. prestongrangemuseum.org. Open Apr–Oct daily 1100–1630. Free.

Seton Collegiate Church £
Longniddry; tel: 01875 813 334; www.historic-scotland. gov.uk. Open Easter–Sep daily 0930–1730.

Myreton Motor Museum ££
Aberlady; tel: 01875 870 288. Open daily mid-Mar–Nov.

home became one of the first country-house hotels in Britain in 1948. Its unusual crescent shape is surrounded by extensive walled gardens, designed by the renowned Gertrude Jekyll, which make a beautiful retreat. The 23 bedrooms are luxuriously appointed and individually decorated with antiques. Public rooms, such as the large panelled library lined with books and warmed by a log fire, are tastefully and comfortably arranged for relaxation. The dining room serves outstanding gourmet cuisine, with a creative table d'hôte menu made from fresh local produce, finished off with hand-made chocolates. Gentlemen are requested to wear a jacket and tie for dinner. Greywalls borders the championship Muirfield golf course.

Suggested tour

Total distance: 75 miles (120km) for the East Lothians and 50 miles (80km) for the West Lothians, both round-trip from Edinburgh.

Time: Driving time for each of the routes is about 2 hours, depending on the traffic around the city. Allow a full day for each if you plan to visit the stately homes and castles.

Links: Ambitious sightseers could combine the East and West Lothians into one long day's drive using the ring roads around the city, although this would only allow time for brief visits to one or two sights. The East Lothian route is easily combined with a longer tour of the Borders region. The West Lothian sights can be seen en route to Stirling or the Kingdom of Fife.

East Lothian route: Leave Edinburgh on the A199 and follow signs for **MUSSELBURGH ❶**. Continue east on the B1348 along the coast to **Prestonpans ❷**, where Bonnie Prince Charlie won a victory over the English in 1745. The market cross, dating from the early 17th century, survives in its original form and position. There is also an industrial heritage museum. Follow the B1348 through the fishing villages of **Cockenzie ❸** and **Port Seton ❹**, with its colourful harbour. One mile (1.6km) southeast is the lovely 15th-century Seton Collegiate Church. Continue on the A198 through **Longniddry ❺**, where Gosford House, designed by Robert Adam (1800), overlooks the Firth of Forth. **Aberlady ❻**, an attractive village and golfing centre, was the 12th-century port for Haddington. The striking neo-Gothic cottages were built in the 19th century. Transport buffs can visit the **Myreton Motor Museum** outside the town. The A198 passes Luffness Castle (13th century) on its way to **Gullane ❼**, famous for its British Open Championship golf course. Continue on the A198 to visit **DIRLETON ❽** and **NORTH BERWICK ❾**. Three miles (5km) beyond the town, the ruins of **TANTALLON CASTLE ❿** (14th century) loom dramatically on the clifftop. The A198 turns inland to **Whitekirk ⓫**. The 15th-century church of St Mary's, with its Norman square tower,

Freeport Shopping and Leisure Village at West Calder in the West Lothians has a range of factory outlet stores for both high-street and independent retailers. Take the M8 to Junction 4 and follow signs for Freeport Leisure Village.

Eyemouth Tourist Information Centre *Auld Kirk, Market Place; tel: 08706 080404; e-mail: info@visitscotland.com. Open Easter–Oct.*

Preston Mill and Phantassie Dovecot *£ East Linton; tel: 01620 860 426; www.nts.org.uk. Open Jun–Sep Thu–Mon 1300–1700.*

National Museum of Flight *££ East Fortune Airfield, East Lothian; tel: 01620 897 240; www.nms.ac.uk. Open daily 1000–1700.*

Below St Abb's Head

had a holy well and was a centre of pilgrimage; the nearby tithe barn is one of the oldest in the country. **Tyninghame** ⑫ is a charming village of pink sandstone cottages with pantiled roofs. At the junction beyond the village, turn left (east) on the A1, then take the A1087 to join the coast again at **DUNBAR** ⑬.

Detour: If you're taken with the splendid ocean scenery, continue south from Dunbar on the A1 along the the Berwickshire coast. Above **Pease Bay** ⑭, with its sandy beach and Pease Dene Nature Reserve, is the clifftop hamlet of **Cove** ⑮; the town's fishermen reached the harbour through a tunnel. Follow the A1107 to **Coldingham** ⑯. The Priory, founded in 1098, is associated with Mary Queen of Scots. It was burned by Cromwell in the 17th century but is now restored. On the coast, beneath 300-ft (91-m) volcanic cliffs, is the little harbour of **St Abbs** ⑰. The dramatic cliffs and offshore stacks of **St Abb's Head** ⑱ are a mecca for birdlife, with huge seabird colonies around the lighthouse. The mile- (1.6km-) long coastal path provides memorable views, and there are regular guided walks from the visitor centre. **Eyemouth** ⑲, 5 miles (8km) north of the English border, has a good museum that commemorates its history as a fishing community. Return to Dunbar on the A1, or follow the B6355 through picturesque Ayton, Preston and across the Lammermuir Hills to Gifford, taking the B6369 to rejoin the route at Haddington.

From Dunbar, follow the A1 inland to **East Linton** ⑳. **Preston Mill** dates from the 16th century and is one of the few working water mills in Scotland. Its red pantiled roof suggests Dutch influence. In the nearby field a few minutes' walk away is the oddly shaped **Phantassie Dovecot**, which has a revolving ladder to reach the nests inside. The B1377 leads to **East Fortune** ㉑, a former RAF airfield. The **National Museum of Flight** here has a huge collection of historic aircraft,

National Flag Heritage Centre
Main Street, Athelstaneford; tel: 01368 863 239. Open Apr–Oct daily 0900–1800. Free.

Maid of the Forth
£££ Haws Pier, under the Forth Rail Bridge, South Queensferry; tel: 0131 331 5000; www.maidoftheforth.co.uk, sails under the bridge to Inchcolm Island, and also offers evening jazz and ceilidh cruises. Open Apr–Dec.

Bo'ness and Kinneil Railway £ *Bo'ness Station, Union Street, Bo'ness; tel: 01506 822 298; www.srps.org.uk. Open Apr–Oct, check timetable locally.*

including Concorde; you can visit the cabin and cockpit in a pre-booked onboard tour. There is also a Sunday market. Scotland's national flag, the Saltire, was created at **Athelstaneford ㉒**, on the B1343. Its story is told in the **National Flag Heritage Centre**. Enjoy the splendid views from the nearby Hopetoun Monument, then take the A6137 south to **HADDINGTON ㉓**. Return to Musselburgh following the A199 through Tranent.

West Lothian route: Leave Edinburgh on the A90 towards the Forth Road Bridge at **SOUTH QUEENSFERRY ❶**. From here follow the Forth Valley national tourist route along the A904 to visit **HOPETOUN HOUSE ❷** and the **House of the Binns ❸**. Nearby, 15th-century **Blackness Castle ❹** commands a rocky promontory on the Firth of Forth. Literally shipshape, it became one of four garrison fortresses following the Union of Parliaments in 1707. Follow B903 and A904 to **Bo'ness ❺** for a ride on the Bo'ness and Kinneil Railway. The Scottish Railway Preservation Society has re-created the station complex in the style of days gone by, while the 3.5-mile (5.5-km) steam train route runs up to Birkhill where you can tour the Fireclay Mine. Turn south on the A706 to **LINLITHGOW ❻**. The Falkirk Wheel (*see page 58*) is a few miles west, on the A803. After visiting the palace, take the A706 and B792 to **Torphichen ❼**, a pretty village with a preceptory founded by the Knights of St John of Jerusalem in 1153. The church's original

Above
Spring at Hopetoun House

Bennie Museum
*9–11 Mansfield Street,
Bathgate; tel: 01506 634
944. Open Apr–Oct
Mon–Sat 1000–1600;
Nov–Mar 1100–1500.*

**Glenkinchie Distillery
Visitor Centre £**
*Pencaitland, Trenent, East
Lothian; tel: 01875 342004;
www.malts.com*

**St Mary's Episcopal
Church** *Dalkeith Country
Park, Dalkeith;
www.stmarysdalkeith.co.uk
Open summer weekends;
see website for events and
activities. Donations
welcome.*

**Scottish Mining
Museum £** *Lady Victoria
Colliery, Newtongrange;
tel: 0131 663 7519. Open
daily Mar–mid-Oct
1000–1700; mid-Oct–Feb
1000–1600. Closed
Christmas and
New Year.*

central tower and transepts still stand, while the nave, rebuilt in the 18th century, is now the parish church. From the town, follow signs for **Cairnpapple Hill** ❽ to see the ruins of a Neolithic temple (*c*2500–2000 BC) with Copper and Bronze Age graves. There are great views of the surrounding Bathgate Hills from here. Nearby, to the northeast, is Beecraigs Country Park. The B792 leads to the busy town of **Bathgate** ❾ . The **Bennie Museum**, in a cottage on Mansefield Street, has displays about the town. Head back east on the A89 through the attractive village of **Dechmont** ❿ and **Broxburn** ⓫, where you can watch glass cutting at Gleneagles of Edinburgh. Cross over the motorway and return to Edinburgh on the A8.

Also worth exploring

From Dunbar, the B6370 leads to **Stenton** and **Garvald**, two picturesque villages with red sandstone houses nestled in the Lammermuir Hills. Look for the tron, an old device for weighing wool, on Stenton's east green. **Gifford**, set beside a stream, has traditional inns and harled houses. The **Glenkinchie Distillery** south of Pencaitland (B6355) makes one of Scotland's classic malt whiskies in the traditional manner and gives guided tours. Lovely **St Mary's Episcopal Church** in Dalkeith Country Park was built in 1843 by Burns and Bryce. It contains the only water-powered Hamilton organ in Scotland. At the **Scottish Mining Museum** at Newtongrange there are talking tableaux and guided tours of the Lady Victoria Colliery with former miners.

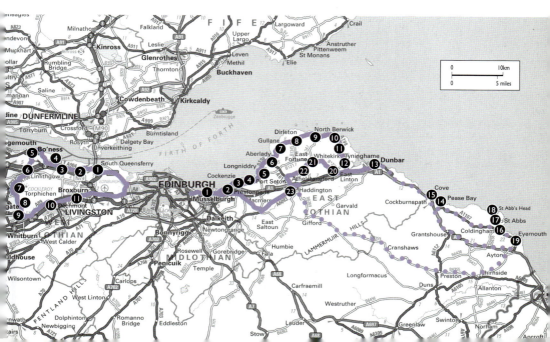

The Borders

Ratings

Abbeys	●●●●●
Castles and stately homes	●●●●●
Outdoor activities	●●●●●
Walking	●●●●●
Historical sights	●●●●○
Children	●●●○○
Scenery	●●●○○
Shopping	●●●○○

Stretching from the Southern Uplands to the Berwickshire coast, the gentle rolling landscape of the Scottish Borders belies its turbulent history. In medieval times, this region was the site of brutal cross-border warfare as invading English kings and noblemen sought to expand their territory, while the grazing lands offered rich pickings for cattle thieves, or reivers. Many towns still celebrate the defence of their territory in annual pageants known as the Common Ridings, when townsfolk gather to patrol their lands on horseback as in the days of old. The ruins of four great medieval abbeys stand within a small radius, another symbol of the region's importance. Running along the banks of the River Tweed is a string of historic mill towns, with good bargains to be found in the factory shops. There are fine stately homes and castles to visit, including the home of Scotland's great novelist and poet, Sir Walter Scott. Cycling and walking routes, riding centres, golf courses and fishing spots provide plenty of opportunity to enjoy the beautiful countryside.

ABBOTSFORD HOUSE

Abbotsford House
££ 3 miles (5km) west of Melrose; tel: 01896 752 043; www.scottsabbotsford.co.uk. Open mid-Mar–Oct daily 0930–1700, also Sun 1400–1700 Mar, Apr, May & Oct.

This splendid mansion on the banks of the River Tweed was the home of Sir Walter Scott, and his descendants still live in a wing of the house today.

On show is the wood-panelled study where he wrote, the dining and drawing rooms and, most impressive of all, his library containing some 7000 volumes. The ornate moulded ceiling was copied from the medieval carving at Rosslyn Chapel (*see page 60*).

Scott was passionate about history and filled his home with relics and mementoes: Rob Roy's *skene-dhu* (dagger), Napoleon's pen case, a lock of Bonnie Prince Charlie's hair. The Armoury fills the entrance hall and smoking corridor. A small chapel was added after his death.

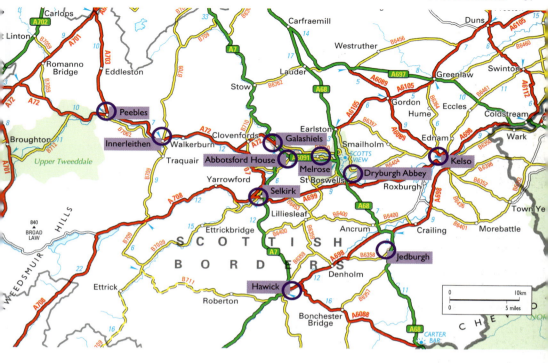

DRYBURGH ABBEY

🏛 **Dryburgh Abbey £**
Near St Boswells on the B6404, 5 miles (8km) southeast of Melrose; tel: 01835 822 381; www. historic-scotland.gov.uk. Open daily Easter–Sep 0930–1730; Oct–Mar 0930–1630.

Dryburgh Abbey, founded in 1150, stands in secluded grounds on the banks of the River Tweed. This peaceful setting makes it one of the most attractive of the abbey group. Much of the church was destroyed during Border warfare, but the cloister and living quarters are well preserved. The abbey is the final resting place of Sir Walter Scott, whose grave is in the north transept. A woodland walk leads to a huge 19th-century sandstone statue of the patriot William Wallace.

GALASHIELS

Set in the narrow valley of the Gala Water, Galashiels is one of the largest Border towns. Its prosperity also came from textiles, and the **Lochcarron Mill Visitor Centre** (*tel: 01750 726 100; open Mon–Sat 0900–1700, Sun 1100–1600, tours Mon–Thu*) gives factory tours showing the process of weaving tartan. The mill also contains a museum with displays on the development of the town and its industries. **Old Gala House** (*Scott Crescent; tel: 01750 20 096; open Apr–Sep Tue–Sat 1000–1600*) is a historic 16th-century house with a museum and art gallery. The town's war memorial has a large figure of a Border reiver (cattle thief).

HAWICK

ℹ Hawick Tourist Information Centre
Drumlanrig's Tower, Tower Knowe; tel: 0870 608 0404; e-mail: hawick@ visitscotland.com. Open Apr–Oct.

Hawick is the largest of the Border towns. It is known for its knitwear factories, and free tours are given at Peter Scott and Wrights of Trowmill. An audio-visual exhibition on the town's turbulent history from medieval times is on view in **Drumlanrig's Tower**, a fortified tower house that was the stronghold of the Douglas family. It also houses the tourist office. There is also a town museum and art gallery. Hawick holds one of the oldest Common Ridings in the Borders in early June, an event that commemorates the defeat of English soldiers by local lads in 1514.

INNERLEITHEN

ℹ St Ronan's Well Interpretive Centre *Wells Brae; tel: 01896 833 583; www.innerleithen.org.uk. Open mid-Mar–mid-Oct Mon–Fri 1000–1300, 1400–1700, Sat–Sun 1400–1700. Free.*

Robert Smail's Printing Works (National Trust for Scotland) ££ *High Street; tel: 01896 830 206; www.nts.org.uk. Open Easter–Oct Thu–Mon 1200–1700, Sun 1300–1700. Last entry 45 minutes before closing.*

Traquair House ££ *1.5 miles (2.5km) from Innerleithen; tel: 01896 830 323; www.traquair.co.uk. Open Apr–May & Sep 1200–1700; Jul–Aug 1030–1700; Oct–Nov 1100–1500; weekends only Apr & Nov.*

This pleasant little mill town became a fashionable spa in the 19th century after its mineral spring, reputed to have healing powers, featured in Sir Walter Scott's novel *St Ronan's Well*. That era is depicted at the **St Ronan's Well Interpretive Centre**, where you can taste the health-giving waters. The legend of St Ronan is commemorated each year in festivities surrounding St Ronan's Border Games, held in the third week in July. **Robert Smail's Printing Works** is a turn-of-the-20th-century print shop where you can try setting type by hand and watch the presses in action. **Traquair House**, said to be the oldest continually inhabited house in Scotland, has many royal connections. Explore the maze and the 18th-century working brewery. Innerleithen's woollen manufactory, built in the late 1780s, still operates today.

Right
Jedburgh Abbey

JEDBURGH

ℹ️ **Jedburgh Tourist Information Centre** *Murrays Green; tel: 0870 608 0404; e-mail: jedburgh@visitscotland.com*

🐌 Try the local delicacy, Jethart Snails, a mint-flavoured boiled sweet shaped like a snail. It was reputedly brought to the town by prisoners of the Napoleonic wars.

Jedburgh Abbey (*tel: 01835 863 331; www.historic-scotland.gov.uk; open Easter–Sep daily 0930–1730, Oct–Mar 0930–1630*) was established in the 12th century by King David for the Augustinians, who were called the 'black canons' because of their black robes. Just 10 miles (16km) from the English border, it was attacked and rebuilt many times, and the vast shell of the Romanesque and early Gothic church commands the site today. Its sheer size makes it the most impressive of the Border abbeys, and it has a good visitor centre. Jedburgh's colourful town centre is worth exploring. The **Mary Queen of Scots House** (*tel: 01835 863 331; open Mar–Nov Mon–Sat 1000–1630, Sun 1100–1630*) is a fine example of a fortified house of the 16th century. Displays tell the story of Mary's tragic life, including her stay here in 1566. Tired of defending their castle from the continual wave of invaders, Jedburgh's townsfolk demolished it in 1409. The **Castle Jail** (*tel: 01835 864 750; open Easter–Oct Mon–Sat 1000–1630, Sun 1300–1600*), a 19th-century prison on the site, has displays on the town's history. South of town is the **Jedforest Deer and Farm Park** (*open May–Oct daily*), a favourite with children.

KELSO

ℹ️ **Kelso Tourist Information Centre** *Town House, The Square; tel: 0870 608 0404; e-mail: kelso@visitscotland.com*

🏰 **Floors Castle ££** *Tel: 01573 223 333; www.floorscastle.com. Open daily May–Oct 1100–1700.*

Kelso Abbey (Historic Scotland) *www.historic-scotland.gov.uk. Open Apr–Dec Mon–Sat and Sun afternoons. Free.*

The rivers Tweed and Teviot meet at Kelso, a beautiful country town set around a large square lined with attractive buildings. The five-arched bridge which spans the Tweed was built between 1800 and 1803 by John Rennie; notice the fine tollhouse on the north bank. From here there is a good view of the pinnacled façade of **Floors Castle**, the largest inhabited castle in the country and home to the Duke of Roxburghe. Designed by William Adam and dating from 1721, it is filled with a fine collection of paintings, tapestries, porcelain and furniture. **Kelso Abbey**, founded in 1128, was once the largest and richest of the Border abbeys. It fell victim to invading forces and only the west front and tower attest to its former glory.

MELROSE

ℹ️ **Melrose Tourist Information Centre** *Abbey House, Abbey Street; tel: 0870 608 0404; e-mail: melrose@visitscotland.com*

The focus of this small, charming town is **Melrose Abbey**, perhaps the best preserved of all the Border abbeys. Although smaller than Jedburgh Abbey, it is very atmospheric, with a fine setting against a scenic backdrop of hills. It was founded in 1136 by the Cistercians. The church, destroyed by Richard II, was rebuilt from 1385. Much carved detail still remains in the arches, fonts and inscriptions by the

Melrose Abbey (Historic Scotland)
££ Tel: 01896 822 562;
www.historic-scotland.gov.uk.
Open daily Easter–Sep
0930–1730; Oct–Mar
0930–1630.

Three Hills Roman Heritage Centre £
The Ormiston, Market
Square; tel: 01896 822 651;
www.trimontium.net.
Open Apr–Oct daily
1030–1630.

Melrose Abbey is the starting point for St Cuthbert's Way, a 62-mile (100-km) walking route across the border to Lindisfarne. There is a waymarked route to the summit of the Eildon Hills (ask at the tourist office).

master builder John Morow. Tradition long held it that Robert the Bruce wanted his heart buried at Melrose Abbey, although his body lay in Dunfermline Abbey with the other Scots kings. In 1921 excavations uncovered a leaden casket containing the heart of the great warrior. Adjacent to the abbey is **Priorwood Garden**; it specialises in plants used for dried flower arranging and has an apple orchard with rare varieties. Also worth a visit is the **Three Hills Roman Heritage Centre**, which chronicles Roman Scotland.

Border walks and cycleways

The Borders is great walking country, and a series of Countryside and Hill Walk leaflets is available from the tourist information centres listing walks mainly of between 5 and 8 miles (8–13km). There are also many forest walks around the region; several start from Harestanes Visitor Centre near Jedburgh (tel: 01835 830 306). A programme of ranger-led walks operates between spring and autumn.

Some 82 miles (132km) of the long-distance coast-to-coast path, the Southern Upland Way, passes through the Borders. You can walk sections of the 212-mile (339-km) waymarked route in a day. Information is available at the tourist offices.

Much of the Borders' 1200 miles (1920km) of roadway lies in peaceful countryside that is perfect for cycling. The Tweed Cycleway is a 90-mile (145-km) signposted route from Berwick-upon-Tweed to Biggar. The Four Abbeys Cycle Route is a splendid ride between Jedburgh, Kelso, Dryburgh and Melrose.

PEEBLES

Peebles Tourist Information Centre High Street;
tel: 0870 608 0404; e-mail:
peebles@visitscotland.com

Neidpath Castle £
Tel: 01721 702 333.
Open Easter and May bank
holidays daily; Jul–mid-Sep
Mon–Sat 1100–1800, Sun
1300–1700.

This attractive market town set among hills alongside the River Tweed is a popular base for exploring the Border towns. The wide High Street, with its 15th-century Mercat Cross, has good shops and fine old buildings. The historic Chambers Institute houses the **Tweeddale Museum and Gallery** (tel: 01721 724 820; open Mon–Fri all year plus Sat Easter–Oct), with local history and contemporary art exhibitions. A mile (1.6km) west of town, **Neidpath Castle** is a medieval tower house set on a rocky crag in a wooded gorge. It contains a pit prison, draw well, and a series of batiks depicting the life of Mary Queen of Scots in the Great Hall. The 13th-century **Old Cross Kirk** is also worth a look. Three miles (5km) east of town, the **Tweed Valley Forest Park** offers forest walks, mountain biking, horse riding and an osprey viewing centre.

SELKIRK

Within easy reach of the abbey towns and other attractions, Selkirk makes a good base for exploring the Borders. Sir Walter Scott was the

ⓘ Selkirk Tourist Information
Centre *Halliwell's House; tel: 0870 608 0404; e-mail: selkirk@visitscotland.com. Open Apr–Oct.*

Ⓝ Sir Walter Scott's Courtroom £
Market Place; tel: 01750 720 761. Open Apr–Sep Mon–Fri 1000–1600, Sat 1000–1400 (and Sun May–Aug); Oct Mon–Sat 1300–1600.

Halliwell's House Museum *Market Place; tel: 01750 20096. Open Apr–Sep Mon–Sat 1000–1700 (1000–1730 Jul–Aug), Sun 1000–1200; Oct Mon– Sat 1000–1600. Free.*

Clapperton's Daylight Photographic Studio £
28 Scotts Place; tel: 01750 20523; www.scottishbordercamera.org.uk. Open May–Aug Fri–Sun 1400–1600 or by appointment.

sheriff here for 33 years, and his **Courtroom** has exhibits relating to his time in office. His statue stands in the marketplace. **Halliwell's House** contains the town museum, with an interesting re-creation of an ironmonger's shop. Photography buffs will enjoy the archive photos and demonstrations of old-fashioned techniques at **Clapperton's Daylight Photographic Studio**, dating from 1867. In June, up to 400 riders take part in the ancient Selkirk Common Riding, a festival that dates back to the Battle of Flodden in 1513.

Accommodation and food

Tontine Hotel ££ *Peebles; tel: 01721 720892; e-mail: stay@tontinehotel.com; www.tontinehotel.com.* Lovely historic hotel, distinguishable on Peebles' High Street because it still has its 19th-century cobbled courtyard at the front. The hotel was built in 1806 and remains at the heart of town life, with a popular bar and well-used restaurant. There are 36 comfortable en-suite rooms; the best are at the back overlooking the River Tweed's valley. The **Adam Room Restaurant** also looks out in this direction and serves creative Scottish cuisine.

Shopping

The Borders offer some of the best bargains in woollens and textiles. Many mills have factory outlet shops, particularly in towns such as Hawick, Selkirk and Peebles. Although the industry is changing and many of the smaller, independent manufacturers are closing or being bought out by the larger mills, they are worth seeking out for the variety and quality of their textiles.

Above
Borders scenery, between Innerleithen and Selkirk

The River Tweed is known as the queen of salmon rivers and its salmon pools attract anglers from around the world; the main season runs from February to November. Brown trout and sea trout are also abundant on the river and its tributaries, and there is sea fishing on the coast.

Keen golfers should check out the 'Freedom of the Fairways' leaflet, available from the tourist information centres, which offers three- and five-day passports giving considerable discounts at the region's 21 golf courses.

Hume Castle
Hume. Open Apr–Oct, daylight hours. In winter the key is available from the large house opposite the castle. Free.

Mellerstain House ££
Gordon, 5 miles (8km) from the A68 at Earlston; tel: 01573 410 225. Open May–Sep 1230–1700 (closed Tue, Fri & Sat).

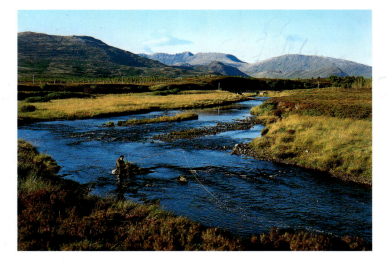

Above
Salmon fishing

Suggested tour

Total distance: 58 miles (93km).

Time: 2.5 hours, not counting stops. If you want to visit all of the abbeys at length, this will take the best part of a day, so head straight to Jedburgh via the A699 and A68. Those with limited time should concentrate on Jedburgh and/or Melrose Abbey.

Links: If you're heading north to Edinburgh and beyond, the A72 is a scenic route along the River Tweed, with stops in the mill towns of Galashiels, Innerleithen, Walkerburn and Peebles. If you're touring southern Scotland and are heading to Dumfries and Galloway, follow the A7 south from Hawick, and at Langholm take the B7068 to Lockerbie, for a scenic route through the rolling hills of Teviotdale and Eskdale.

Route: From **SELKIRK** ❶ take the A7 south to **HAWICK** ❷. Then take the A698 and B6358 to **JEDBURGH** ❸ for a visit to the abbey. Leave town on the A68 (signposted Edinburgh), and after 2 miles (3km) take the A698 to **KELSO** ❹.

Detour: From Kelso take the A6089/B6364 to the imposing ruins of **Hume Castle** ❺, from which there are splendid views over the Merse of Berwickshire. The A6089 also leads to **Mellerstain House** ❻, considered by many to be the finest mansion designed by Robert Adam, with outstanding decorative plasterwork and coloured ceilings. From here you can connect to the main route on the B6397, or carry on along the A6089 to Gordon to see the ruins of **Greenknowe Tower** ❼, a 16th-century tower house with corbelled turrets and crow-stepped gables.

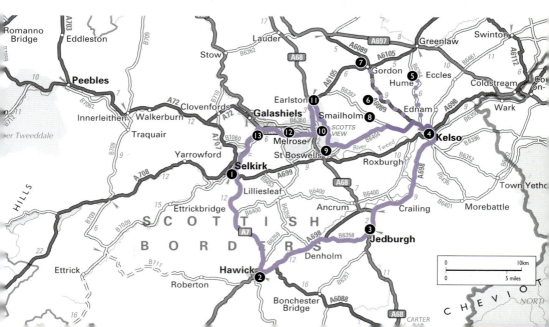

**Smailholm Tower
(Historic Scotland)**
*£ 6 miles (9.5km) west of
Kelso on the B6937;
tel: 01573 460 364;
www.historic-scotland.gov.uk.
Open Apr–Sep daily
0930–1730; Oct–Mar
weekends 0930–1630.*

**Hermitage Castle
(Historic Scotland) £**
*15 miles (24km) south of
Hawick on the B6399;
tel: 01387 376 222;
www.historic-scotland.gov.uk.
Open Easter–Sep daily
0930–1730.*

Thirlestane Castle ££
*Lauder; tel: 01578 722 430;
www.thirlestanecastle.co.uk.
Open Easter weekend and
May–Jun & Sep Sun, Wed,
Thu 1000–1500, Jul–Aug
Sun–Thu 1000–1500.*

For the main route, leave Kelso on the A6089 and after 1.5 miles (2.4km) turn left on the B6397 towards Smailholm. After 2.5 miles (4km) turn left on the B6404, following the small sign for **Smailholm Tower ❽** (note that the tower is not actually in the town, and you will drive through a farmyard to reach the car park). This characterful 16th-century defensive tower, standing a lonely guard on a windy hilltop, captures the essence of the Borders history when constant watch was kept for reivers (cattle thieves) and invading forces. Return to the B6404 (signposted St Boswells) and drive 4 miles (6.5km) following signs to **DRYBURGH ABBEY ❾**. A short way up the hill on the B6356 is **Scott's View❿**, with a wonderful panorama overlooking the River Tweed across to the Eildon Hills. Sir Walter often stopped here to admire the view, and it is said that, as his funeral cortège made its way to Dryburgh Abbey, his horses paused here of their own accord. Continue north to **Earlston ⓫**, with its ruined Rhymer's Tower; this was the home of a 13th-century poet and seer, Thomas the Rhymer. From here take the A68 back south, turning right on the A6091 to **MELROSE ⓬**. Return to Selkirk (7 miles, 11km), taking the B6360 past **ABBOTSFORD HOUSE ⓭**, which connects to the A7.

Also worth exploring

Hermitage Castle looms large on an isolated moor off the B6399 south of Hawick. Mary Queen of Scots rode to this grim fortress to visit her wounded lover, the Earl of Bothwell. **Thirlestane Castle**, with fine Restoration period plasterwork ceilings and a historic toy collection, is located in the medieval town of Lauder.

Dumfries and Galloway

Ratings

Outdoor activities	●●●●●
Wildlife	●●●●●
Abbeys	●●●●○
Children	●●●●○
Museums and galleries	●●●●○
Castles	●●●○○
Scenery	●●●○○
Walking	●●●○○
Archaeology	●●○○○

Tucked away in the southwest corner of Scotland, Dumfries and Galloway is a holiday region often overlooked by visitors speeding northwards on the A74 to the city centres or the Highlands. Those who pause to explore it will find this gentle landscape offers a number of surprises: 200 miles (322km) of beautiful coastline bordering the Irish Sea and the Solway Firth, a forest park with herds of red deer and wild goats, an artists' colony and the highest village in Scotland. The region is characterised by bright green rolling hills and pastureland, all the more beautiful in autumn when tinged with the reds, golds and browns of changing foliage. Driving is relaxing and lends a sense of wellbeing. This is the land of Robert Burns, and the region's capital, Dumfries, contains many tributes to the nation's favourite poet. With its mild climate warmed by the Gulf Stream, peaceful villages, recreational pursuits and easy access to Glasgow and Edinburgh, more than a few incomers from south of the border have chosen to relocate here.

CASTLE DOUGLAS

ⓘ Castle Douglas Tourist Information Centre *Markethill Car Park; tel: 01556 502 611. Open Apr–Oct.*

ⓝ Ken-Dee Marshes Nature Reserve RSPB. With a nature trail and viewing hide among the marshes and woodland along Loch Ken and the River Dee. *Open all year. Free.*

Castle Douglas is a fair-sized market town whose distinguishing feature is an odd dome-topped clock tower. It was named after William Douglas, a wealthy local merchant who founded the town's 18th-century cotton mills. The cattle market here, which began in 1819, is the world centre for the sale of Galloway cattle, a unique breed having no horns. The town is pleasant enough with lots of shopping, but the main attraction is **Threave Garden and Estate** (*tel: 01556 502 575; www.nts.org.uk; estate and garden open all year, house Apr–Oct*), a mile (1.6km) to the west. It is particularly beautiful in springtime, with an extensive display of daffodils. The 14th-century **castle**, whose remains stand on an island in the River Dee, was the stronghold of the powerful Black Douglases. It was sacked by the Covenanters in 1640.

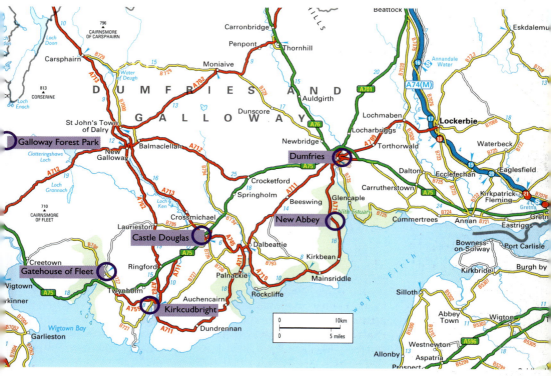

DUMFRIES

ⓘ Dumfries Tourist Information Centre 64 *Whitesands*; tel: 01387 245 555; *www. visitdumfriesandgalloway. co.uk.* Open all year.

ⓗ Robert Burns Centre £ *Mill Road*; tel: 01387 264 808. Open Apr–Sep Mon–Sat 1000– 2000, Sun 1400–1700; Oct–Mar Tue–Sat 1000– 1300, 1400–1700.

Dumfries Museum (free) and Camera Obscura (£) *The Observatory*; tel: 01387 253 374. Open Apr–Sep Mon–Sat 1000–1700, Sun 1400–1700; Oct–Mar Tue–Sat 1000–1300, 1400–1700.

Dumfries, a handsome town of pink-hued sandstone buildings straddling the River Nith, is the largest town in the southwest and an important tourist centre. The Queen of the South, as she is called, dates back to the 12th century and witnessed an important scene in Scottish history. Robert the Bruce fatally stabbed his rival, the Red Comyn, here at the old Greyfriars Kirk in 1306, an event that sparked the Scottish Wars of Independence. There are many tributes to Robert Burns, who lived here from 1791 until his death in 1796, writing many of his best-known poems while working as an excise officer. You can visit the **Burns House**, where the poet spent his last years, and his **mausoleum** in the churchyard, or have a drink in the **Globe Inn**, his favourite pub. The churchyard in which Burns is buried also has the mass grave of victims of the 1832 cholera epidemic. The **Robert Burns Centre**, in a restored mill near the river, examines Burns's Dumfries connections. His memorial statue stands in the High Street, north of the striking **Midsteeple**, erected in 1707 as a prison and courthouse. Also of interest are the **Dumfries Museum**, whose windmill tower is topped by the **Camera Obscura**, and the **Old Bridge House Museum** (*tel: 01387 256 904; open Apr–Sep daily; afternoons only on Sun*) in the town's oldest house, built into the Devorgilla Bridge in 1660.

GALLOWAY FOREST PARK

ⓘ The Kirroughtree Visitor Centre
off the A75 at Palnure, 3 miles (5km) east of Newton Stewart, is the southern gateway to Galloway Forest Park, with a tearoom and information on cycle routes and forest trails. Tel: 01671 402 165. Open daily mid-Apr–Oct.

ⓘ Glen Trool Visitor Centre
Tel: 01671 840302. Open daily 1030–1630 (until 1730 Jul–mid-Sep).

Galloway Red Deer Range £ Tel: 01671 402420. Check locally for tours.

Raiders Road £ Open mid-Apr–Oct.

Clatteringshaws Visitor Centre Tel: 01644 420 285. Open 1030–1630 (until 1730 Jul–mid-Sep).

Golden eagles and peregrine falcons can be seen in the Galloway Forest Park. A birdwatching guide is available from the tourist offices detailing nature reserves such as the Wood of Cree near Newton Stewart, where you can see many native and migratory species.

Covering some 300 square miles (777sq km), Galloway Forest Park is a scenic mixture of the woodlands, lochs and moorlands that characterise the Southern Uplands landscape. The area's native trees were felled long ago, and today's Sitka spruces were introduced in a reforestation project that resulted in the founding of the park in 1943. It is a haven for wildlife, including several endangered species such as the golden eagle, hen harrier and wildcat. One of the most scenic spots in the park is **Glen Trool**, off the A714 at Bargrennan, 12 miles (19km) north of Newton Stewart. The **Queen's Way** is a 19-mile (30.5-km) route through the park along the A712, passing many points of interest. The **Glen of the Bar** viewpoint overlooks a waterfall where a hoard of Dark Ages jewellery was found. At the **Wild Goat Park** you can observe the thriving herd of native animals grazing along the roadside. To protect the forest, the park's herd of native deer is enclosed within the **Red Deer Range**; you can observe them from a viewing platform atop a hill or close up on ranger-guided tours during the high season. **Raider's Road** is a 10-mile (16-km) unsurfaced timber road along the river that follows an old cattle-rustler's route; it has good picnic and swimming spots, but may be closed out of season. **Clatteringshaws Loch** is a man-made reservoir across from the entrance to Raider's Road. There is a Forest Wildlife Centre here and, a short walk away, **Bruce's Stone**, commemorating an early victory by the great warrior in the Wars of Independence. Hiking routes abound. To celebrate the 50th anniversary of Galloway Forest Park, a series of contemporary artworks was installed throughout the park, some along

Right
Sweetheart Abbey

popular routes, others hidden in more remote parts of the forest. Maps are available at visitor centres to guide you to the sculptures.

GATEHOUSE OF FLEET

Mill on the Fleet £
High Street, by the
river; tel: 01557 814 099.
Open Easter–Oct daily
1000–1700.

This pretty town, a mixture of whitewashed and pastel-painted cottages with a commanding granite clock tower (1871), was an important mill town in the late 18th century. Its **Mill on the Fleet** was named 'Roaring Birtwhistle' by Robert Burns on his visit in 1795. Today it is an impressive visitor centre, with a working water wheel and a clever exhibition on local life in a textile town. An audiovisual presentation presents a buzzard's-eye view of the Galloway landscape.

KIRKCUDBRIGHT

Harbour Square;
tel: 01557 330 494;
www.kirkcudbright.co.uk.
Open Feb–Nov.

**Tolbooth Art
Centre £** High Street;
tel: 01557 331 556. Open
May–Sep Mon–Sat 1100–
1700, Sun 1400–1700
(Jul–Aug 1000–1700); Oct–
Apr Mon–Sat 1100–1600.

**Broughton House
(National Trust for
Scotland) ££** 12 High Street;
tel: 01557 330 437. Open
Easter–Sep Thu–Mon
1200–1700; garden only
Jul–Aug daily 1100–1600;
Feb–Mar Mon–Fri 1100–1600.

Stewartry Museum £
St Mary Street; tel: 01557 331
643; www.dumgal.gov.uk/
museums. Open May–Sep
Mon–Sat 1100–1700 (Jul–Aug
1000–1700), Sun 1400–1700;
Oct–Apr Mon–Sat 1100–1600.

'In Kirkcudbright one either fishes or paints' wrote Dorothy Sayers in her detective novel *Five Red Herrings*, which is set in the town in the 1920s. This delightful burgh (pronounced 'kir-koo-bree'), set alongside a picturesque harbour, is lined with colourful, well-kept 17th- and 18th-century buildings and medieval closes, many housing art galleries and craft shops. In the late 19th century well-known artists came to Kirkcudbright, attracted by the splendid light and scenery of the Galloway countryside. At the **Tolbooth Art Centre** it's well worth watching the 15-minute audiovisual show telling the story of the artist's colony, and there is a small gallery of their works. After undergoing major conservation work you can now visit **Broughton House**, studio home of the painter E A Hornel, with a collection of his works, a magnificent garden and enormous library of Scottish literature and history books. Also on the High Street, look out for the homes of artists Jessie M King and E A Tayler at Greengate, Charles Oppenheimer at No 14 and Tim and Mary Jeffs at No 9. Their works are on display at the **Stewartry Museum**, while contemporary exhibitions are held at the charming **Harbour Cottage Gallery** (*tel: 01557 330 073*).

NEW ABBEY

This quaint village on a narrow, winding main street has three attractions. **Sweetheart Abbey** was established in 1273 by Lady

Sweetheart Abbey (Historic Scotland)
£ Tel: 01387 850 397;
www.historic-scotland.gov.uk.
Open Apr–Sep daily
0930–1730; Oct–Mar Mon–
Wed and Sat–Sun
0930–1630.

New Abbey Corn Mill (Historic Scotland) £
Tel: 01387 850 260;
www.historic-scotland.gov.uk.
Open same hours as
Sweetheart Abbey.

Shambellie House Museum of Costume £
Tel: 01387 850 375. Open
Apr–Oct daily 1000–1700.

At **Gatehouse of Fleet**, drop in for a wee dram at the Murray Arms Hotel, where Robbie Burns wrote Scots wha hae.

Gael Force is Dumfries and Galloway's arts and entertainment festival, with a varied programme of music and cultural events running mid-Aug–Oct (tel: 01387 262 084 for more information; www.gaelforcefestival.co.uk).

At the Moffat Pottery you can visit the studio of the singing potter, Gerard Lyons (20 High Street, Moffat; open Mon–Sat).
Keen gardeners will enjoy a visit to Cally Gardens at Gatehouse of Fleet, a nursery where you can buy plant stock which is grown from seed from botanic gardens worldwide.

Devorgilla in memory of her husband John Balliol, founder of the Oxford college. The red sandstone Cistercian abbey was the last of any size built in Scotland. The couple were devoted lovers, and when he died she had his heart embalmed and placed in an ivory and silver casket. She kept it with her always and called it her 'sweet, silent companion'. The monks named the abbey 'Sweetheart' in honour of her undying love. Lady Devorgilla is buried, with the heart, in front of the High Altar. The **New Abbey Corn Mill** is a renovated 18th-century mill, still in working order. Nearby, in attractive wooded grounds, is the **Shambellie House Museum of Costume**.

The Killing Times

The Covenanters were Scottish Presbyterians who protested against attempts by Charles I to impose an Anglican prayer book and structure on their church services. They signed a National Covenant declaring their resistance at Greyfriars Kirk in Edinburgh in 1638 and, in 1639, joined the English Parliamentarians in a revolt that led to the execution of the king. When the monarchy was restored in 1660 Charles II, in spite of having signed the Covenant prior to his coronation at Scone, again instituted episcopal rule. Resistance was particularly strong in the southwest of Scotland, leading to a period of persecution and violence known as 'the killing times'. After the Covenanters were defeated at Bothwell Brig in 1679, more than 1000 were imprisoned in a field at Greyfriars Kirkyard. In 1690, under William of Orange, the Presbyterian kirk was accepted as the national church of Scotland.

Accommodation and food

The Edenbank Hotel £ *17 Laurieknowe, Dumfries; tel: 01387 252 759; e-mail: enquiries@edenbank.fsbusiness.co.uk; www.edenbankhotel.co.uk.* The Bishop of Dumfries and Galloway once lived in this handsome sandstone house that was built in 1867 and is only five minutes' walk from the town centre. It's now a small and very friendly family-run hotel with just ten rooms, all en suite, and with its own lounge bar and restaurant.

The Globe Inn £ *56 High Street, Dumfries; tel: 01387 252 335; www.globeinndumfries.co.uk.* The favourite watering hole of Robert Burns dates from 1610. Atmospheric bar, dining room lunches served *1000–1500 Mon–Sat,* suppers by appointment.

The Smithy £ *High Street, New Galloway; tel: 01644 420 269. Open Mar–Oct from 1000, closed Wed.* Delightful restaurant with delicious home baking, serving scones, shortbread, snacks and full meals.

Baytree House ££ *110 High Street, Kirkcudbright; tel/fax: 01557 330 824; e-mail: info@baytreekirkcudbright.co.uk; www.baytreekirkcudbright.co.uk.*

**Dundrennan Abbey
(Historic Scotland)** £
Tel: 01557 500 262; www.historic-scotland.gov.uk. Open Easter–Sep daily 0930–1730; Oct–Mar weekends 0930–1630.

Rough Island can be reached at low tide from Kippford Causeway or by walking across the mud from Rockcliffe. Because of ground-nesting terns and oystercatchers, people are asked not to visit the island in May or June, and to keep to central paths during July. Take care because the estuary floods very quickly when the tide comes in and the causeway is covered for about 5 hours at high tide.

Elegant Georgian townhouse in the conservation area of town, near the picturesque harbour and main attractions. The three large bedrooms are beautifully furnished, one with a four-poster bed and antique bath. Guests are welcomed with a glass of sherry in the drawing room.

Suggested tour

Total distance: 120 miles (193km) for main route, the detour only adds a few extra miles.

Time: Allow a full day.

Links: Dumfries is only 14 miles (22.5km) west of Lockerbie, which is on the main A74(M) motorway connecting Scotland and England. You can reach Hawick in the Borders from Dumfries in about an hour and a half, taking the A709 to Lockerbie, then following the scenic B7068 to Langholm and north on the A7.

Route: Leave Dumfries on the A710 south to **NEW ABBEY ❶**, 7 miles (11km) away. A couple of miles (3km) further outside the town, the coastline of the Solway Firth comes into view. The road meanders through pasture and woodland, with parts of the English coast visible across the water. At **Kirkbean ❷**, naval buffs can visit the cottage where John Paul Jones, 'father of the American Navy', was born in 1747. If the day is warm, stop off at **Sandyhills ❸** after 18 miles (29km) for a barefoot stroll on the sandy beach. This stretch of the shoreline, known as the Colvend Coast, is one of the most scenic in the region.

Detour: Two miles (3km) further on, a side road leads to the shore at **Rockcliffe ❹**. Note that parking alongside the shore is limited. This is a good place for kids to splash around in the rock pools and look for cockles in the mud when the tide is out. Out in the estuary is **Rough Island**, a bird sanctuary. A short path leads to the top of the Mote of Mark hill fort, a Celtic stronghold dating from the 5th century AD. The Jubilee Footpath carries on to the next village of **Kippford ❺**, about a mile (1.6km) away. To reach Kippford by car, return to the main road and take the next signposted turning. This is a good place to stop for a drink or a pub meal, and to admire the boats bobbing in the inlet against the pretty backdrop of hills.

Continue on the A710 to **Dalbeattie ❻**. Its sparkling grey granite cottages were built from the local stone which was exported worldwide in the 19th century. Two and a half miles (4km) north of town is the Mote of Urr, an extensive Saxon motte-and-bailey earthwork fortification. Take the A711 to Kirkcudbright, 18 miles (29km) away. When driving this stretch, notice the venerable huge-trunked trees standing sentinel in the fields. Along the way you'll pass the sweet village of **Palnackie ❼**; the Orchardton Tower nearby is a rare circular tower house. A striking cast-iron fountain stands in the

Cardoness Castle (Historic Scotland)
£ *Tel: 01557 814 427; www.historic-scotland.gov.uk. Open Easter–Sep daily 0930–1730; Oct–Mar weekends 0930–1630.*

Creetown Gem Rock Museum £ *Chain Road; tel: 01671 820357; www.gemrock.net. Open Easter–Sep daily 0930–1730; Oct–Easter 1000–1600; closed 23 Dec–Jan.*

village square at **Auchencairn** ❽ , situated on a hillside with fine views across the bay. The ruins of **Dundrennan Abbey** ❾ , built in the 12th century, are worth a visit for their austere Gothic beauty set against the pastoral landscape. Mary Queen of Scots spent her last night in her homeland here before fleeing to England.

After a visit to **KIRKCUDBRIGHT** ❿ , cross its picturesque bridge and continue on the A755, turning left on the A75. At **Cardoness Castle** ⓫ , a 15th-century ruin, turn right on B796 for 1 mile (1.6km) to **GATEHOUSE OF FLEET** ⓬ . Six miles (9.5km) further along the A75 is the turn-off for the **Cairn Holy** ⓭ Neolithic chambered cairns, and a mile (1.6km) beyond are the roadside ruins of **Carsluith Castle** ⓮ , a 16th-century tower house. At this point the A75 affords beautiful sweeping views over the coast.

Detour: An alternative scenic route between Gatehouse of Fleet and Creetown leads inland on the B796 through the high hills along the Big Water of Fleet.

Creetown ⓯ was another important granite quarry and thus is a town of grey stone buildings. It is best known today as the home of the **Gem Rock Museum** with excellent specimens of mineral and fossils from around the world. **Newton Stewart** ⓰ , an attractive market town on the River Cree, is known for its mohair rugs and its salmon fishing. The town is the starting point of the scenic road A712 through **GALLOWAY FOREST PARK** ⓱ , where there is a variety of hiking trails, three visitor centres and a chance to see wildlife including wild goats, red deer and birds of prey.

Above
Dumfries on the River Nith

Newton Stewart Tourist Information Centre
Dashwood Square;
tel: 01671 402 431.
Open Apr–Oct.

The Dumfries and Galloway countryside offers a wide range of recreational pursuits, from its 31 golf courses to salmon rivers and lochs and burns with native brown, rainbow and sea trout. The Southern Upland Way long-distance walking path runs through the region. Cyclists can pick up a guide to cycle routes from the tourist offices.

At the other end is the pleasant village of **New Galloway** 18, which is the smallest royal burgh in Scotland. Located at the northern end of Loch Ken, it is a popular base for anglers. Take the A713 along the shores of **Loch Ken** 19, which was created by the damming of the rivers Ken and Dee for the Galloway hydroelectric scheme; 9 miles (14.5km) long, it is a centre for fishing, sailing, watersports and birdwatching. Follow the Red Kite Trail signs for a rare chance to see this mighty bird of prey up close. After 13 miles (21km) you reach **CASTLE DOUGLAS** 20. From here it is 18 miles (29km) along the A75 back to Dumfries.

Also worth exploring

Caerlaverock Castle, 8 miles (13km) southeast of Dumfries on B725, is a picture-postcard medieval castle on the shores of the Solway Firth. Built in the late 13th century, it has a moat and an outstanding Renaissance façade on the inner courtyard. **Drumlanrig Castle**, 4 miles (6.5km) north of Thornhill on A76, is an impressive 17th-century pile in a splendid setting, filled with a fine collection of paintings and a bicycle museum. **Moffat**, a famous Victorian spa town, is a popular tourist centre with shopping for crafts, textiles and tartans. The Moffat Ram adorning the high-street fountain signifies the town's importance as a sheep and wool trading centre. Nearby are the **Devil's Beef Tub**, where the Border Reivers hid stolen cattle, and the waterfall called the **Grey Mare's Tail. Wanlockhead**, an old lead-mining centre sitting at 1,533ft (467m), is Scotland's highest village. The **Museum of Lead Mining** gives tours of the mine and period cottages; you can even pan for Scottish gold.

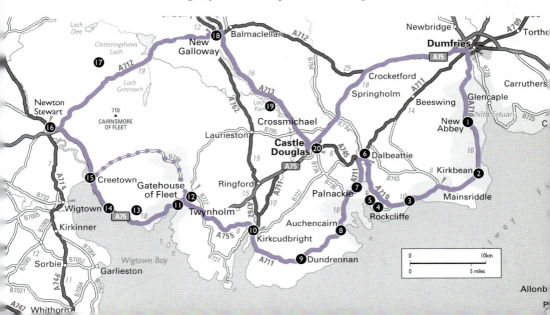

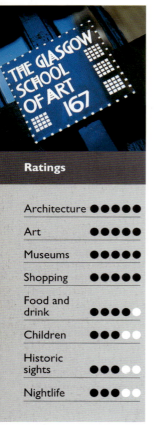

Glasgow

Ratings

Architecture	●●●●●
Art	●●●●●
Museums	●●●●●
Shopping	●●●●●
Food and drink	●●●●○
Children	●●●○○
Historic sights	●●●○○
Nightlife	●●●○○

Scotland's largest city has many faces. Its Gaelic name, Glasghu, means 'dear green place', and indeed it boasts more than 70 parks and gardens. Yet outsiders, particularly those who haven't been there, often associate it with the grimy industrial visage for which it was long known. Until recently, that is. Following a design-led renaissance in which the old sandstone warehouses were cleaned up and converted to fashionable shops, restaurants and flats, Glasgow made an all-out effort to change its image. Its appointment as the UK City of Architecture and Design 1999 was a fitting accolade, but it was not all that surprising, for Glasgow has been at the cutting edge for centuries. It has tremendous architectural riches, generated in part by the 18th-century 'tobacco lords', whose wealth from trade funded the move into manufacturing and heavy industry in the following century. Glasgow today is stylish yet laid-back, fashionable yet friendly, forward-thinking yet down-to-earth. It holds its own with any European city.

Getting there and getting around

ⓘ Glasgow Tourist Information Centre 11 George Square; tel: 0141 204 4400; e-mail: glasgow@visitscotland.com. Open all year.

Glasgow Airport Tourist Information Desk International Arrivals Hall; tel: 0141 848 4440. Open all year.

Airport: Glasgow International Airport is located at Paisley, 8 miles (13km) from the city centre (*tel: 0870 040 0008*). An express connection into the city takes half an hour and is reasonably priced.

Rail: Glasgow Central Station is in the heart of the city centre (*24-hour National Rail Enquiries, tel: 08457 484 950*).

Parking: Glasgow has a good number of car parks in or near the city centre. Among the most convenient are the parking areas at the Cathedral, the large High Street car park at High and Duke streets, the St Enoch's Centre car park and the Concert Square car park at the top of Buchanan Street. There are also NCP car parks at the Anderston Centre on Argyle Street, Mitchell Street, George Street, Oswald Street and Ingram Street, across from City Halls. A brochure and map with these and other locations is available from the tourist information centre.

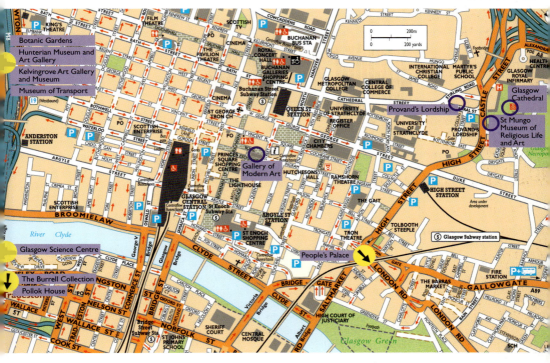

Botanic Gardens
730 Great Western
Road; tel: 0141 276 1614;
www.glasgow.gov.uk. Open
dawn–dusk. Free.

The Burrell Collection
2060 Pollokshaws Road,
Pollok Country Park;
tel: 0141 287 2550;
www.glasgowmuseums.com.
Open Mon–Thu and Sat
1000–1700, Fri and Sun
1100–1700. Free.

**Gallery of Modern
Art** Queen Street;
tel: 0141 229 1996;
www.glasgowmuseums.com.
Open Mon–Wed and Sat
1000–1700, Thu
1000–2000, Fri and Sun
1100–1700. Free.

Driving: With Glasgow's excellent public transport system and with most of the main sights within walking distance of each other, there is no need to drive in the city.

Public Transport: Glasgow is the only city in Scotland with an underground train service, which travels in one circuit around the city. You can buy single-journey tickets at the stations. A variety of day-tripper tickets for individuals or families is also available, as well as Zonecards which can cover the whole Strathclyde area (economical if you are going to be in Glasgow for a week or longer). Some tickets offer a combined bus and rail service. For enquiries ring Traveline Scotland (tel: 0871 200 2233; www.travelinescotland.com) or visit the Travel Centre at Buchanan Bus Station (Killermont Street; tel: 0141 333 3708; open Mon–Sat 0630–2230, Sun 0700–2230).

Sights

Botanic Gardens

Glasgow's Botanic Gardens wind along the River Kelvin. The focal point is the Kibble Palace, built in 1863 for John Kibble, a Glasgow merchant, and moved here in 1871. It contains a lush variety of ferns and exotic temperate plants. Other glasshouses harbour orchids, ferns and begonias. The grounds feature themed gardens such as the chronological garden, and paths lead down to the riverside walk.

Glasgow Cathedral
Castle Street; tel: 0141 552 6891; www.historic-scotland.gov.uk. Open Oct–Mar Mon–Sat 0930–1630, Sun 1300–1630; Easter–Sep Mon–Sat 0930–1730, Sun 1300–1700.

Glasgow Science Centre £–££
50 Pacific Quay; tel: 0871-540 1000; www.gsc.org.uk. Open mid-Mar–Oct daily 1000–1700; Nov–mid-Mar Tue–Sun 1000–1700; some evening IMAX films.

Opposite
Glasgow's Gothic cathedral

Below
Detail from Felipe Linores' *Seven Deadly Sins*, in the Gallery of Modern Art

The Burrell Collection

The Burrell Collection (4 miles, 6.5km southwest of Glasgow) is one of the finest art collections in Europe. It was acquired by one man, Sir William Burrell, a prosperous Glaswegian shipowner. Although wealthy, he had nowhere near the resources of Getty, Frick or other millionaire collectors, and this collection of over 8000 items represents his personal taste, foresight and achievement. Among the highlights are artefacts from ancient Egypt and Greece, Oriental art, Near Eastern carpets and ceramics, exquisite medieval tapestries, needlework, religious art and stained glass. There are period galleries and entire rooms from Burrell's Hutton Castle, as well as paintings and sculpture. The splendid building in its woodland setting was designed to enhance the beautiful objects within.

Gallery of Modern Art

Among Scotland's top venues for contemporary art, the gallery is housed in the former Royal Exchange, built in 1780 as a neoclassical mansion for a rich Glasgow tobacco lord. It features the works of artists from 1950 to the present, particularly those who have achieved international acclaim. Along with the paintings there are mobiles, sculptures, photographs and installations. There is a pleasant café and art book shop in the basement.

Glasgow Cathedral

Dating back to the 12th century, this beautiful Gothic building is a gem. The cathedral is associated with St Mungo, Glasgow's patron saint, who founded a church here in the 7th century, and contains his tomb. It boasts one of the country's finest displays of post-war stained-

glass windows. The nave has a medieval open timber roof, and is separated from the Quire by a unique 15th-century stone screen, or *pulpitum*. The sacristy (mid-13th century), in the northeast corner, was the bishops' apartment. The Blacader Aisle, a 15th-century addition, has fine carved bosses on the ceiling.

Glasgow Science Centre

This award-winning science and technology centre on the banks of the River Clyde is Glasgow's newest attraction. Its futuristic design incorporates the science mall, with interactive exhibits, the Space Theatre planetarium and a Virtual Science theatre that presents high-tech demonstrations of the wonders of science. There is also an IMAX theatre and the rotating Glasgow Tower, which houses galleries on the city's past and future and offers superb views over the city.

Hunterian Art Gallery University of Glasgow, 82 Hillhead Street; tel: 0141 330 5431; www.hunterian.gla.ac.uk. Open Mon–Sat 0930–1700. Mackintosh House closed daily 1230–1330. Free.

Hunterian Museum University of Glasgow, University Avenue; tel: 0141 330 4221; www.hunterian.gla.ac.uk. Open Mon–Sat 0930–1700, closed public holidays. Free.

Kelvingrove Art Gallery and Museum Kelvingrove, Argyle Street; tel: 0141 276 9599; www. glasgowmuseums.com. Open Mon–Thu and Sat 1000–1700, Fri and Sun 1100–1700. Free.

Hunterian Art Gallery

The Hunterian contains the former home – or parts of it – of the famous Glaswegian architect, Charles Rennie Mackintosh. The original terraced house was demolished in 1963, but many of the original fitments were salvaged for the reconstruction within the gallery. The dining room, studio-drawing room and main bedroom cover three floors, with the original furniture Mackintosh himself designed. The Hunterian is also worth a visit for its fine collection of paintings. The **Whistler Collection** was bequeathed to the city by the artist's estate. There are also fine works by the landscape painter William McTaggart, the Glasgow Boys and the Scottish Colourists.

Hunterian Museum

The collections of Dr William Hunter formed the basis of Scotland's first public museum, which opened in 1807. Hunter had trained at Glasgow University before moving to London, where he became a successful physician. He bequeathed his entire private collection to his alma mater, including not only anatomical and zoological specimens, but also coins, archaeological and geological finds, artworks and manuscripts.

Kelvingrove Art Gallery and Museum

Reopened in 2006 after a major renovation, this massive red sandstone building which dates from 1902 holds a wealth of treasures. The main public entrance is on the lower ground floor, along with the

Museum of Transport

1 Bunhouse Road; tel: 0141 287 2720; www.glasgowmuseums.com. Open Mon–Thu and Sat 1000–1700, Fri and Sun 1100–1700. Free.

Above
Brutalism with Mackintosh allusions – the buildings of the Hunterian Museum and Art Gallery

exhibition gallery. Among the ground-floor galleries which are spread over two wings of the museum are displays on Scottish natural history, archaeology, ancient Egypt, Mackintosh and the Glasgow style and Scottish art. The top floor galleries contain a wonderful collection of British and European paintings and sculpture. The Glasgow Boys and Scottish Colourists are well represented, as are works by the French Impressionists and Dutch old masters.

Museum of Transport

This popular museum has a delightful array of trains, trams, buses, automobiles, fire-fighting equipment, bicycles and horse-drawn vehicles. The motorcar collection highlights famous models produced by Scottish manufacturers. The Clyde Room of Ship Models has a splendid collection of boats built in Scotland's shipyards, including sailing ships, steamers and passenger liners. There is also a reconstruction of a typical Glasgow Street in 1938, lined with shops and a subway station.

For a pleasant stroll along one of Glasgow's main thoroughfares, you can walk from the Art Gallery and Museum down Sauchiehall Street to the city centre at Buchanan Street in about an hour. Stop off at the Willow Tea Room for refreshments (see below and page 91).

 People's Palace
Glasgow Green;
tel: 0141 271 2962;
www.glasgowmuseums.com.
Open Mon–Thu and Sat
1000–1700, Fri and Sun
1100–1700. Free.

Pollok House (National Trust for Scotland) ££
2060 Pollockshaws Road;
tel: 0141 616 6410;
www.nts.org.uk. Open daily
1000–1700.

Provand's Lordship
3 Castle Street;
tel: 0141 552 8819;
www.glasgowmuseums.com.
Open Mon–Thu and Sat
1000–1700, Fri and Sun
1100–1700. Free.

St Mungo Museum of Religious Life and Art
2 Castle Street;
tel: 0141 553 2557;
www.glasgowmuseums.com.
Open Mon–Thu and Sat
1000–1700, Fri and Sun
1100–1700. Free.

People's Palace
This entertaining and enlightening museum tells the story of the people of Glasgow and looks at popular culture and working-class life. Exhibits examine such aspects as 'The Patter' (Glaswegian speech), life in Glasgow during the war, housing, holidays and industry. There are charming re-creations of the Buttercup Dairy shop and the Steamie (laundry). Adjoining the Victorian building is the Winter Gardens, a large glass conservatory with palms and temperate plants.

Pollok House
This 18th-century mansion, once the private home of Sir William Stirling Maxwell, houses his excellent collection of Spanish paintings, including two outstanding portraits by El Greco. Other European artists are represented as well, and there are collections of fine furniture, silver, ceramics and glass. The house is set in parkland, near the Burrell Collection.

Provand's Lordship
Built in 1471, this is Glasgow's oldest domestic building. It was built as a clergyman's house (the word 'provand' has the same meaning as 'prebend'), next to the old St Nicholas Hospital, long gone. It is filled with period furniture dating from the 16th to 20th centuries, and displays on the house's long history. There is a lovely medieval garden outside.

St Mungo Museum of Religious Life and Art
This highly interesting and admirable small museum has provoked controversy since its opening in 1993, for its portrayal of religious and spiritual beliefs and symbols across the world's cultures. Christian stained glass stands side by side with Dali's *St John of the Cross*, Aboriginal painting and an Islamic prayer rug. The Religious Life room looks at local customs from Scandinavian trolls to African initiation masks, and you can lift handsets to hear people of different faiths talking about creation, marriage and ways of worship. Upstairs, the Religion in Scotland exhibits trace the history of worship since earliest times.

Accommodation and food

Willow Tea Room £ *217 Sauchiehall Street, above Hendersons jewellery and gift shop; tel: 0141 332 0521; www.willowtearooms.co.uk; open 0900–1700, Sun 1100–1615.* Charles Rennie Mackintosh designed both the building and its interiors, including the furniture, for Catherine Cranston's tearoom in 1903. It has been re-created here to its original design. Breakfast is served all day, along with sandwiches, soups, cakes and a wide selection of teas and coffees. There is another branch at 97 Buchanan Street, with a re-creation of the White Dining Room from another of her tearooms nearby.

⚫ **City Halls**
(*Candleriggs; tel: 0141 353 8000;
www.glasgowcityhalls.com*),
together with the adjacent
Old Fruitmarket (Albion
Street), is one of the
country's most exciting
music venues. The BBC
Scottish Symphony
Orchestra, the Scottish
Chamber Orchestra and the
Scottish Music Centre are
based here. Celtic
Connections and other
popular music festivals are
held in the Old Fruitmarket.
The Royal Scottish National
Orchestra (RSNO), the
country's leading symphony
orchestra, performs at the
**Glasgow Royal Concert
Hall** (*2 Sauchiehall Street;
tel: 0141 353 8000;
www.grch.com*). **Theatre
Royal** (*282 Hope Street;
tel: 0870 060 6647;
www.theambassadors.com*) is
the home of Scottish Opera
and presents opera, ballet
and children's theatre.

Glasgow's top theatres
include **King's Theatre**
(*297 Bath Street; tel: 0870
060 6648;
www.theambassadors.com*),
which presents touring
musicals; **Tron Theatre**
(*63 Trongate; tel: 0141 552
4267; www.tron.co.uk*), and
The Citizens' Theatre
(*119 Gorbals Street; tel:
0141 429 0022;
www.citz.co.uk*).

**Glasgow Film Theatre
(GFT)** (*12 Rose Street;
tel: 0141 332 6535;
www.gft.org.uk*) presents
films and events in an art-
deco building.

Left
The Mackintosh-designed
Glasgow School of Art

Radisson SAS Hotel ££ *301 Argyle Street; tel: 0141 204 3333; fax: 0141 204 3344; e-mail: info.glasgow@radissonsas.com; www.glasgow. radissonsas.com.* This stylish hotel in the city centre is sleek and impressive, more like a boutique hotel than an international chain. The 250 guest rooms are beautifully designed, with contemporary décor and amenities. There are two good restaurants, two bars and a health club. It's two minutes' walk from Glasgow Central Station, close to shopping and attractions.

St Jude's Hotel ££ *190 Bath St; tel: 041 352 8800; e-mail: info@saintjudes.com; www.saintjudes.com.* The St Jude's boutique hotel has just six rooms, with a fashionable bar/lounge and very popular restaurant attached. Although there are only six rooms (one standard, four deluxe and one penthouse suite), they are all spacious and come with such amenities as fresh fruit and flowers daily, complimentary wifi, iPod docking stations, and you can even borrow an iPod pre-loaded with music and videos if you've left yours at home. Definitely a touch of class.

Chardon d'Or ££–£££ *176 West Regent Street; tel: 0141 248 3801; www.brianmaule.com.* Formerly head chef at the Michelin-starred Le Gavroche in London, Scottish chef Brian Maule opened his own elegant restaurant in this city-centre townhouse. He combines French techniques with the finest Scottish ingredients to produce superior food. The pre-theatre menu is excellent value. Booking advised.

Suggested tour

Length: The main route covers about a mile (1.6km), with the detour adding another half mile (0.8km).

Time: You can walk the main route in an hour and a half, not counting stops. The detour takes another 15 minutes each way.

Route: This walking tour centres on the Merchant City, taking in the Cathedral with an optional detour to Glasgow Green. Begin at **George Square ❶**, laid out in 1782, and the city's main square with statues and civic buildings. It is adorned with floral displays throughout the year. Commanding the east side of the square are the **City Chambers ❷**, opened in 1888. Built in the Italian Renaissance style, it is one of the grandest structures in Britain. Guided tours of the opulent interiors are given on weekdays at 1030 and 1430, when the council is not in session. From the west side of the square, walk south on Queen Street. On your right, in the former Royal Exchange, is the **GALLERY OF MODERN ART ❸**. Head west on Ingram Street. **Hutchesons' Hall ❹** (1802) sits at the top of Hutcheson Street, its creamy white walls and graceful spire looking very stately when viewed from the opposite end. It is now the offices and shop of the National Trust for Scotland. Next door is the **Italian Centre ❺**, best entered through its smart

Glasgow is the UK's biggest retail centre outside London. You'll find everything from designer names to flea markets. Buchanan Street is an attractive, pedestrianised street with branches of the main high-street chains and other shops. The most famous shopping centre in Glasgow is Princes Square, An outdoor square was enclosed to create a very stylish mall on several levels; the shops are generally upmarket.

Nearby, the long L-shaped Argyle Arcade is a brightly lit promenade of jewellery shops. Over the road is another mall, the St Enoch Centre, which is less upmarket. The Italian Centre, off Ingram Street, boasts the UK's first Versace outlet, in company with other designer names.

At the other end of the scale, the Barras, just east of Glasgow Cross, is Glasgow's famous weekend flea market (*Sat and Sun 0900–1700*) with hundreds of traders.

 The Tramway *25 Albert Drive; tel: 0141 276 0950; www.tramway.org* is one of Europe's best spaces for contemporary art exhibitions.

Above
Highlight of the Mackintosh itinerary – the Willow Tea Rooms

courtyard off the pedestrianised John Street, which is decorated with metalwork sculptures and surrounded by cafés. The centre is typical of the Glasgow renaissance, with remodelled warehouses now housing designer shops. Continue east on Ingram Street to the top of Candleriggs. On the left, **Ramshorn Kirk** ❻ is one of the earliest Gothic Revival churches in Scotland, and is now used as a theatre by Strathclyde University. Turn right on Candleriggs. The **City Halls** ❼ are the old Victorian market halls, and these splendid buildings are now used for concerts. You will notice the fruitmarket and, round the corner on Bell and Albion streets, the **Café Gandolfi** ❽ in the old cheesemarket, one of the first Merchant City revamps. Continue south on Albion to Trongate. To the left is **Glasgow Cross** ❾, the centre of the city until Victorian times. In the middle of this junction is the **Tolbooth Steeple** ❿, a seven-storey tower with a crown built in 1626.

Detour: Walk south on Saltmarket to the entrance to Glasgow Green on the north bank of the River Clyde. The road through the centre leads past the crumbling Doulton Fountain and the Nelson Monument to the **PEOPLE'S PALACE** ⓫. Beyond the museum, off Glasgow Green, is the former **Templeton's Carpet Factory** ⓬, built in 1889; its multicoloured brick-and-tile façade is one of the city's architectural highlights. It now houses a business centre. Return to Glasgow Cross to continue the tour.

Now walk north on High Street, which becomes Castle Street. On the left as you approach the cathedral is **PROVAND'S LORDSHIP** ⓭ and, opposite, the **ST MUNGO MUSEUM OF RELIGIOUS LIFE AND ART** ⓮. Just beyond is **GLASGOW CATHEDRAL** ⓯. Walk west on Cathedral Street past Strathclyde University, and turn left on North Hanover Street to return to George Square.

Admission is free to most Glasgow museums. **The Centre for Contemporary Arts (CCA)** (*350 Sauchiehall Street; tel: 0141 352 4900; www.cca-glasgow.com*) presents changing exhibitions and has a regular programme of theatre, dance and other events.

Also worth exploring

Glasgow School of Art (*167 Renfrew Street; tel: 0141 353 4526; admission by guided tour only*) is one of Charles Rennie Mackintosh's finest buildings, designed when he was just 28. The Clydebuilt, the Scottish Maritime Museum at Braehead (*1 King's Inch Road; tel: 0141 886 1013*), has displays and interactive exhibits on Glasgow's shipbuilding history and the River Clyde. One of the main features of Victoria Park (*1 Victoria Park Drive North*) is the **Fossil Grove**, with fossils some 350 million years old. **Crookston Castle** (*off Brockburn Road, Pollok*) is a tower house dating from the 12th century.

Charles Rennie Mackintosh

Charles Rennie Mackintosh was one of the 20th century's most important architects and designers. He was born in Glasgow in 1868, and studied at the Glasgow School of Art, where he met his wife, Margaret Macdonald. Their experiments with crafts and design gained critical favour, and they were instrumental in developing the 'Glasgow Style'. Mackintosh designed public buildings and private houses, and is perhaps best known for the interiors he created for Miss Cranston's four tearooms in the city. After his death in 1927, Mackintosh's work was largely forgotten, but in recent years there has been a revival of interest. The tourist information centre provides a list of Mackintosh-designed sights around the city, which include the Glasgow School of Art, the Willow Tea Rooms, Queen's Cross Church and Scotland Street School, as well as the Mackintosh House at the Hunterian Art Gallery.

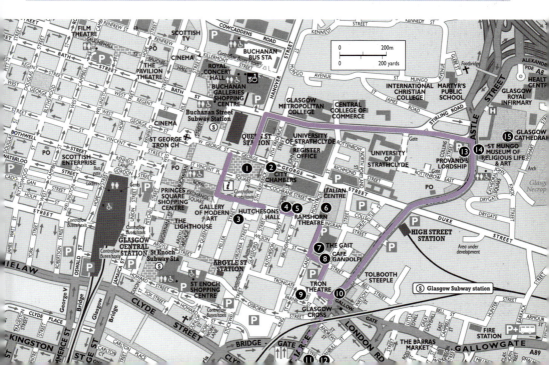

Stirling and the Mill Trail

Ratings

Castles	●●●●●
Historical sights	●●●●●
Walking	●●●●○
Scenery	●●●○○
Children	●●○○○
Museums	●○○○○
Shopping	●○○○○
Wildlife	●○○○○

Stirling, one of the first royal burghs, is among Scotland's most historic cities. The great battles of the Wars of Independence – Bannockburn and Stirling Bridge – were fought here, and Stirling Castle, favoured residence of the Stuart monarchs, remains the centrepiece of the attractive Old Town with its fine cathedral. Stirling stands at the centre of several tourist routes, one of which is the Mill Trail to the east. Known as the 'wee country', Clackmannanshire is the smallest county in Scotland. In the 19th century it was the country's second-largest textile producer. The mills were powered by streams rushing down the steep slopes of the Ochil Hills, and the string of towns backed up against them – Alva, Tillicoultry and Dollar among them – are known as the Hillfoots villages. The Ochil Hills offer pleasant walks, scenic drives through the beautiful glens of Glendevon and Gleneagles and splendid panoramic views from the peaks.

ALVA

ⓘ **Mill Trail Visitor Centre** *West Stirling Street (A91), Alva; tel: 01259 763 100. Open all year.*

Situated at the foot of Silver Glen, Alva is the centre for the Hillfoots towns today. Its Mill Trail Visitor Centre has an exhibition and audio-visual show that takes you through the history of the mills and the life of the people who worked in them. Adjoining the centre is the Maddy Moss Mill Shop, where you can watch the production of fine knitwear. From Alva you can reach Ben Cleuch, the highest peak in the Ochils at 2363ft (720m).

BANNOCKBURN

Ⓗ **Bannockburn £** *Junction 9, off M80/M9; tel: 01786 812 664, www.nts.org.uk. Grounds open all year; Heritage Centre Mar–Oct daily 1000–1730.*

This historic battlefield was the site of Robert the Bruce's victory over Edward II's army in 1314, freeing Scotland from English domination. An audiovisual presentation tells the story of the battle, and the grounds include Bruce's command post, the Borestone site, enclosed by a Rotunda and a towering equestrian statue of Bruce in his armour.

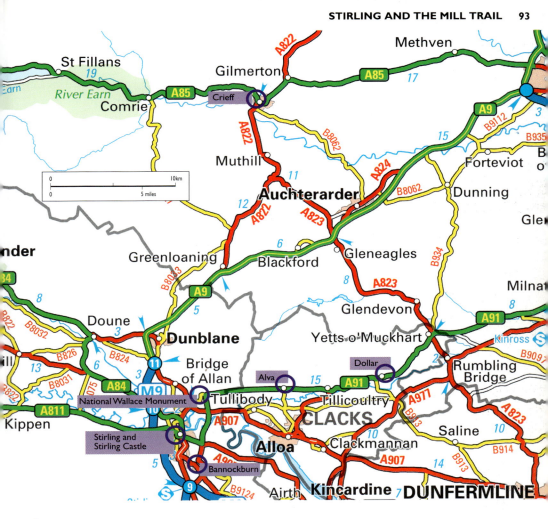

CRIEFF

ⓘ Crieff Tourist Information Centre *Town Hall, High Street; tel: 01764 652 578; e-mail: crieff@visitscotland.com. Open all year.*

ⓘ Crieff Visitor Centre *Muthill Road; tel: 01764 654 014; e-mail: info@crieff.co.uk; www.crieff.co.uk. Open all year.*

Crieff, once the venue for Scotland's largest cattle market, became a popular resort with the coming of the railway in Victorian times and thus it has remained. This attractive town, set on the south slope of the Grampian foothills, has several tourist attractions and is a good base for walkers, anglers and golfers. It is home to the **Glenturret Distillery** (*on the A85 towards Comrice; tel: 01764 656 565; www.glenturret.com; open daily*), Scotland's oldest, which puts on a good tour and free tastings. At the **Crieff Visitor Centre** you can watch the production of the distinctive *millefiori* (the name means 'a thousand flowers') glass paperweights and tour the Buchan pottery factory. South of town are the formal, terraced **Drummond Castle Gardens** (*tel: 01764 681 257; open Easter and May–Oct daily 1300–1800*).

DOLLAR

Castle Campbell (Historic Scotland)
£ Tel: 01259 742 408;
www.historic-scotland.gov.uk.
Open Apr–Sep daily
0930–1730; Oct–Mar
Sat–Wed 0930–1630.

Dollar is one of the more attractive Hillfoots towns, with its cherry-lined burn and Academy. **Dollar Glen**, a 54-acre (22-ha) area of woodland managed by the National Trust for Scotland, has a splendid scenic path up to **Castle Campbell**. Built in the late 15th century, the tower house was the Lowland home of the Campbell clan chiefs, the Earls of Argyll. The castle's finest feature is its impressive location rising above the hills, and there are fantastic views from the parapet walk extending as far as the Forth Valley and Pentland hills.

STIRLING

Stirling Visitor Centre Castle Esplanade; tel: 08707 200 622. Open all year. There is a good audiovisual programme about the town and its history.

Church of the Holy Rude St John Street; tel: 01786 475 275. Open May–Sep 1100–1600.

Argyll's Lodging (Historic Scotland) £ Castle Wynd; tel: 01786 431 319; www.historic-scotland.gov.uk. Open daily Apr–Sep 0930–1730; Oct–Mar 0930–1630.

Stirling Castle (Historic Scotland) ££ Tel: 01786 450 000; www.historic-scotland.gov.uk. Open daily Apr–Sep 0930–1800; Oct–Mar 0930–1700; last entrance 45 minutes before closing.

In medieval times Stirling was known as the brooch or clasp of Scotland, due to its strategic position on the River Forth at the crossroads of north-south routes. It plays a similar role for visitors today. This historic city never fails to delight with its awesome castle and impressive Old Town. The **Stirling Visitor Centre** at the castle esplanade presents a good, free film about the town's history. As you wander through the streets, information plaques point out the historic buildings along the way. Highlights include the **Church of the Holy Rude** with exquisite stained

glass and timber roof, the striking Renaissance façade of **Mar's Wark**, the 17th-century mansion **Argyll's Lodging** and the amusing **Old Town Jail** (St John Street; tel: 01786 450 050; open daily Apr–Sep 0930–1700; Oct and Mar 0930–1630; Nov–Feb 0930–1530), not to mention many restaurants and shops.

Stirling Castle

Dominating the town and countryside from atop a volcanic crag, Stirling Castle was one of Scotland's most important strongholds. It dates from 1496 and was the royal court of the Stuart monarchs. Among the highlights are the Royal Apartments with the rare carved oak medallions known as the Stirling Heads, the Chapel Royal and the Great Kitchens with their amusing displays of 16th-century fare – you might even take home a recipe or two! The views from the ramparts are magnificent. While much of the splendid Renaissance architecture has been restored, some parts of the castle are undergoing renovation. Many rooms are now empty, but will in time be furnished with specially woven tapestries and period furniture reproductions to re-create the palace ambience.

Above
Mar's Wark

National Wallace Monument ££
Abbey Craig, Hillfoot Road; tel: 01786 472 140; www. nationalwallacemonument.com. Open Jan–Feb and Nov–Dec 1030–1600; Mar–May and Oct 1000–1700; Jun 1000–1800; Jul–Aug 0930–1830; Sep 0930–1700.

Right
Stirling Castle

National Wallace Monument

This 220-ft (67-m) Gothic tower, completed in 1869, commemorates William Wallace, Scotland's national hero, whose clever tactics defeated the English army at the Battle of Stirling Bridge in 1297. There is a dramatisation of this historic event in the battle tent, a Hall of Heroes and spectacular views from the top of the tower (246 steps to the top!). The walk up from the car park takes 10–15 minutes and is quite steep in places; a shuttle bus runs every 15–20 minutes.

Accommodation and food

The Barnton Bar & Bistro £ *3½ Barnton Street, Stirling; tel: 01786 461698; www.thebistro.co.uk.* Café and bar opposite the main post office serving meals and snacks.

Castlecroft B&B £ *Ballengeich Road, Stirling; tel: 01786 474 933; e-mail: castlecroft@gmail.com; www.castlecroft.uk.com.* Pleasant and comfortable rooms in a friendly guesthouse nestled on the hill beneath Stirling Castle. There are splendid panoramic views of the Grampians and Trossachs from the large lounge. Convenient for the castle and town centre.

Merlindale £ *Perth Road, Crieff; tel/fax: 01764 655 205; e-mail: info@merlindale.co.uk; www.merlindale.co.uk.* You couldn't ask for a finer Highland welcome than at this lovely Georgian home at the foot of the Grampians. Rooms are beautifully decorated, two with large sunken bathrooms; one has a whirlpool. Dinners here feature superb Cordon Bleu cooking with the cordial hosts. Guests can also relax in the library or garden.

**Alloa Tower
(National Trust for
Scotland)** £ *Tel: 01259
211 701; www.nts.org.uk.
Open Apr–Oct daily
1300–1700.*

The River House ££ *Castle Business Park, Stirling; tel: 01786 465 577;
www.riverhouserestaurant.co.uk.* Informal restaurant beside the loch at
the foot of Stirling Castle. The changing menu fuses French and
Scottish cuisine using fresh local produce, from steaks, poultry and fish
to vegetarian entrées. The lunchtime and early evening menus are good
value, with two courses and a complimentary drink in the evening.

Suggested tour

Total distance: The main route is 55 miles (88.5km). The detour to
Alloa Tower is 6 miles (9.5km). The longer route, returning from Crieff
to Stirling via Lochearnhead, is 78 miles (125.5km).

Time: The main route will take 2 hours to drive. The return via
Lochearnhead will take about half an hour longer. Those with little
time should concentrate on Stirling, with perhaps a visit to Crieff.

Links: The A822 north from Crieff through Sma' Glen is a scenic route
to Dunkeld (*see page 204*) and Aberfeldy (*see page 146*). This route
adjoins the Trossachs tour (*see page 102*), while the A91 continues east
to Fife (*see page 212*). Stirling is a quick drive from Glasgow on the
M80 and from Edinburgh on the M9.

Route: From the **WALLACE MONUMENT** ❶, continue along
Hillsfoot Road and at the junction take the A91 for 4 miles (6.5km) to
ALVA ❷, passing Menstrie Castle, 16th-century home of the first Earl
of Stirling, who was the main founder of the colony of Nova Scotia in
Canada. Continue east on the A91 through Tillicoultry, another
historic mill town, to **DOLLAR** ❸.

Detour: From Alva, take the B908 (signposted) south 3 miles (5km) to
Alloa ❹. The Alloa Tower, which dates from 1497, is all that remains of
the ancestral seat of the Earls of Mar; it has rare medieval features such
as the timber roof. Return to the main road at Tillicoultry via the A908.

From Dollar, continue 4 miles (6.5km) to the Yetts o' Muckhart and
the junction for the A823. Just over a mile (1.6km) to the right is
Rumbling Bridge ❺, where the River Devon tumbles through a deep
gorge. There's a walkway and viewing platform, but only a handful of
parking spots on the busy roadside, making the effort to see it more
trouble than it's worth.

The A823 leads north through the beautiful countryside of **Glendevon**
❻ and **Gleneagles** ❼, surrounded by the Ochil Hills. Incidentally, the
name 'eagles' refers to churches, not birds of prey. The famous golf
course and hotel of Gleneagles is nearby at Auchterarder. After about
13 miles (21km) you reach the junction with the A822. Turn right,
passing through Muthill with its striking church, and continue 5 miles
(8km) to **CRIEFF** ❽.

**Auchingarrich
Wildlife Centre ££**
*Tel: 01764 679 469. Open
1000–dusk.*

Take the A822 south for about 10 miles (16km) to Braco, and turn
right onto the B8033 for 7 miles (11km) to **Dunblane** ➒. The
magnificent 13th-century **cathedral** ➓ is the centrepiece of this
peaceful town on the Allan Water. Among its many fine features
are the west front and the choir. Stirling is about 5 miles (8km) south
on the A9.

Detour: To lengthen the tour, take the A85 from Crieff to the pretty
village of **Comrie** ⓫, 6 miles (9.5km) west. Situated on the Highland
Boundary Fault, it has the strange distinction of being the earthquake
centre of Scotland, with an Earthquake House (*open Apr–Oct*) built in
1874 to record earth tremors. Children will enjoy the **Auchingarrich
Wildlife Centre** here. Continue on the A85 for 11 more miles
(17.5km), along the shores of Loch Earn, to Lochearnhead ⓬. Return
to Stirling via Callander (*see page 100*) on the A84, a distance of
28 miles (45km).

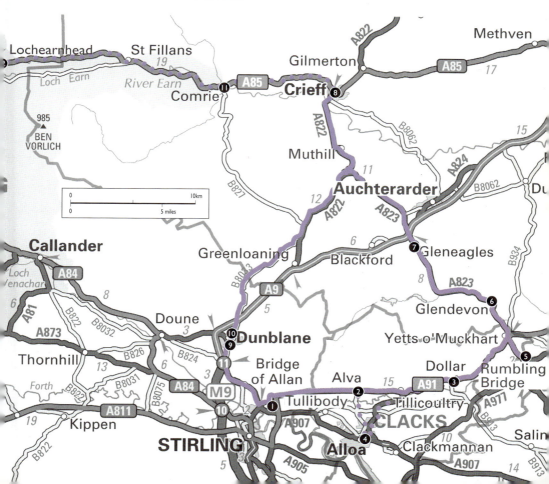

The Trossachs

Ratings

Outdoor activities	●●●●●
Walking	●●●●●
Scenery	●●●●○
Children	●●●○○
Wildlife	●●●○○
Mountains	●●○○○
Museums	●●○○○
Castles	●○○○○

The Trossachs have been called 'Scotland in miniature' and indeed this small region contains mountains, lochs, forests and pastoral lowlands, from its highest peak, Ben Lomond – at 3192ft (973m) the most southerly of the Highland Munros – to Scotland's only lake (as opposed to loch), Menteith. Add to this its proximity to Glasgow (less than an hour's drive) and Edinburgh, and its popularity with day-trippers, weekenders and tourists alike is not surprising. In fact, the Trossachs have been a tourist destination since the end of the 18th century. The best time to visit here is in the early morning, when the natural peace and beauty of the region prevail. The Trossachs' greatest tourism booster is the legendary reiver Rob Roy MacGregor. This is MacGregor country, and whatever the true story of this Scottish Robin Hood, so much romanticised in literature and film, may be, it is hard to dismiss the daring tales amid the magnificent scenery of his homeland.

ABERFOYLE

ⓘ Trossachs Discovery Centre *Main Street; tel: 08707 200 604. Open daily Apr–Oct, weekends only Nov–Mar.*

Ⓣ The Scottish Wool Centre *Main Street; tel: 01877 382 850. Open daily Apr–Sep 0930–1730; Oct–Mar 1000–1630. Charge for shows £.*

Set in lovely foothills at the start of the Highlands, Aberfoyle is the southern entrance to the Trossachs. It is a picture-postcard town geared towards tourism, with pleasant cafés, restaurants and shops. Local legends abound with tales of the 'fairy folk' that inhabit these parts, and in 1691 the town's minister published *The Secret Commonwealth of Elfs, Fawns and Fairies*, following an alleged holiday in their realm. The **Trossachs Discovery Centre** gives a good overview of the area's natural history. A popular attraction is the **Scottish Wool Centre**, with sheep shows, working sheepdogs and spinning demonstrations.

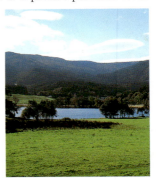

Right
View of the Trossachs

CALLANDER

Callander Tourist Information Centre (£ for exhibition)
Ancaster Square; tel: 01877 330342. Open all year.

Hamilton Toy Collection £
111 Main Street; tel: 01877 330 004. Open Easter–Oct Mon–Sat 1000–1630, Sun 1200–1630.

Factory shops and showrooms where you can watch the stages of production include **Kilmahog Woollen Mill**, with a traditional weaving shed, and **Mounter Pottery**.

Callander, the main town of the Trossachs region, has a long, attractive main street with good shops, restaurants and hotels. Just a few yards away are the Callander Meadows, a quiet spot for relaxing on the banks of the River Teith, while the Callander Crags, above the town, offer woodland walks with beautiful views. The exhibition at the **Rob Roy and Trossachs Visitor Centre**, housed beneath the Gothic spire of the old parish church, is an entertaining insight into the true life story of Scotland's outlaw-hero, and has excellent displays on Highland life. Nearby, the **Hamilton Toy Collection** makes nostalgic browsing for big kids as well as little ones.

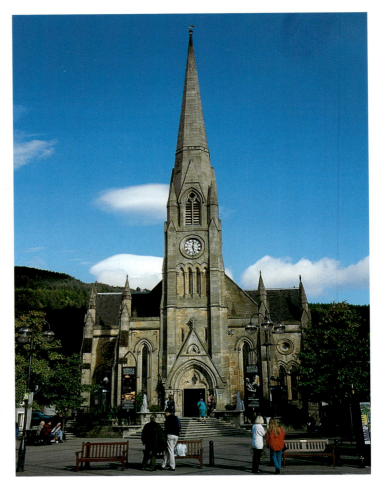

Right
Callander Tourist Information Centre

LAKE OF MENTEITH

Lake of Menteith Fishery *Port of Menteith, Stirling FK8 3RA; tel: 01877 385 664. Open Apr–Oct.*

Inchmahome Priory (Historic Scotland) £ *Tel: 01877 385 294; www.historic-scotland.gov.uk. Open Apr–Sep daily 0930–1630 (last sailing).*

Scotland's only true 'lake' (as opposed to the usual Scottish styling of 'loch') is a beauty spot with a wealth of flora and fauna. Its stock of rainbow trout makes it a fine fishing hole, not only for anglers but also for ospreys and herons. The largest of its three islands is Inchmahome, sometimes also known as the 'Isle of Rest'. On the island is a beautifully situated   Augustinian priory founded in 1238. Now in ruins, the priory witnessed the wedding of King David II of Scotland to his second wife, Margaret. Mary Queen of Scots took refuge here as a child before she left for France. A ferry from the Port of Menteith takes visitors to the island.

LOCH KATRINE

SS *Sir Walter Scott* ££ *Tel: 01877 376 316; www.lochkatrine.com. Morning and afternoon cruises Easter–Oct.*

Trossachs Cycle Hire *at Loch Katrine has a range of children's and adults' mountain bikes for hire by the hour or by the day. Tel: 01877 382 614; www.trossachsholidays.co.uk*

Beautiful Loch Katrine was the inspiration for Sir Walter Scott's poem *The Lady of the Lake*. However, it is not named after a woman but derives from the Gaelic word 'cateran', a Highland robber. The loch is nearly 10 miles (16km) long and more than a mile (1.6km) wide. From the pier there are cruises on the steamship *Sir Walter Scott* across to Stronachlachar. Near the head of the loch is the MacGregor clan graveyard and Glengyle House, birthplace of Rob Roy. A lovely lochside road, open only to walkers and cyclists, runs along the north bank. As long ago as 1859, the pure waters of Loch Katrine began to be piped 35 miles (56km) to the city of Glasgow, as they are today.

Rob Roy MacGregor

The real Rob Roy was born in 1671 near Loch Katrine, the 'roy' (the Gaelic *ruadh*, or red) a reference to the colour of his hair. He was the son of a MacGregor chieftain and fought alongside his father at the Battle of Killiecrankie, where he distinguished himself as a skilled swordsman. The MacGregors were notorious reivers, or cattle raiders, and Rob Roy organised a kind of blackmail in exchange for a 'watch' over his neighbours' herds. In those days when cattle roamed wild in the hills, reiving was not seen as a dishonourable profession among the clans. Nevertheless, the MacGregor name was proscribed more than once. After his father's death in 1702, Rob Roy became acting chief of the clan as well as a prosperous cattle drover. But in 1713 he was falsely accused of stealing £1000 from the Duke of Montrose and was forced to flee to the hills, thus beginning his life as an outlaw. In 1725 he was pardoned and died peacefully at his home in Balquhidder in 1734. Defiant to the end, his grave is marked with the epitaph 'MacGregor Despite Them'.

QUEEN ELIZABETH FOREST PARK

ⓘ David Marshall Lodge Visitor Centre *Queen Elizabeth Forest Park, 1 mile (1.6km) from Aberfoyle; tel: 01877 382 258; www.forestry.gov.uk/qefp. Open daily Mar–Oct; weekends Jan–Feb.*

Covering some 65 square miles (168 sq km), Queen Elizabeth Forest Park has a beautiful landscape of forest, lochs, mountains and open hills that provides a habitat for many wildlife species as well as miles of wooded trails for visitors. The visitor centre has information and maps of the cycle routes and waymarked footpaths and the Achray Forest Drive, plus an exhibition area and crafts. There are extensive views over the lowlands of the Forth Valley from the picnic area.

Accommodation and food

Brig o' Turk Tearoom £ *On the A821 at Brig o'Turk; tel: 01877 376 267.* Rustic tearoom and licensed restaurant serving home-cooked meals – venison stew, cottage pie, Trossachs trout, soups and vegetarian dishes.

Glenbruach Country House B&B £ *Loch Achray; tel: 01877 376 216; e-mail: james.lindsay5@btinternet.com; www.nationalparkscotland.com.* Victorian mansion in secluded grounds on a hill overlooking Loch Achray and the Trossachs Church. Spacious rooms with original features, interesting books and collections, and gardens. Evening meals available.

The Roman Camp Country House Hotel £££ *Callander; tel: 01877 330 003; fax: 01877 331 533; e-mail: mail@romancamphotel.co.uk; www.romancamphotel.co.uk.* Set off Callander's main street on the banks of the River Teith, this pink turreted hotel was built as a hunting lodge in the 17th century, near the site of a Roman camp. Bedrooms are attractively furnished and vary in size and style. Features include a gracious fire-lit lounge, conservatory and a large library full of character with a secret chapel. Outside is a beautiful walled garden set in 20 acres (8ha) of grounds. Elegant restaurant with innovative cuisine.

The Roman Camp is open to non-residents for meals. It is a popular spot for a formal tea on Sunday afternoons – a great way to enjoy the atmosphere if you're passing through. Booking is advised, but not essential.

Suggested tour

Total distance: The main route is 34 miles (55km). The detour to Inversnaid is 15 miles (24km) each way.

Time: The main route around the Trossachs takes about 1.5 hours, not counting stops, although the actual length of time depends on the amount of traffic. The detour to Inversnaid takes about 40 minutes each way.

Above
Pretty Loch Katrine with its
lochside road.

Links: The Trossachs route can easily be done as a day-trip from Glasgow (*see pages 82–91*). It links naturally with Stirling and the Mill Trail (*see pages 92–97*), Breadalbane via Killin (*see page 152*), and Mid-Argyll via A84/A85 through Crianlarich (*see page 130*).

Route: From CALLANDER ❶ take the main street (A84) 1 mile (1.6km) north of town to **Kilmahog** ❷, known for its woollen mills. Turn left on the A821 (signposted 'The Trossachs Trail'). Continue along the shores of Loch Venachar, with picnic areas along the shore, to **Brig o' Turk** ❸, a pleasant hamlet where there is a nice café, and on to Loch Achray. The pseudo-castle building here, a former hotel, has been taken over by a time-share development which, in the usual spirit of such ventures, has fenced off the best open views of the loch for private access. Fortunately there's a (small) forestry commission car park just past here on the left for those who want to scramble up the trail to the top of Ben A'an and into Glen Finglas, an old cattle droving route through the hills. Carry on to the shores of **LOCH KATRINE** ❹, 10 miles (16km) from Callander.

Continue south on the A821. This is a pretty route through the high, forested ground known as the **Duke's Pass** ❺, particularly beautiful in autumn. A viewpoint about halfway along affords a splendid vista out over the treetops to the lowlands beyond. Near here is the entrance to the **Achray Forest Drive** ❻ (£), 7 miles (11km) of forest road through Queen Elizabeth Forest Park. There are parking areas where you can stop for a picnic or just to enjoy the woodland environment. Continue on the A821, descending to the visitor centre for the **QUEEN ELIZABETH FOREST PARK** ❼. Just beyond is **ABERFOYLE** ❽, the other main Trossachs town, 9 miles (14.5km) from Loch Katrine.

Detour: From Aberfoyle, a 15-mile (24-km) detour on the B829 leads to Inversnaid, on the shores of Loch Lomond, where Rob Roy went to live after his marriage to Mary in 1693. This is a splendid scenic drive that is less touristy and in many ways nicer than the Trossachs heartland. The narrow road winds along the shores of Loch Ard with nothing between you and the water but a low dry-stone wall. It passes through forest around Loch Chon, which means 'loch of the dogs', where there is access for small boats and picnic spots. As it emerges from the woodland there are stunning views of the distant Arrochar Alps, and you can almost see Rob Roy himself running his cattle through this wild land. At Stronachlachar, at the end of the B829 – Rob Roy was born in nearby Glen Gyle – there is a viewpoint over Loch Katrine. From here a single track continues for the last

Above
Rob Roy's view

4 miles (6.5km) past the Loch Arklet Reservoir; to the right are the ruins of an 18th-century barracks, built for troops sent in (without success) to control the troublesome MacGregors. Just before the descent to Inversnaid, a left turn over a wooden suspension bridge leads to a small car park and a path to a lookout called Rob Roy's View. Park in the village below for walks along the banks of Loch Lomond.

Right
Rob Roy's grave

From Aberfoyle, continue around on the A821/A81 for 3.5 miles (5.5km) to the **LAKE OF MENTEITH** ❾. About a mile (1.6km) beyond, at the junction take the right-hand fork onto the A873. The scenery here is strikingly different from the wooded hills you've just come through. Now it opens out into the green rolling hills and pastoral fields of the Forth Valley, as the road follows the river towards

**Doune Castle
(Historic Scotland)**
£ Just east of Doune; tel:
01786 841742. Open daily
Apr–Sep 0930–1700;
Oct–Mar Sat–Wed
0930–1600 (last admission).

Stirling. After passing the village of Ruskie, in another 4.5 miles (7km), turn left at Thornhill onto the B822 which, after 6 miles (9.5km), brings you back to Callander.

Also worth exploring

North of Callander, the A84 leads past the Falls of Leny to lovely Loch Earn and Lochearnhead. On the way you can pay your respects at **Rob Roy's Grave** by following a minor road to the left to Balquhidder. There are fine walks in Balquhidder Glen, below the rugged mountain terrain of the Braes of Balquhidder. Also from Callander, Bracklinn Road takes you above the town to the **Bracklinn Falls**, a dramatic plunge into a deep gorge. They can also be reached on foot from town on a pleasant woodland walk. You may also like to visit the ruins of **Doune Castle**, location for the filming of *Monty Python and the Holy Grail*. From Aberfoyle you can continue south on the A81/A811 through Drymen, where the B837 takes you to picnic and camping spots on the east shores of Loch Lomond.

Argyll

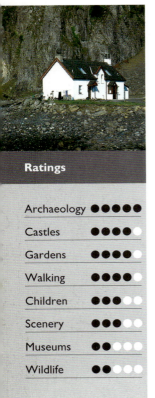

Ratings

Archaeology	●●●●●
Castles	●●●●○
Gardens	●●●●○
Walking	●●●●○
Children	●●●○○
Scenery	●●●○○
Museums	●●○○○
Wildlife	●●○○○

Argyll's scenery is quintessential Scotland, with wooded slopes bordering delightful lochs and glens. The mountains of Lorn sweep down to the coast around Oban, with magnificent views of the islands offshore, while to the south, sea lochs burrow into the coastline. With the mild climate brought by the Gulf Stream, rare and exotic species flourish and beautiful gardens have been developed around the county since the beginning of the 18th century. The hills and glens of Argyll have been settled since ancient times, as attested to by the wealth of prehistoric standing stones, carvings and burial cairns in Kilmartin Glen. Argyll was the stepping stone for a turning point in Scottish history when, at the end of the 5th century, the Irish Gaels established their kingdom of Dalriada at Dunadd Fort. From here their power and influence spread throughout the land and these settlers, the Scots, gave the country its name.

CARNASSERIE CASTLE

Carnasserie Castle (Historic Scotland)
Off the A816. Open at all times. Free.

The well-preserved ruins of Carnasserie Castle, which date from the latter part of the 16th century, were purposely built with a medieval look – notice the arrow slits in the lower walls of the tower, built less for defence than for show. The castle was the home of John Carsewell, Bishop of the Isles, who translated Knox's liturgy into Gaelic.

CLACHAN BRIDGE

The Tigh-na-Truish is an atmospheric spot for a drink or a bar meal. These days you can wear what you like!

The delightful, humpbacked Clachan Bridge holds a title far weightier than its small size would suggest: The Bridge Over the Atlantic. It was built by Thomas Telford in 1792 to link the island of Seil to the mainland across Seil Sound, which is indeed a narrow finger of the ocean. In the days of proscription the old Tigh-na-Truish inn here was known as the House of the Trousers, where Highlanders returning to the island would change back into their forbidden kilts.

DUNADD FORT

Dunadd Fort
Kilmartin Glen.
Access at all times. Free.

Dunadd Fort was the capital of the Scots kingdom of Dalriada from around AD 500 and was occupied intermittently until the mid-9th century. It is a superb example of a Dark Ages fortification, defended by a series of ramparts built into the natural features of the hill. These enclosed the timber buildings of the inhabitants, no trace of which survives. The climb up is less difficult than it looks from below, and at the top are the site's most remarkable features: a rock slab with the carving of a boar, the outline of a footprint and a rock-cut basin, as well as several lines of ogham inscription. These were believed to have been used in the kingship rituals of the day. The strategic importance of the site is easily apparent from the sweeping views over the countryside, including a fine view of the **Moine Mhor**, or Great Moss, one of the last wild raised bogs left in Britain.

ISLAND OF SEIL

The Island of Seil is a captivating spot, so peaceful and charming that you can while away an hour here before you realise it. It is a former slate quarrying centre, and the rows of whitewashed cottages along the shore at **Easdale**, its main village, are all the more picturesque against the chunky grey backdrop. There are boat trips to its off-lying island, also called Easdale, where you can visit the former slate quarries, now sea lagoons, and a fine folk museum. The village is a centre for local crafts and has a number of cute gift shops. The Highland Arts Exhibition is a shop with artworks by the local painter John Taylor. The lovely gardens of **An Cala** are nearby.

Right
Fishermen's cottages line the harbour at Easdale on the Island of Seil

Above
Ihid burial cairn near Kilmartin

KILMARTIN

The café at **Kilmartin House,** which features wild foods and local produce, is a pleasant spot for lunch or a coffee, with a great view of the cairn.

Kilmartin House £
On the A816;
tel: 01546 510 278;
www.kilmartin.org.
Open daily Mar–Oct
1000–1730; Nov–Dec, call
for times.

Some 150 prehistoric sites lie within 6 miles (9.5km) of the small village of Kilmartin. A fascinating overview of the area and its rich remains of standing stones, burial cairns and mysterious carvings can be seen at **Kilmartin House**. It begins with a superb 12-projector audiovisual show, *Valley of Ghosts*, with music performed on reconstructed ancient instruments. The Museum of Ancient Culture contains artefacts from the sites in Kilmartin Glen, reconstructions of ancient boats and musical instruments, and interesting explanations of prehistoric life, enhanced by models, listening posts and video sequences. The graveyard at **Kilmartin Church** contains one of the largest groups of medieval carved grave-slabs; many are unique to the West Highlands. Dating from the 9th to 16th centuries, the finest are the Poltalloch Stones of the Malcolm chiefs. Inside the church are the large carved Kilmartin Crosses.

Most prehistoric sites lie on private land amid livestock pastures and are accessible thanks to the goodwill of the owner. Always be sure to shut gates behind you in order to protect the animals and ensure access for future visitors.

Linear Cemetery (Historic Scotland)
Access at all times. Free.

The Linear Cemetery

Among the numerous archaeological sites in Kilmartin Glen, the most famous is the so-called Linear Cemetery, a line of burial cairns stretching southward from the village for 1.25 miles (2km). The easiest way to access some of the sites is from the Lady Glassary Wood car park just off the main road to the right, south of the village. In a field across the footbridge are the **Nether Largie Standing Stones**, whose alignment remains a mystery. Follow the path to the **Temple Wood Stone Circles**, built before 3000 BC. Nearby is the oldest cairn in the linear cemetery, **Nether Largie South Cairn**. The old coach road leads past the Mid, North and Glebe cairns back up the hill to Kilmartin, or you can return along the path to the car park.

LOCH AWE

The Forestry Commission has leaflets on walks of various lengths from Loch Awe, including the Dalavich Oakwood Trail, Inverinan Glen and Loch Avich. Ask at tourist information centres or contact *West Argyll Forest District, Lochgilphead PA31 8RS; tel: 01546 602 518; www.forestry.gov.uk*

Stretching over 25 miles (40km), Loch Awe is Scotland's longest loch. Until the last Ice Age it drained south, with an outlet where the village of Ford is today, but glacial action reversed this and it now flows north into the River Awe at the Pass of Brander, site of the Cruachan Dam hydroelectric project. Above it towers Ben Cruachan at 3695ft (1126m). There are scenic roads along both sides of the loch, though the unclassified road on the western side is arguably the finer one as it

Right
Oban dominated by McCaig's Folly, a replica of the Roman Colosseum

is less developed and runs along higher ground, with fantastic vistas over the forest and water. Much of the land on this side is managed by the forest service, and there are numerous woodland walks and picnic areas.

OBAN

① Tourist Information Centre *Argyll Square; tel: 01631 563 122. Open all year.*

Set around its picturesque harbour, **Oban** is an important ferry terminal, with car and passenger services to Mull, Coll, Tiree, Barra, South Uist, Colonsay and Islay, as well as Kerrera, Lismore, Luing and Easdale. Oban is a pleasant and popular tourist centre. It developed as a fishing port in the 18th century, and took off as a resort in Victorian times with the arrival of the railway and steamboat trips to the islands. Oban's unmissable landmark is **McCaig's Tower**, sometimes called McCaig's Folly, a replica of the Roman Colosseum. Intended as a family memorial, it was built by a local banker to provide work for unemployed stonemasons in 1897–1900. When the banker died, so did the project, and it remains unfinished. Other attractions include the **Oban Distillery** (*Stafford Street; tel: 01631 572 004; guided tours weekdays Feb–Dec and also Sat Jun–Oct and Sun Jul–Sep*). The **Oban War and Peace Museum** (*Old Oban Times Building, Corran Esplanade; tel: 01631 570 007; open daily Mar–Sep*) tells the story of local life and the region's strategic role during World War II through its collection of photographs and memorabilia.

Accommodation and food

The Barriemore Hotel ££ *Corran Esplanade, Oban; tel/fax: 01631 566 356; e-mail: reception@barriemore-hotel.co.uk; www.barriemore-hotel.co.uk.* Fifteen beautifully appointed rooms in a Victorian stone-built house overlooking Oban Bay and Kerrera Island. Dating from 1895, it was the home of the McCaig family, who built the landmark McCaig's Tower. Situated at a quiet end of the esplanade, about 10 minutes' walk from the town centre. Follow signs for Ganavan. Free parking.

The Waterfront Restaurant ££ *No 1, The Waterfront, Railway Pier, Oban; tel: 01631 563 110.* Fresh fish and seafood are the specialities at this attractive harbourside restaurant. Modern Scottish cooking with a Mediterranean influence.

The Gathering Restaurant ££–£££ *Breadalbane Street, Oban; tel: 01631 564 849. Open Easter–Christmas.* This Taste of Scotland restaurant is one of the oldest in Oban, an authentic Scottish banqueting hall built in 1882 to serve visiting royalty and noblemen. Downstairs, O'Donnell's Irish Pub features Celtic music and dance most evenings.

Arduaine Garden (National Trust for Scotland) £ *Arduaine, near Oban, on the A816; tel: 01852 200 366; www.nts.org.uk. Open daily 0930–sunset.*

Taychreggan Hotel £££ *Kilchrenan, near Taynuilt; tel: 01866 833 211; fax: 01866 833 244; e-mail: enquiries@taychregganhotel.co.uk; www.taychregganhotel.co.uk.* This is one of Britain's most romantic hotels, stunningly situated in 40 acres (16ha) of garden and woodland on the shores of Loch Awe. The old stone house, set round a cobbled courtyard, was built as a drover's inn over 300 years ago. Most of the 20 rooms and suites – beautifully decorated with every comfort – have loch views. The hotel also has fishing rights, boats and a ghillie. The restaurant is superb, and has won accolades for its innovative preparation and presentation of fresh Scottish fare. It is open to non-residents (booking essential). There is also an extensive selection of malt whiskies to try.

Suggested tour

Total distance: The main route is 70 miles (112.5km). The detour to the Isle of Seil is an 18-mile (29-km) round-trip. The detour to the archaeological sites between Kilmartin and Dunadd will add about 8 miles (13km).

Time: It will take roughly 2.5 hours for the main route, not counting stops. The detour for the Isle of Seil will take 20 minutes each way. Driving time for the archaeological sites is minimal.

Links: This route is a natural link with the tour of Mid-Argyll (*see page 128*). It also links with the Road to the Isles tour via Glen Orchy and Glencoe (*see page 141*). Oban is the port for ferries to the Isle of Mull (*see page 116*).

Route: From **OBAN** ❶ head south on the A816. After 8 miles (13km) you reach the junction for the B844.

Detour: Turn right on the B844 and go 5 miles (8km) to the **CLACHAN BRIDGE** ❷. Continue 4 miles (6.5km) to **Easdale** ❸ on the **ISLAND OF SEIL**. Return to the main road.

Continue on the A816. Near Kilmelford, on a promontory overlooking Asknish Bay, **Arduaine Garden** ❹ is known for its outstanding range of rhododendrons, azaleas and magnolias. After 19 miles (30.5km) you reach **CARNASSERIE CASTLE** ❺. A mile (1.6km) further on is **KILMARTIN** ❻.

Detour: Several of the ancient sites lie within 5 miles (8km) of Kilmartin. About a mile (1.6km) south on the main road, turn right to the Lady Glassary Wood car park for a short walk to see the sites at the **LINEAR CEMETERY.** ❼ A mile (1.6km) or so further along the A816 is another easily accessed site at **Dunchraigaig** ❽ (car park on the left), with a Bronze Age cairn and standing stones. Follow the path to the **Baluachraig rock carvings** ❾ with their strange cup-and-ring markings. About 4 miles (6.5km) from Kilmartin is the turn-off (to

The First Scots

The colonisation of Argyll by Gaels from Ireland was one of the most decisive events in Scottish history. It began in around AD 500, when Fergus Mor mac Eric moved his base of power here from Antrim. From their stronghold at Dunadd, the Scotti, or Scots, expanded throughout the country. Archaeological studies have provided some clues about the ancient rituals that took place here. At that time, the High King was the overlord of the rulers of separate Scots kingdoms. The footprint carved into the rock was a sign of allegiance. Each ruler poured a bit of earth from his own land into the footprint. The king sat on the Stone of Destiny (see page 208) and established his sovereignty by putting his foot over this symbolic joining of the kingdoms. The basin served as an anointing stoup.

Right
The 5000-year-old Nether Largie Stones, part of the Linear Cemetery in Kilmartin Glen

F **Ardanaiseig Gardens** *Ardanaiseig Hotel, Kilchrenan, on the B845. Open mid-Feb–Dec daily 0900–dusk. Free.*

the right) for **DUNADD FORT** **10** . Return to Kilmartin to rejoin the main route.

Head back north on the A816 and after about a mile (1.6km) turn right on the B840. At Ford, take the left-hand fork on the unclassified road that leads up the west side of **LOCH AWE** **11** . The Kilmaha viewpoint, about 8 miles (13km) along, has spectacular views up and down the loch in both directions. At the top end of the road turn left to Kilchrenan. Follow signs for **Ardanaiseig Gardens** **12** , with a variety of species covering 100 acres (40.5ha) of Victorian woodland on the shores of Loch Awe. Continue 6 miles (9.5km) on the B845 to **Taynuilt** **13** . Here you can visit the **Inverawe Fisheries and**

Inverawe Fisheries and Smokery
Tel: 01866 822 777. Open
Mar–Dec 0800–dusk.

**Bonawe Iron Furnace
(Historic Scotland) £**
Tel: 01866 822 432;
www.historic-scotland.gov.uk.
Open Apr–Sep daily
0930–1730.

**Cruachan Power
Station £**
Tel: 01866 822 618. Open
Easter–Oct 0930–1700;
Nov–Dec and Mar–Easter
call for opening times.
Closed Jan.

**Dunstaffnage Castle
(Historic Scotland) £**
Off the A85 north of Oban;
tel: 01631 562 465;
www.historic-scotland.gov.uk.
Open daily Apr–Sep
0930–1730; Oct–Mar
0930–1630.

Crinan Wood, at the
west end of the Crinan
Canal, has walks in the
ancient wildwood and
splendid views out to the
islands of Jura and Mull.

Above
Clachan Bridge, on the Isle
of Seil

Smokery ⑭ surrounded by a country park. Nearby at Loch Etive is the
Bonawe Iron Furnace ⑮, the remains of an 18th-century charcoal
furnace for iron smelting, with restored sheds and workmen's cottages.
To the east on the A85 is the **Cruachan Visitor Centre** ⑯, with tours
inside the underground power station on Loch Awe. Go west on the
A85 for 7 miles (11km) to **Connel** ⑰. The cantilevered bridge is one
of the largest of its type in Europe. Beneath the bridge is the
phenomenal Falls of Lora, a tidal waterfall whose direction changes
with the tide. From here it is 5 miles (8km) further on to Oban. On the
way, at Dunbeg, a side road to the right leads to **Dunstaffnage Castle**
⑱, which stands on a promontory at the entrance to Loch Etive. The
castle dates from the 13th century (the 17th-century tower house was
the home of the MacDougalls), but Dunstaffnage is believed to have
been the seat of the early Scots court until Kenneth MacAlpine moved
it to Scone following the unification with the Picts.

Also worth exploring

The 9-mile (14.5-km) **Crinan Canal**, between Crinan and
Lochgilphead, was built by Thomas Telford in the late 18th century as
a commercial waterway but is now a scenic spot used by fishing boats
and pleasure craft.

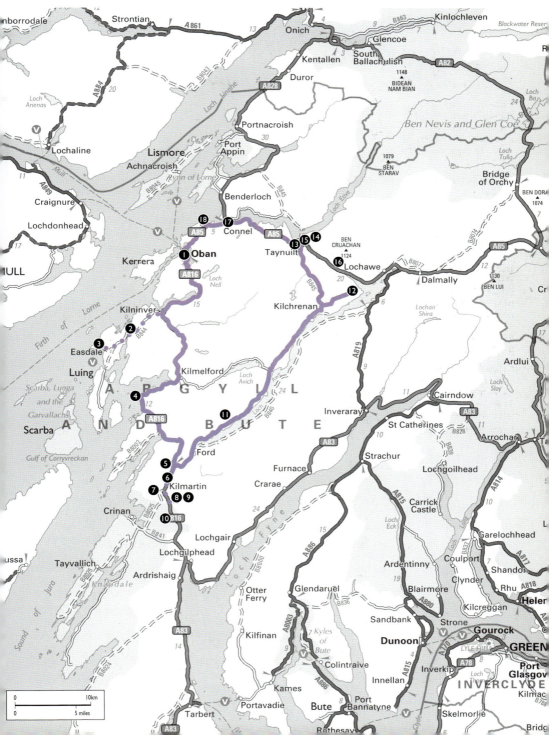

Ratings

Abbeys	●●●●●
Scenery	●●●●○
Beaches	●●●○○
Children	●●●○○
Walking	●●●○○
Watersport	●●●○○
Wildlife	●●●○○
Museums	●●○○○

Mull and Iona

Mull is the second-largest island of the Inner Hebrides. Its 300 miles (483km) of coastline are rocky, jagged and cut by deep sea lochs. Inland it is marked by a solitary Munro, Ben More, which rises to 3171ft (966m). Mull has some beautiful stretches of coastline, but the overall impression here is one of emptiness. Much of the interior is moorland, and most of the settlements, like the island's one main road, hug the shore. This road is single-track for all but 13 miles (21km), and it is narrow with tortuous stretches and hairpin bends around Dervaig. Your impression of Mull will depend largely on where else in Scotland you've been. If you're going no farther north and you want a bit of rugged road and remote landscape, then you'll probably enjoy it. But if you've seen the more dramatic scenery of the Highlands, you may wonder if the tiring road was worth the effort. Either way, Mull is a necessary stepping stone to Iona, the real gem.

CRAIGNURE

ⓘ Tourist Information Centre *The Pier, Isle of Mull; tel: 08707 200 610. Open all year.*

Ⓗ Torosay Castle and Gardens ££ *Tel: 01680 812 421. Open end Mar–Oct daily 1030–1700; garden open all year.*

Wings Over Mull £
Auchnacroish House, Torosay; tel: 01680 812 594; www.wingsovermull.com. Open Easter–Oct 1030–1730.

Craignure is the main ferry terminal for the island. There's little more here than the pier, the visitor centre and a couple of shops, but just down the road are two of the island's main sights. **Torosay Castle**, built in 1856, is actually a Victorian mansion. Its highlight is the Italian terraced gardens, designed by Robert Lorimer and graced with statues, which cover 12 acres (5ha). Also at Torosay, **Wings Over Mull** is a birds of prey and conservation centre, with exhibits and daily flying displays. A good way to get from Craignure to Torosay Castle is to take the miniature railway, with splendid views along the way (*departures daily Apr–Oct from the Old Pier Station, Mull Rail; tel: 01680 812 494*). Further down the road is **Duart Castle** (*off the A489; tel: 01680 812 309; www.duartcastle.com; open Apr Sun–Thu 1100–1600 and May–mid-Oct daily 1030–1730*), built in the 13th century and home of the Maclean clan chiefs. Perched on a clifftop overlooking the Sound of Mull, it affords fine views from the ramparts. The state rooms, dungeons and clan memorabilia are on show.

DERVAIG

The Old Byre Heritage Centre £
Tel: 01688 400 229. Open Apr–Oct Wed–Sun 1030–1830.

Mull Little Theatre
Tel: 01688 302 828; www.mulltheatre.org.uk. Open Apr–Sep.

Seven miles (11km) from Tobermory, Dervaig is home to the **Mull Little Theatre**. Once known as the smallest professional theatre in the country with only 37 seats, by adding half-a-dozen more it forfeited the title. Its productions are varied and highly acclaimed; needless to say, space is limited so book early. Nearby in Glen Bellart is the **Old Byre Heritage Centre**, with tableaux depicting island life through the ages, natural history exhibits and a film about the island.

The Tour of Mull Rally

Each year in October Mull becomes the racecourse for the Tour of Mull Rally, which gives you some idea of the nature of the driving here. The three-day event, which began in 1969, attracts around 2000 visitors, nearly doubling the island's population. Roads are closed to the public for the duration, so it is vital that you check with the area tourist board as to the exact dates if you plan on doing any sightseeing. Actually, the island is best avoided during the week prior to the rally as well, as there are plenty of Subarus and flashy Fords tearing around on test runs.

IONA

**Iona Abbey
(Historic Scotland)**
£ Tel: 01681 700 512.
Open all year.

**Iona Heritage
Centre** £ Tel: 01681 700
576. Open Apr–Oct
Mon–Sat 1030–1630.

The passenger ferry
from Fionnphort runs
continually throughout the
day and the crossing takes
5 minutes. The fare is
inexpensive.

Various tour operators
run **day cruises** from
Oban to Iona, Mull and the
tiny island of Staffa, with
the legendary Fingal's
Cave. Try Gordon Grant
Tours, Waterfront, Railway
Pier, Oban; tel: 01631 562
842.

Below
Iona's abbey church

This small island – just 3 miles (5km) long and a mile (1.6km) wide – is known as 'the cradle of Scottish Christianity'. St Columba landed here from Ireland in 563 and set up a monastery whose influence spread throughout the land. It is said that Columba chose Iona because it was the first point from which he could not see his native land. But archaeological evidence suggests that the island had long been a pagan centre of worship. Iona's importance was such that it became the burial place of Scottish kings. The island was viciously sacked by Viking raiders in the 8th century; Columba's original wooden monastery was destroyed and the community was forced to return to Kells, in Ireland. The Benedictines established an abbey here in 1203, which fell into ruins after the Reformation. Restoration of the buildings began in the early 20th century.

The most amazing thing about Iona is that it maintains its peaceful ambience despite the stream of visitors ferrying across each day. The first historic buildings you see are the ruins of the early 13th-century Augustinian **nunnery**, the finest example of a medieval nunnery in Britain. The **abbey church**, about 10 minutes' walk away, is beautifully restored. The tiny **St Columba's Shrine** is said to be the saint's original burial place. Of the 300 high crosses that surrounded the abbey before the Reformation, St Martin's Cross, outside the entrance, is the only original one left standing. The Cross of St John and other outstanding medieval carved stones can be seen in the **Infirmary Museum**. Iona's oldest building is

St Oran's Chapel, set in the early Christian graveyard where kings from Kenneth MacAlpine to Malcolm III are reputedly buried. Between the abbey and the nunnery is the **Iona Heritage Centre**, housed in the Old Manse, with displays on crofting, fishing and island life, and the 15th-century **MacLean's Cross**, carved in the Celtic tradition by the Iona school of carvers.

The most spiritual part of Iona is perhaps to be found away from the abbey and its crowds, in its tranquil machair landscape and shell beaches; it is best surveyed from atop the low hill, Dun I, north of the abbey.

Above
St Oran's Chapel

St Columba

St Colum Cille, the venerable St Columba, was born to an aristocratic family in Donegal, Ireland in AD 521. A natural scholar, he became an accomplished musician, poet, mathematician and scribe and founded several monasteries in Ireland. Then, in 561, he was exiled for his part in a family conflict that had led to a bloody battle. Columba and his followers sailed to Iona to pursue a monastic and missionary life. Because of his family standing, Columba was influential in the political life of the Celts. He arbitrated disputes among the Irish and Scots at Dalriada, and promoted the kingship of Aidan, crowning him at Dunadd. The saint was one of the foremost scholars of his day, and is said to have produced over 300 books as well as calculating solar and lunar cycles to determine the date of Easter and other Christian holy days. He died at Iona at the age of 75.

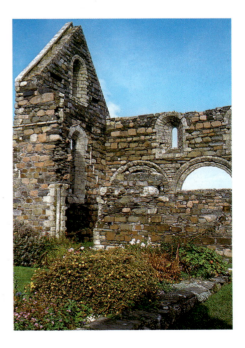

Right
Iona's 13th-century nunnery

TOBERMORY

Tourist Information Centre Main Street; tel: 0845 225 5121. Open Apr–Oct.

Tobermory Distillery £
Tel: 01688 302 645. Open Easter–Oct Mon–Fri 1000–1700, other times by appointment.

Hebridean Whale and Dolphin Trust Visitor Centre 28 Main Street, opposite the beach; tel: 01688 302 620; www.hwdt.org. Open all year. Free.

Columba Centre Fionnphort; tel: 01681 700 640. Open Apr–Oct daily 1000–1300 and 1400–1730. Free.

An Tobar Arts Centre has a summer programme of music, exhibitions and workshops for children. Tel: 01688 302 211; www.antobar.co.uk

Right
Coastal scenery on Mull

Tobermory, the main town on the island, has a lovely sheltered harbour lined with tall, brightly painted houses, photos of which grace many a travel brochure. From here the town climbs up the steep slopes of the surrounding hills. It can be very busy in summer. The harbour is a popular yachting centre, as well as a fishing, diving and cruising port. It also contains a lost treasure. In 1588 a Spanish galleon was blown up in the harbour along with its hoard of gold, most of which has never been found. The **Tobermory Distillery**, the only one on the island, gives tours. The **Hebridean Whale and Dolphin Trust Visitor Centre** has displays and information about these marine animals.

Accommodation and food

MacGochans £ Ledaig, Tobermory; tel: 01688 302 350. Pleasant harbourside pub adjacent to the distillery with a nautical theme and live music at the weekends. Good food, meals served 1200–2200 daily.

Highland Cottage ££ Breadalbane Street, Tobermory; tel: 01688 302 030; e-mail: davidandjo@highlandcottage.co.uk; www.highlandcottage.co.uk. Small, quality hotel built in the conservation area in Upper Tobermory, a few minutes' walk from the harbour. Comfortable, well-appointed rooms decorated with antique or four-poster beds and period furniture. Satellite TV and other amenities. Informal dining and well-presented fresh local fare.

The Tobermory Hotel ££ Waterfront, Tobermory; tel: 01688 302091; e-mail: tobhotel@tinyworld.co.uk; www.thetobermoryhotel.com. This family-run hotel overlooking the harbour was once a row of fishermen's cottages, but today it offers 15 cosy en-suite bedrooms and its Water's Edge restaurant is highly rated by local foodies.

Opposite
A replica of the 10th-century St John's Cross on Iona (the original is in the Infirmary Museum)

Try to avoid driving up and around the northwest coast into the setting sun, as the blinding light makes the hairpins around Dervaig all the more hellish.

Right
Visitors to Iona heading for a tour of Staffa and Fingal's Cave

Suggested tour

Total distance: The main route around the island is 130 miles (209km), including the leg to Fionnphort for the Iona ferry.

Time: Allow one very long day to see the entire island. Even if you catch the first ferry, you will be hard pressed to do the main route and see Iona as well before the last ferry back, so you will need to spend the night. Those with little time should concentrate on seeing Iona (best done on an organised tour from Oban, as it is much cheaper).

Route: Begin at the ferry landing at **CRAIGNURE** ❶. Follow the A849 for 37 miles (59.5km) to **Fionnphort** ❷. Be sure to visit the **Columba Centre** ❸, just off the main road, for an insight into Celtic Christianity and the life of St Columba, illustrated with artefacts and models. Park the car and take the passenger ferry to **IONA** ❹. From Fionnphort return on the same road to the junction with the B8035; turn left and continue to **Gruline** ❺, 39 miles (63km) away. The National Trust of Australia maintains the mausoleum of Major-General Lachlan Macquarie, a native son whose career in the British army led to his post as Governor-General of New South Wales, 1810–20. If you're running late or simply want to avoid the strenuous driving ahead, the B8035 cuts across the island's corset-like waist to Salen, where you can easily connect with Tobermory to the north or Craignure to the south. Otherwise, turn left on the B8073. For the next 13 miles (21km) there are beautiful views over Loch na Keal and Loch Tuath to Ulva and the other offshore islands. The small church, dating from 1755, overlooking the sea at **Kilninian** ❻, has a churchyard with carved gravestones from the early 16th century. The ruins of the Dun Aisgain stronghold lie on the coast to the north. **Calgary** ❼, 7 miles (11km) on, is known for its sandy beach. This was a prosperous crofting township until evictions in 1884 forced the people to emigrate to Canada, where they founded the town of Calgary, Alberta. The Carthouse Gallery at the Calgary Farmhouse Hotel has exhibitions of local artists in a lovely stone-arch gallery. About 7 miles (11km) beyond Calgary are some extremely steep and narrow hairpin-bends to negotiate, just before the town of **DERVAIG** ❽. There are more hairpins on the opposite end of town climbing up and over a bracken-covered ridge, and after 7 miles (11km) you will reach **TOBERMORY** ❾. From here it is 21 miles (34km) back to Craignure. Just before **Salen** ❿ you pass a ruined tower, part of Aros Castle, a 14th-century stronghold of the Lords of the Isles.

Also worth exploring

On the northeast coast, a 3-mile (5-km) walk from Carsaig leads to the **Carsaig Arches**, a natural archway carved through the rock below lava cliffs.

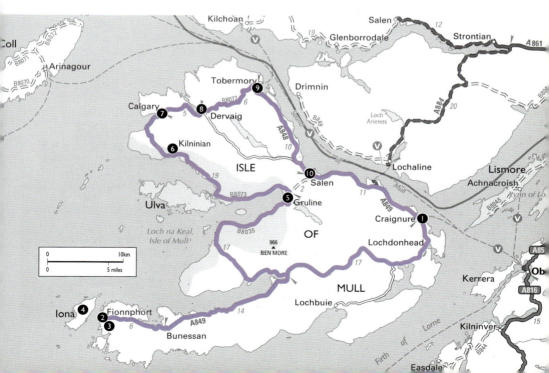

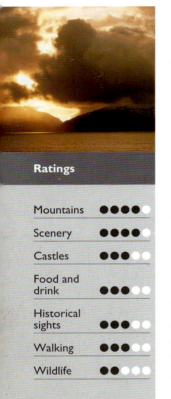

Ratings

Mountains	●●●●○
Scenery	●●●●○
Castles	●●●○○
Food and drink	●●●○○
Historical sights	●●●○○
Walking	●●●○○
Wildlife	●●○○○

Along the Argyll Lochs

From Loch Linnhe in the north to the Firth of Clyde, the coast of Argyll is sliced by sounds and sea lochs, with some, such as Loch Fyne and Loch Long, carving deep into the shoreline and shaping the dangling appendages of Cowal and Kintyre. Thus an inland town like Inveraray, seat of the Campbell clan chiefs, the dukes of Argyll, is known for its fresh seafood. Loch Fyne kippers grace breakfast menus throughout the country, and barrels of its famous herrings were once bestowed in gratitude for service to the town. At the tip of the loch, rugged mountains loom, with the dramatic road through Glen Croe winding down to Loch Long, which points a crooked fingertip at its inland neighbour, Loch Lomond. This is Britain's largest body of fresh water, and after a drive along its scenic shores, you can circle around to the top of its longest stretch, Loch Awe.

INVERARAY

ℹ Inveraray Tourist Information Centre
Front Street; tel: 0845 225 5121. Open all year.

🏰 Inveraray Castle ££
Tel: 01499 302 203; www.inveraray-castle.com. Open Apr–Oct 1000–1745, Sun 1200–1745.

Inveraray Jail ££
Church Square; tel: 01499 302 381. Open Apr–Oct daily 0930–1800; Nov–Mar 1000–1700.

Inveraray's original castle and the village that surrounded it were torched in 1644 during a military campaign, and nearly a century later work began on their replacements. It was worth the wait. The village that stands today on the shores of Loch Fyne is well planned and attractive, if somewhat touristy, with a fine parish church. **Inveraray Castle**, the home of the Duke of Argyll, head of the Campbells, now stands aloof among formal gardens, each corner guarded by a witch's-hat tower. The lofty

central hall with its impressive display of arms recalls the might of this Highland clan. There are also fine tapestries, portraits and memorabilia including Rob Roy artefacts. Other attractions include the **Inveraray Jail**, the **Argyll Wildlife Park** (*at Dalchenna, on the A83; open Apr–Oct*) and the *Arctic Penguin* iron sailing ship, the centrepiece of the **Inveraray Maritime Museum** (*The Pier; open daily*).

LOCH FYNE

Auchindrain Township £
6 miles (9.5km) south of Inveraray on the A83; tel: 01499 500 235. Open Apr–Oct daily 1000–1700.

Crarae Gardens £
10 miles (16km) south of Inveraray on the A83; tel: 01546 886 614. Open daily 0930–sunset; visitor centre Apr–Sep 1000–1700.

Loch Fyne, one of the country's largest salt-water lochs, is famous for its seafood and exports oysters and shellfish. There are excellent views of its lovely slate-blue waters from either shore. South of Inveraray, **Auchindrain Township** is an original West Highland village, the only communal tenancy township to have survived on its native site. The buildings have been preserved largely in their original form and offer a fascinating look at everyday life in times past. **Crarae Gardens** (National Trust for Scotland) has hundreds of species of rhododendrons and azaleas, exotic plants and native oaks set among a beautiful gorge.

LOCH LOMOND

The Drover's Inn
at Inverarnan at the top of the loch, is an atmospheric re-creation of the old 18th-century inn that once stood here. Serves traditional Scottish food and drink throughout the day.

The bonnie banks of Britain's largest expanse of fresh water have earned it the title 'Queen of Scottish Lochs' and made it the heart of Scotland's first national park, Loch Lomond and Trossachs National Park (*see page 132*). It covers more than 27 square miles (70sq km), measuring 23 miles (37km) long and more than 5 miles (8km) wide at its southern end. Here, it is dotted with some 38 islands, called 'inches', from the Gaelic word *innis*. All have names and were once inhabited, by everyone from saints to whisky smugglers. These are best seen on pleasure cruises from Tarbet, Luss, Balloch and Balmaha. The loch is surrounded by mountain scenery in the north, softening to pastoral green hills in the south. Only 20 miles (32km) from Glasgow, it is a busy weekend retreat.

Right
Loch Lomond

Right
Inveraray Castle and town

REST AND BE THANKFUL

The mountain pass at the top of Glen Croe is known in Argyll as 'The Rest'. In 1748, a detachment of soldiers, upon completing the old military road, erected a stone at its 800-ft (244-m) summit inscribed 'Rest and Be Thankful'. The present granite headstone is a replacement for the original, which disappeared. From here, hill walkers ascend Beinn Ime (3318 ft, 1011m).

Accommodation and food

Loch Fyne Oyster Bar £–££ *Tel: 01499 600 236. Open daily 0900–2030.* Set in an old farm building at Cairndow, this restaurant near the head of the loch is famous for its seafood and fine wines. The seafood chowder and home baking are excellent. It also has a shop selling fresh seafood and smoked fish, including salmon, mussels and, of course, oysters. Eight miles (13km) from Inveraray, beside the A83/A815 junction.

Suggested tour

Total distance: The main route is 75 miles (120km). The detour around Loch Awe will add an extra 45 miles (72km).

Time: The main route will take about 2 hours, not counting stops. The detour around Loch Awe will add 1 hour 20 minutes.

Links: The route is a natural link with the tour of Argyll (*see page 112*). From Crianlarich the A85 east takes you to Killin (*see page 149*) and then south to the Trossachs (*see page 98*), while the A82 north leads up through Glencoe (*see page 135*).

Below
Loch Fyne

Take care on the northern stretch of the A82 along Loch Lomond. The road is very narrow and twisty, and traffic can be frustrating here in summer.

Route: From **INVERARAY ❶** take the A83 east for 9 miles (14.5km) to the junction with the A815. Turn right and continue 2 miles (3km) to the B839.

Turn left on the B839 and begin the descent into **Hell's Glen ❷**. Perhaps it's the name that makes this road seem so scary, though it's really no worse than any other single-track. But the steep descent into the dark hanging valley keeps you on the lookout for goblins round every bend. After about 3.5 miles (5.5km), take the left-hand turn onto the B828, which climbs 1000ft (300m) in 3 miles (5km) up a dramatic mountain glen to a parking area where you can **REST AND BE THANKFUL ❸**.

Crianlarich, a pit-stop on the West Highland Way, and Tyndrum, with its proximity to a fortnight's worth of Munros, are popular bases for climbers and hill walkers.

Tarbet Tourist Information Centre *Main Street; tel: 08707 200 623. Open Apr–Oct.*

Detour: At the junction in Hell's Glen, you can continue on the B839 (right fork) to **Lochgoilhead** ❹, a whitewashed village now somewhat overtaken by a watersports centre. There are cruises on Loch Goil, or you can continue for 5 miles (8km) on a minor road to the ruins of Carrick Castle, a 14th-century Campbell stronghold.

Turn right on the A83, passing through **Glen Croe** ❺ for 7 miles (11km) to **Arrochar** ❻ on Loch Long. Set below the so-called Arrochar Alps, it is a popular base for climbers and walkers, as well as sea-anglers. **Tarbet** ❼, on the shores of **LOCH LOMOND** ❽, is 2 miles (3km) beyond. The town's name means 'isthmus', for in 1263 the Vikings dragged their boats across the narrow strip of land that separates Loch Lomond from Loch Long. At the junction, turn left on the A82 for a scenic drive up the west bank. **Ardlui** ❾, 8 miles (13km) north, with its mountain backdrop and pretty marina, is one of the most attractive resorts on the loch. In another 8 miles (13km) you reach **Crianlarich** ❿ and the junction with the A85. Turn left for 5 miles (8km) to **Tyndrum** ⓫ and continue west for 12 miles (19km) on A85 to **Dalmally** ⓬. About a mile (1.6km) past town, turn left on the A819. Just after the turn, on your right, you will have a fine view of the atmospheric ruins of **Kilchurn Castle** ⓭. From here it's a scenic 15 miles (24km) back to Inveraray.

Right
Ancient lookout tower on the hill above Inveraray

Opposite
The Scots pine, Scotland's native tree

Lochgilphead Tourist Information Centre
Lochnell Street;
tel: 0845 225 5121. Open
Apr–Oct.

Loch Lomond Shores ££ *Balloch;*
tel: 0845 345 4978;
www.lochlomondshores.com.
Open summer 0930–1800;
winter 1000–1700.

Detour: For a longer route, 6 miles (9.5km) past Dalmally take the B840 down the east side of Loch Awe. It is a scenic 21 miles (34km) to Ford, and just past the village turn left on the A816 for 9 miles (14.5km) to **Lochgilphead** ⑭ . Its attractions include Kilmory Castle Gardens, part of Kilmory Woodland Park, with walking trails and picnic sites; and the Highbank Pottery where you can watch porcelain production. From Lochgilphead take the A83 (signposted Glasgow) along the shores of Loch Fyne 23 miles (37km) back to Inveraray.

Also worth exploring

South from Tarbet, the road along Loch Lomond is smoother and gives fine views of the islands and Ben Lomond rising above the opposite shore. **Luss** is an attractive village with flower-strewn cottages and an old churchyard.

At Balloch, on the loch's southern edge, is **Loch Lomond Shores**, the visitor centre for the Loch Lomond and Trossachs National Park. The castle-like building has huge windows affording spectacular views over the loch, while two audiovisual shows tell the story of the loch and its famous song, 'The Bonnie Banks'.

Rob Roy fans can seek out the ruined cottage in **Glen Shira**, said to be the home of the outlaw hero at one time. It can be reached on a rough track north of Inveraray, although the trail through the woodland and past a waterfall also makes a fine hike.

The Bonnie Banks

'Oh, I'll tak the high road,
An you'll tak the low road
An I'll be in Scotland afore ye
But me and my true love will never meet again
On the bonnie, bonnie banks o' Loch Lomond.'

This famous song is known the world over, but few are aware of its real meaning. Most innocently believe that it refers to two alternative roads to Scotland – the hilltop route and the valley road – with an allusion to the basic geographic division of Scotland into Highland and Lowland regions. All this is fine, of course, but there is a darker side to the simple poem. It was composed by a Jacobite prisoner, Donald MacDonell, while awaiting his execution in a Carlisle jail following the battle of Culloden. The sentences dispensed by the English were arbitrary: some prisoners were hanged while others were freed and told to walk home. MacDonell, sensing his fate, told his companions that his spirit would reach Scotland on the 'high' road to heaven before they returned to the land of their birth on the 'low', or earthly, road.

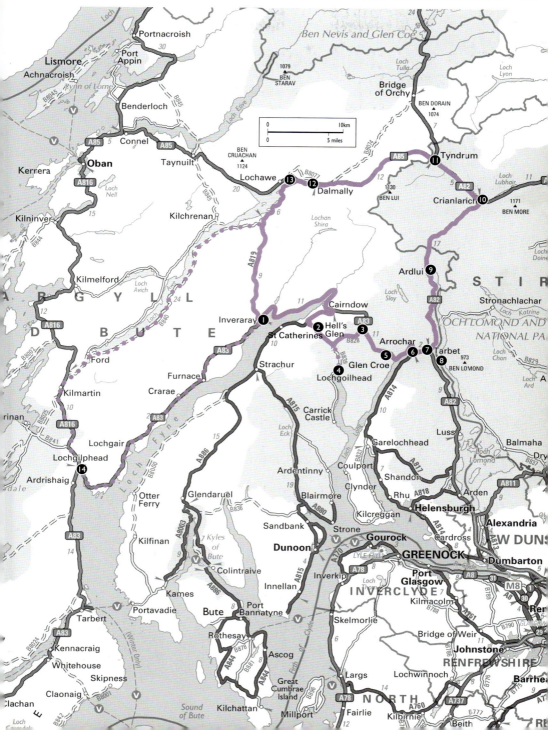

The Road to the Isles

The southwestern corner of the Highlands, between Loch Hourn in the north and Loch Sunart in the south, has long been known in Gaelic as 'The Rough Bounds'. This was the realm of staunchly Jacobite clans, remote and dangerous in its day, and even now traversed by and large only by rough tracks. Fort William is the centre of this western region of Lochaber, set at the foot of Ben Nevis, Britain's highest peak. From here the famous Road to the Isles leads to Mallaig, ferry port for the Hebrides, passing the glorious monument at Glenfinnan where, on 19 August 1745, Prince Charles Edward Stuart raised the standard that launched the last Jacobite rebellion. It is easy to imagine the Bonnie Prince's feelings when he sailed into the timeless beauty of Loch Shiel and saw his lost homeland for the first time. To the south are the wild peninsulas of Moidart and Ardnamurchan, the westernmost point on the British mainland. Inland lies one of Scotland's most famous places, dark and haunting Glencoe.

ARDNAMURCHAN POINT

ℹ Ardnamurchan Point Visitor Centre £
Tel: 01972 510 210; www. ardnamurchan.u-net.com. Open Apr–Oct daily 1000–1700.

Ardnamurchan Point is the westernmost point on mainland Britain. Populated only by sea birds, a lighthouse and the few tourists who venture out this far, it is a place of special beauty and calm. The views are amazing, taking in the island panorama of Muck, Eigg, Rum, Canna, Skye, South Uist, Barra, Mull and Coll. The Egyptian-style **lighthouse** contains an exhibition in the pump room and there are displays and computer interactives in the keepers' cottages. The viewing platform around the enormous red foghorn is known as a place to spot whales and dolphins. An old stone stable block houses a shop and café.

Right
Rugged terrain

FORT WILLIAM

Tourist Information Centre
Cameron Square; tel: 0845 225 5121; e-mail: info@visitscotland.com. Open all year.

The Nevis Range gondola on Aonach Mor takes you up to 2150ft (655m) for fantastic views year-round. Tel: 01397 705 825; www.nevisrange.co.uk

Fort William, capital of the Lochaber region, stretches along the shores of Loch Linnhe, near the southern entrance to the Caledonian Canal (*see page 224*). It lies at the foot of Britain's highest mountain, Ben Nevis, and thus is a popular base for climbers and hill walkers as well as for holidaymakers touring the region. The fort for which the town was named, first erected in 1655 and later strengthened against the Jacobite risings and named after William of Orange, is long gone, replaced by the train station and the Victorian town which grew up around it. The **West Highland Museum** (*Cameron Square; open Mon–Sat year-round and Sunday afternoons in Jul–Aug*) is well laid out and worth a visit, particularly to see the strange 'anamorphic' portrait of Bonnie Prince Charlie used in secret toasts.

GLENCOE

Glencoe will forever be known for the bloody massacre that took place here in 1692 (*see page 144*). Yet, had that shocking event never taken place, Glencoe would still be one of the most haunting and evocative places in all of Scotland. The brooding mountains and the lonely

Glencoe Visitor Centre (National Trust for Scotland) £
Tel: 01855 811 307; www.nts.org.uk. Open all year.

Glencoe Ski Centre Chairlift ££
Tel: 01855 851 226; e-mail: info@glencoemountain.com; www.glencoemountain.com. The chairlift at the Glencoe Ski Centre operates in summer, giving breathtaking views of the mountains and moorlands from 2400ft (731m).

Those with a sweet tooth should visit the Confectionery Factory nearby at Ballachulish Bridge where you can watch tablet (a kind of fudge) and other sweets being made. A range of wicked goodies is on sale in the shop. Open Mon–Sat all year and Sun Easter–Oct.

moorland form a landscape that feels ominous and melancholy even in sunlight. Watch the film about the massacre at the National Trust for Scotland Visitor Centre. Then drive through the glen itself, past the dramatic peaks of the Three Sisters and the ski area and along the bleak expanse of Rannoch Moor.

Right
The path to Ben Nevis

GLENFINNAN

Glenfinnan holds its very traditional Highland Games on the Saturday closest to 19 August, the day of the raising of the Jacobite standard in 1745.

Glenfinnan is one of the most moving and memorable spots in the Highlands. The **Glenfinnan Monument**, a memorial to the sacrifice of the Highlanders in the Jacobite cause, was erected here in 1815 at the head of Loch Shiel, near the place where Prince Charles Edward Stuart landed in 1745 and raised his standard. From the viewpoint above the visitor centre, the vista down the loch, surrounded by misty mountains, is achingly beautiful. The visitor centre exhibition gives an excellent background to the Rising, its battles and its aftermath. You can climb a winding staircase to the top of the monument. It is surrounded by plants adopted as plant badges, or *suaichanteas*, by the Jacobite clans.

GLEN NEVIS

Glen Nevis Visitor Centre *Tel: 01397 705 922. Open Easter–Sep 0900–1700, Jun–Aug 0800–1800; reduced hours rest of the year.*

Ben Nevis is Britain's highest mountain at 4406ft (1343m). Beneath its southern and western slopes is the beautiful valley of Glen Nevis. From Fort William there is a pretty 7-mile (11-km) drive up through the glen that makes an easy foray into these mountains. A visitor centre at the foot of the road has information about length and difficulty of various walks. Near the first car park, about 4 miles (6.5km) up, there is a lovely waterfall. As you climb to the end of the road there are stunning views of the high mountains closing in all around. This is the starting point for serious walks stretching 25 miles (40km) across the range to Rannoch Moor (*see page 152*).

LOCH LEVEN

If you're driving to Glencoe from Fort William, a scenic 14-mile (22.5-km) diversion on the B863 can be made around Loch Leven. The road hugs the loch to the village of **Kinlochleven**, site of an aluminium works; the visitor centre tells the story. From here there are walking trails into the mountains, including one to a spectacular waterfall. The main road circles around the other side of the loch on high ground with gorgeous views of the surrounding mountains.

Torr a'Choit

Many believe that Torr a'Choit, the hill behind the Glenfinnan visitor centre, was the actual point where the standard was raised. That morning the Prince had picked a white rose from the garden of his host, and thus it became the symbol of the Jacobites during the rising. It was made up in cloth and worn on the bonnet and became known as the 'white cockade'.

Mallaig

When heading for Mallaig to catch a ferry, leave plenty of time. The 20-mile (32-km) stretch from Lochailort to Mallaig is tortuously winding and must be taken slowly.

Mallaig is a busy fishing harbour, railway terminus and ferry port for boats to the Small Isles, the Outer Islands and Skye. It is attractive in a workaday way, and busy with ferry passengers and day-trippers. The only attractions to entertain them are the Marine World aquarium and fishing exhibition and the Heritage Centre with displays on local history. There are fine views across to the Isle of Skye.

The Small Isles

The four Hebridean islands lying off the coast of Lochaber – Eigg, Muck, Rum and Canna – are known as the Small Isles. Eigg is a scenic island, settled since prehistoric times, which gained much notoriety in recent years as residents campaigned, successfully, to buy the island. Muck, the smallest island, has sandy beaches and has been owned by the MacEwans since 1879. Rum also had prehistoric settlements and is now owned by Scottish Natural Heritage. It has much wildlife, including wild ponies thought to be descended from ancestors carried on ships of the Spanish Armada, which sank off these shores in the 16th century. Canna belongs to the National Trust for Scotland and has a centre for advanced Gaelic and Celtic studies.

Opposite and below
Different faces of Glencoe

Accommodation and food

Ben Nevis Bar £ *103–109 High Street, Fort William; tel: 01397 702 295.* The restaurant upstairs prepares some of the best haggis around. This is the place to give Scotland's national dish a try. Also steaks, lamb, fish, seafood and other specials, in a busy, friendly setting. *Open daily.*

St Andrews Guest House £ *Fassifern Road, Fort William; tel: 01397 703 038; e-mail: info@standrewsguesthouse.co.uk; www.standrewsguesthouse.co.uk.* Built in 1880, this characterful listed building was the rectory and choir school for St Andrew's Church and has many original features. Six comfortable rooms, friendly welcome, 3 minutes' walk to the town centre. Off-street parking.

Crannog Seafood Restaurant ££ *Fort William Town Pier, Fort William; tel: 01397 705 589; www.oceanandoak.co.uk.* The Crannog has a wonderful loch-side setting and from the window tables you might even see a fishing boat pulling up and delivering the catch of the day fresh to the kitchen. Their own oak-smoked salmon is delicious, or you can indulge yourself with fresh lobster, or Mallaig monkfish served with a chilli and ginger relish. There are meat dishes and vegetarian options too.

Suggested tour

The Jacobite steam train takes you on a nostalgic and highly scenic journey on the West Highland Line between Fort William and Mallaig. There is a stop at the Glenfinnan Monument. *Regular service mid-May–mid-Oct. Tel: 01524 737751; www.steamtrain.info*

Bruce Watt Sea Cruises has day-trips from Mallaig to Loch Nevis, Inverie and Tarbet *5 days a week mid-May–mid-Sep; tel: 01687 462 320; e-mail: brucewattcruises@aol.com; www.knoydart-ferry.co.uk*

Crannog Cruises has seal cruises on Loch Linnhe, leaving from the pier at Fort William *daily Mar–Oct; tel: 01397 700 714; www.oceanandoak.co.uk*

Total distance: The main route around the Moidart peninsula is about 70 miles (112km) if you take the Corran ferry across Loch Linnhe to return to Fort William. The detour to Mallaig adds 39 miles (63km) and the detour to Ardnamurchan Point adds another 50 miles (80km).

Time: If you want to do the entire route and take both detours, start early and plan on a very long day. These are some of the narrowest and curviest roads in the Highlands, so don't underestimate the time it will take to drive them. Allow half a day for the main route. On a good day with no traffic, the Mallaig detour will take 40 minutes each way. The 25 miles (40km) from Salen to Ardnamurchan Point will take at least an hour and 10 minutes each way.

Links: From Fort William, the A82 north through Spean Bridge and Invergarry connects with Inverness (*see page 226*) and the A87 to the Isle of Skye (*see pages 272–281*). To the south it connects with Loch Lomond via Crianlarich (*see page 130*).

Route: From Fort William, turn left on the A830. Just after the turn stop at Banavie and **Neptune's Staircase** ❶ (signposted to the right) for a good view of the boats making their way through the locks of the Caledonian Canal (*see page 224*). Fom here it is 14 miles (22.5km) to **GLENFINNAN** ❷. Continue west for 9.5 miles (15km) to the junction at Lochailort.

Left
Loch Sunart viewed from Ardnamurchan

Right
Scenic Ardnamurchan Point

Detour: The A830 continues for 19 miles (30.5km) to **MALLAIG** ❸. The road is paved but single-track for much of the way, winding through woodland with fine views of the mountains and lochs. Highlights along this very pretty drive include **Loch nan Uamh** ❹ (pronounced 'naan ooa'), about 4 miles (6.5km) from the turn-off. This is where Bonnie Prince Charlie arrived from France in July 1745 with seven companions to begin his campaign, and where he left, defeated, a year later. The Prince's Cairn honours his memory. **Arisaig** ❺, 7 miles (11km) on, is a small holiday resort on the shores of Loch nan Ceall with lovely views of the offshore islands. The great Gaelic poet Alasdair MacMhaigstir Alasdair, bard to the bonnie prince, is

Below
Magnificent Glencoe

buried in the graveyard of its ruined medieval church. Round the crest of a hill soon after leaving town you come upon one of the most spectacular views in Scotland, looking out across the sea to Skye and the dark peaks of the Cuillins. Then you drop down to the splendid 'silver sands' of **Morar** ❻ which extend around the bay. The road crosses the narrow strip of land that separates the bay from **Loch Morar** ❼ , the deepest freshwater loch in Britain, complete with its own monster called Morag. The 9-mile (14.5-km) stretch between Arisaig and Mallaig is a real 'roader-coaster' with lots of dips and curves, and will take some time. Return to Lochailort to continue the main tour.

The Glencoe Massacre

In an attempt to subdue the threat of the Jacobite Highland clans, William of Orange decreed on penalty of death that the chiefs must sign an oath of allegiance to the Crown by 1 January 1692. With much reluctance most obeyed, except for Maclain of Glencoe, head of a small branch of the Clan Donald. Eventually the obstinate old man conceded and set off for Fort William, only to be told he must go to Inveraray. He was then delayed by a blizzard, but eventually the oath was sworn and accepted, albeit late. The government, however, leapt at the excuse to deal the Highland chiefs a blow and despatched a company of Campbell soldiers to Glencoe. Although there was no love lost between the two clans, under the rules of Highland hospitality, and in the dead of winter, the Campbells were accommodated by the MacDonalds. After two weeks, having received their final orders, the Campbells fell upon their hosts as they lay sleeping. Maclain and 37 of his clan were slaughtered, though many escaped having been secretly warned by the Campbells. History has often portrayed the massacre as a disgraceful battle between rival clans, but the shocking murder and betrayal of trust was in fact an act of government-sponsored genocide.

Head south along the coast on the A861. One stunning view after another is revealed as the road winds around the sparsely populated Moidart peninsula. Along the shores of Loch Moidart at **Kinlochmoidart** ❽ is an idyllic spot where seven beech trees were planted to commemorate the 'Seven Men of Moidart' who landed with Charlie in 1745. Only five survive, but saplings have been planted to replace those destroyed by gales. The road is single-track from here. At **Mingarry** ❾, the Illegal Moidart Museum makes the only tongue-in-cheek concession to tourism, with ceilidh music, crafts and an old illegal whisky still. **Salen** ❿, 17 miles (27km) from the junction, is a small fishing resort in a scenic spot on the north shore of Loch Sunart.

Detour: From Salen, the B8007 runs along the loch out onto the **Ardnamurchan** ⓫ (pronounced 'Ard-na-múr-kan') peninsula to Ardnamurchan Point, the most westerly point on the British mainland. Do not take this road if you are timid, impatient or easily frustrated. It is extremely narrow and winding with lots of blind curves, and requires frequent pulling over and much care. However, every tortuous mile will be rewarded with incredible scenery. After 9 miles (14.5km) the **Ardnamurchan Natural History and Visitor Centre** ⓬ is a welcome break, with a shop where you can buy snacks and drinks and enjoy the views from picnic tables outside. The road then climbs inland through a gentler stretch, passing the ruins of **Mingary Castle** ⓭ about 7 miles (11km) further on. **Kilchoan** ⓮, the peninsula's largest village, has a beach and a ferry crossing to Tobermory on Mull.

It is 6 more masochistically thrilling miles (9.5km) out to **ARDNAMURCHAN POINT** ⓯ along an extremely twisty, dipping, thread of track through remote moorland you pray you won't get stuck in. Needless to say, it's unsuitable for caravans. The drive is

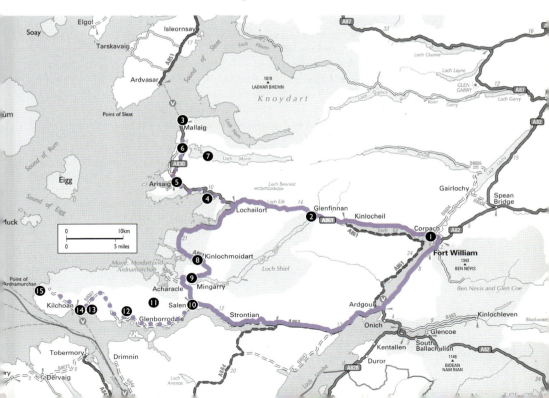 **The Corran ferry**, cheap at thrice the price as it saves a 30-mile (48-km) drive around the loch, runs until around 2030 or 2100, later in summer at weekends. The crossing takes less than 10 minutes and the fare is £6.20.

worth every gut-pinching minute, for at the end is the most peaceful and awe-inspiring place one could hope to find at the edge of a country. Eventually, tear yourself away from the view and retrace the route to Salen (it's easier this time now that you know what to expect...).

Back on the A861, the beauty rolls on past the village of Strontian towards the peak of Garbh Bheinn, almost a Munro at 2903ft (885m), which glows with ever deepening shades of pink at sunset. After 22 miles (35km) you will reach the Corran ferry at Ardgour. If you *really* want to, carry on driving around the lochs for 30 more miles (48km), or queue up, call it a day and once across Loch Linnhe you'll be back in Fort William in 8 easy miles (13km).

Also worth exploring

If you're heading south to Oban from Fort William, there is an alternative scenic route through Glencoe. Continue on the A82 through the glen and just after the Bridge of Orchy take the right-hand turn onto the B8074. This scenic 12-mile (19-km) shortcut through Glen Orchy is a gentle, peaceful antidote to the drama of Glencoe. Turn right on the A85 for 27 miles (43.5km) to Oban.

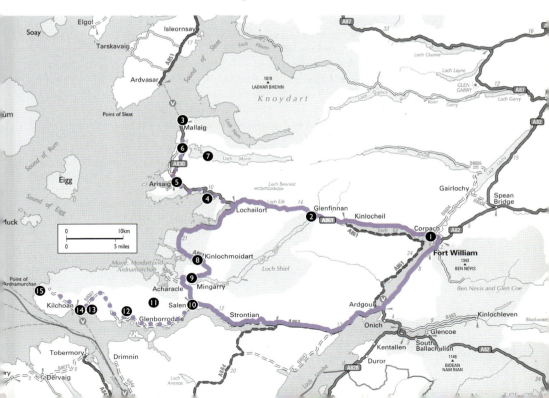

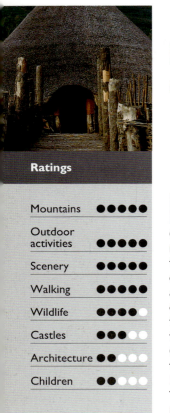

Breadalbane and the Central Highlands

Ratings

Mountains	●●●●●
Outdoor activities	●●●●●
Scenery	●●●●●
Walking	●●●●●
Wildlife	●●●●○
Castles	●●●○○
Architecture	●●○○○
Children	●●○○○

Breadalbane is a scenic upland region stretching from Aberfeldy west to Killen and Crianlarich. Its lyrical name (pronounced 'Bread-dáhl-ben') is derived from Gaelic words meaning 'the high country of Scotland'. This land is rife with folk traditions, with tales of saints and seers, fairies and kelpies, outlaw clans and Celtic heroes. At its heart is Loch Tay, site of ancient platform dwellings called crannogs. The rushing waters of the Falls of Dochart flow into the loch from the west, while from its eastern end the mighty River Tay flows seaward to the firth, a waterway for the famous Tay salmon. Since the time of Queen Victoria, the Central Highlands have been popular with those who enjoy the great outdoors. They encompass Ben Lawers, nearly 4000ft (1219m) high, beautiful Glen Lyon, the Tummel Valley and the historic pass of Killiecrankie. Just 39 miles (63km) from the bustling tourist centre of Pitlochry lies the remote and desolate wilderness of Rannoch Moor.

ABERFELDY

ℹ **Aberfeldy Tourist Information Centre**
The Square; tel: 01887 820 276; e-mail: aberfeldy@ visitscotland.com; www.perthshire.co.uk. Open all year.

The attractive town of Aberfeldy offers plenty of shops, restaurants and services. It centres around the stone bridge built by General Wade in 1733 – at that time the only crossing over the River Tay. The **Aberfeldy Birks** – the old Scots for 'birches' – were made famous by Robert Burns. The town's main attraction is **Castle Menzies** (pronounced 'Ming-ies'), a 16th-century fortified tower, seat of the Clan Menzies chiefs until 1918 (*tel: 01887 820 982; open daily Apr–mid-Oct*).

BLAIR CASTLE

The white walls and turrets of the enormous home of the dukes of Atholl stand out against the green Perthshire hills. The castle dates from 1269 and some 32 exquisitely furnished rooms filled with

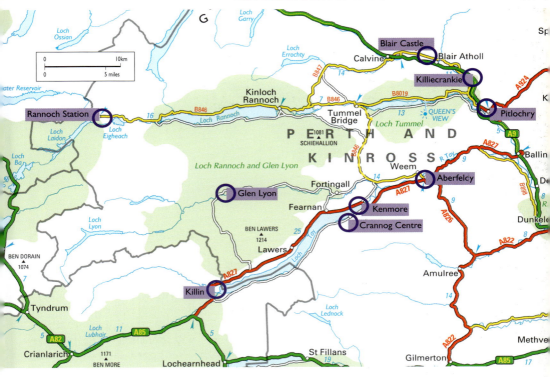

Blair Castle ££
*Blair Atholl, 7 miles
(11km) north of Pitlochry, off
the A9; tel: 01796 481 207;
www.blair-castle.co.uk. Open
Apr–Oct daily 0930–1630
(last admission).*

collections and memorabilia recall its long history, particularly stories of the clan's role in the Jacobite rebellion. The extensive grounds contain a deer park, walled garden and other features. The village of **Blair Atholl** that grew up near the castle is geared to tourists and has a corn mill and country museum. Three miles (5km) north of the castle, the **Falls of Bruar** is an impressive beauty spot reached by a steep walk (about 40 minutes round-trip) from the car park at the House of Bruar.

CRANNOG CENTRE

Crannog Centre ££
*Croft-na-Caber,
Kenmore, Loch Tay;
tel: 01887 830 583;
www.crannog.co.uk.
Open daily mid-Mar–Oct
1000–1730; Nov
1000–1600 weekends.*

Crannogs are ancient loch dwellings, dating back to 3000 BC, that were built on stilt platforms offshore. The remains of 18 crannogs have so far been discovered on Loch Tay. A team of underwater archaeologists excavating the sites has reconstructed a crannog here using ancient methods and materials. The remains of household items such as utensils, cloth and, amazingly, bits of food were discovered, enabling a fascinating re-creation of crannog life. Archaeologists believe that crannog dwellers built these island homes to protect themselves from attack by potential enemies. Romantics might prefer to see them as Scotland's first yuppies with an enviable property on the loch!

Right
The Crannog Centre on Loch
Tay shows how people lived
5000 years ago

GLEN LYON

With its steep sides and fast-flowing river, Glen Lyon is one of the prettiest glens in Scotland. It is also the longest enclosed glen, with a full length of 34 miles (55km). Its name in Gaelic means 'Crooked Glen of Stones', and legend has it that the Celtic hero Fingal had 12 castles here. The ruins of ancient ring forts may have something to do with the story. In more recent history, Glen Lyon was the home of Captain Robert Campbell, who carried out the massacre at Glencoe. Keep an eye out for deer and golden eagles.

KENMORE

Set on the shores of Loch Tay, Kenmore has long been welcoming visitors; its hotel was licensed more than 400 years ago. Distinguished guests included Robert Burns, who was inspired by the views from the bridge over the river's head. The village, with its charming

Loch Tay Boating Centre next to the beach hires canoes, boats and fishing by the hour or the day. *Tel: 01887 830 291; www.loch-tay.co.uk. Open daily Apr–mid-Oct.*

whitewashed cottages, is a popular small resort and watersports centre. The rather incongruous arch is the gateway to Taymouth Castle. This was the seat of the Earls of Breadalbane and was once a grand neo-Gothic palace when Queen Victoria visited in 1842. Now surrounded by a golf course, it has been sadly neglected for many years.

KILLIECRANKIE

Killiecrankie Visitor Centre (National Trust for Scotland) *Tel: 01796 473 233; www.nts.org.uk. Open Easter–Oct daily 1000–1730; site open all year.*

This beautiful river gorge 3 miles (5km) north of Pitlochry was the scene of a fearsome battle in the first Jacobite uprising of 1689. The Highlanders won the day but their leader, John Graham of Claverhouse, the 'Bonnie Dundee', was killed by a stray bullet and the rebellion floundered. The National Trust has set up a visitor centre here, telling the story of the battle and the gorge. There are woodland walks, including one to Soldier's Leap, where a government soldier is said to have jumped 18ft (5.5m) across the river to escape the Highlanders hot on his heels.

KILLIN

Killin Tourist Information Centre *In Breadalbane Folklore Centre; tel: 0845 225 5121. Open Apr–Oct.*

The **Falls of Dochart** tumble through the centre of this pleasant village at the head of Loch Tay. Always a pretty spot, this wide waterway of rocks and rapids can be most impressive when the water is high. The **Breadalbane Folklore Centre** (*tel: 01567 820 254; open daily Mar–Oct*), housed in a historic mill by the water's edge, is dedicated to the region's rich tradition of facts and fables. Many of the tales concern St Fillin, a mystical Irish monk who settled here, the magical deeds of the giant Fingal, and the outlawed Clan MacGregor. With its lovely mountain backdrop, Killin is a popular centre for hill walking and a variety of sports.

PITLOCHRY

Pitlochry Tourist Information Centre *22 Atholl Road; tel: 01796 472 215 or 472 751; e-mail: pitlochry@ visitscotland.com. Open all year.*

Pitlochry's Highland Games are held on the second Sat in Sep. Contact tourist information for details.

Despite a lack of visitor attractions in its own right, Pitlochry is a highly popular tourist centre that shot to fame in the days of Queen Victoria. A pleasant and attractive town, it has many shops and restaurants and makes a good base for exploring the region. Walk across the suspension bridge to the **Pitlochry Dam and Fish Ladder**. When this hydroelectric project threatened to cut off the salmon's route to their spawning grounds, a ladder of 31 stepped pools was created to help them over the dam. You might spot one in the murky viewing chamber. To the west of town is the **Dunfallandy Stone**, a fine Pictish cross-slab carved around the 9th century. There are also two distilleries open to visitors.

RANNOCH STATION

Rannoch Station is a stop on the West Highland Railway line between Glasgow and Fort William. The Caledonian Sleeper also takes this route to Fort William.

The tearoom on the platform at Rannoch Station £ is cosy, busy and, unlike your usual station café, serves good food, in particular the home-baked cakes! Breakfasts, sandwiches, fish and chips and a selection of meals are served between 1000 and 1700 daily.

Right
Rannoch Station

Below
Rannoch Moor

No roads, and only a solitary railway line, traverse the heart of the vast Rannoch Moor. This little outpost is a moody, atmospheric place where you can get a sense of the isolation of the Highlands before the construction of Wade's military roads. The views across the moorland grasses – shimmering in sunlight, ominous in cloud or rain – to the mountains beyond are singular and dramatic, taking in an environment that is bleak and windswept but with its own delicate beauty. Despite the desolation of the surrounding landscape, there is a jolly camaraderie among the people – and there are many – who have ventured out this far. There is a hotel bar and an excellent tearoom on the station platform.

Accommodation and food

Easter Dunfallandy Country House £ *Pitlochry; tel: 01796 474 128; e-mail: sue@dunfallandy.co.uk; www.dunfallandy.co.uk.* From the main road, turn onto Bridge Road and turn left at the caravan park road. The house (signposted to the right) is 1 mile (1.6km) from here, past the Dunfallandy House Hotel and Dunfallandy Stone. A warm welcome at this large, beautifully decorated Victorian house. Bedrooms have tasteful country-living décor. Peaceful countryside location overlooking a large garden.

Victoria's £ *45 Atholl Road, Pitlochry; tel: 01796 472 670.* Bright, pleasant coffee shop and licensed restaurant serving a good range of meals: lasagne, pizza, salmon, steaks, burgers, salads and vegetarian choices.

Wild Rannoch Moor

Rannoch Moor is one of the last remaining wilderness areas in Europe. Sitting on a granite plateau 1000ft (305m) high, it is a vast blanket bog dotted with *lochans* (small lochs) and hummocks stretching over some 60 square miles (155.5sq km). In places the peat is as deep as 20ft (6m). During the Ice Age, great glaciers spread out through Rannoch Moor to carve out the Tummel Valley to the east and Glencoe to the west. Its lifeless appearance belies a wealth of deer, birdlife and boggy plants.

Suggested tour

The highly acclaimed **Pitlochry Festival Theatre** on the banks of the river has a varied season of drama, comedy, concerts and events. *Box office tel: 01796 484 626; www.pitlochry.org.uk*

You can buy walking guides to the Pitlochry area from the visitor centres. You can also pick up a leaflet at the **Killicrankie Visitor Centre** on the **Linn of Tummel Nature Trail**.

Total distance: The main route around Loch Tay and past the Queen's View is 79 miles (127km). The detour through Glen Lyon is 22 miles (35km). The round trip to Rannoch Station from Tummel Bridge is 50 miles (80.5km).

Time: The main route will take 2 hours 45 minutes. On a good day with little traffic, the detour through Glen Lyon will take about 45 minutes, while the drive from Tummel Bridge to Rannoch Station takes 45 minutes each way.

Links: This central region connects with several other tours, including Perth and the Angus Glens (*see page 209*); The Mill Trail via Crieff (*see page 96*); Mid-Argyll via Crianlarich (*see page 130*); and the Trossachs via Lochearnhead. The A9 north of Pitlochry, though busy, has to be one of the most exciting stretches of main road in Scotland, with thrilling views of the Monadhliath Mountains as you approach the junction for Dalwhinnie. Follow the A889 and A86 from here for a spectacular drive to Fort William.

Route: Leave **PITLOCHRY** ❶ on the A9 and travel 5 miles (8km) south to Ballinluig, where you exit for the A827 to **ABERFELDY** ❷,

Ben Lawers Visitor Centre (National Trust for Scotland) £
Off the A827; tel: 01567 820 397; www.nts.org.uk. Open Easter–Sep daily 1000–1700. Audiovisual presentation (£).

The summit of **Ben Lawers** can be reached on a moderate climb of about 3 hours, though you must be properly equipped, as ever. The views over Breadalbane to the Grampian range and, on a clear day, even to both coasts, are spectacular.

Drive carefully on the road to Kinloch Rannoch, for although it has two lanes, it is very narrow with many curves and blind ridges and is heavily travelled.

Right
Prehistoric weaving at the Crannog Centre

9 miles (14.5km) away. Continue west 6 more miles (9.5km) to **KENMORE ❸**. Leave town on the unclassified road that runs along the south side of Loch Tay, stopping just outside of town at the **CRANNOG CENTRE ❹**. This is a very scenic but very narrow little single-track road (unsuitable for caravans) that rises into the hills with lovely views down over the loch and across to the opposite shore. It is altogether delightful, winding largely through woodland broken by small patches of pastureland, though there are plenty of roller-coaster dips and some blind curves and crests. After 17 miles (27km) you reach **KILLIN ❺** and the **Falls of Dochart ❻**.

Return to Kenmore (17 miles, 27km) on the A827 along the north side of Loch Tay. This road is two-lane but still narrow, and although it's pretty, you are further away from the loch for half the drive. As you enter Kenmore take the turning signposted to Tummel Bridge, which leads past the golf course and Taymouth Castle. In a couple of miles (3km) you reach the junction with B846; turn left and continue north 9 miles (14.5km) to Tummel Bridge.

Detour: About 4.5 miles (7km) from Killin, turn left on the minor road (signposted) to **Ben Lawers ❼**, the region's highest mountain at 3984ft (1214m). There is a visitor centre 2 miles (3km) along with displays on the environment and the area's unique proliferation of alpine plants. The narrow road climbs up through desolate mountain moorland for 7 more miles (11km) to the Bridge of Balgie. Turn right for the 13-mile (21-km) drive through pretty **GLEN LYON ❽**. Among the quaint thatched cottages of **Fortingall ❾**, have a look at the yew tree in the churchyard, a decrepit yet admirable survivor which is said to be 3000 years old. Some believe that earthworks on the edge of the village are the remains of a Roman outpost, and a dubious legend claims that it is the birthplace of Pontius Pilate. Soon after the village, rejoin the main route at the B846 and continue north to Tummel Bridge.

Detour: A second detour through a very different but equally awesome landscape can be made from Tummel Bridge to lonely Rannoch Station in the wilds of Rannoch Moor. Turn left and continue on the B846 through lush forest for 7 miles (11km) to Kinloch Rannoch. **Ben Schiehallion ❿**, with its 3554-ft (1083-m)

ⓘ Queen's View Visitor Centre £

Tay Forest Park, on the B8019; tel: 01796 473 123. Open end Mar–mid-Nov daily 1000–1800.

cone, towers on your left. In the 18th century it figured in scientific experiments to estimate the earth's mass and was the inspiration for using contour lines to show map elevations. **Kinloch Rannoch ⓫** is a small fishing resort at the edge of Loch Rannoch. From here there are splendid views across the loch to the distant peaks of Glencoe, and walks in the Black Wood of Rannoch, the old Caledonian pine forest. From here it is 18 miles (29km) to the end of the road at **RANNOCH STATION ⓬**. The only way out is to retrace the route to Tummel Bridge.

From Tummel Bridge, continue east on B8019 towards Pitlochry. After about 7 miles (11km) you come to the turn-off for the **Queen's View ⓭**, a splendid viewpoint looking west up the Tummel Valley, made famous by Queen Victoria's visit in 1866. You'll pay a royal parking fee of £1 for the privilege, so get your money's worth and take a good long look, use their loo, and visit the small exhibition in the visitor centre. The junction with the B8079 is 4 miles (6.5km) on; turn right and Pitlochry is 3 miles (5km) ahead.

Also worth exploring

If you drive from Pitlochry to Fort William you will pass **Dalwhinnie**, at 1188ft (362m) the highest village in the Highlands. It grew up around an inn built in 1729 and was a meeting place for drovers; you can walk the old drove road to Kinloch Laggan.

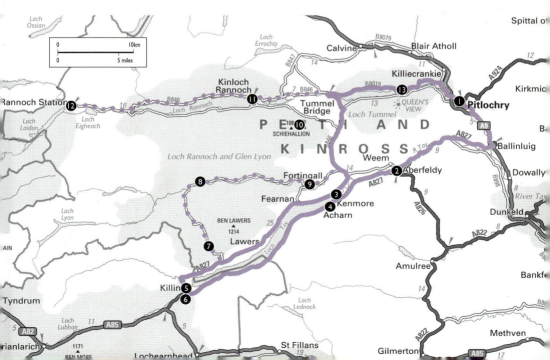

Strathspey and the Cairngorms

Ratings

Children	●●●●●
Outdoor activities	●●●●●
Walking	●●●●●
Wildlife	●●●●●
Mountains	●●●●○
Scenery	●●●●○
Sport	●●●○○
Shopping	●●○○○

Strathspey, or the Spey Valley, is quilted with a patchwork of Highland scenery – forests and moorland, hills and glens, lochs and rivers – that changes colour with every season. The area nestles in the big rounded bosom of the Cairngorms, some of the most rugged mountains in Scotland. This is Britain's prime ski area, but even if you don't take to the slopes you can ride the chairlift for incredible views. Otherwise, keep your feet firmly on the ground on a woodland walk. In August and September, vast undulating fields of heather empurple the hillsides, while autumn turns the forests and fields russet and gold. The River Spey is one of Scotland's most famous salmon rivers with an abundance of sport on offer: golf, fishing, pony-trekking, hiking and watersports. With several theme parks and wildlife centres, this is a good area for children. The region became increasingly popular after 1860 when Queen Victoria proclaimed her visit here to be 'very amusing and never to be forgotten'. You may well agree.

AVIEMORE

ℹ️ **Aviemore Tourist Information Centre** *Grampian Road; tel: 0845 225 5121; e-mail: aviemore@host.co.uk. Open all year.*

🚶 There are woodland walks of 30 minutes to an hour in the Craigellachie National Nature Reserve behind Aviemore.

Right
Aviemore environs

Aviemore was merely a small railway village until the 1960s when the skiing boom hit. Since then it has grown into a sprawling tourist centre with mountain sports shops, supermarkets, large hotels and apartments, and now caters for visitors year-round with a host of summer activities. It is the southern terminus for the **Strathspey Steam Railway**. Signposted off the main road on the north end of town, in an incongruous location in a residential neighbourhood behind the fire station, the small **Aviemore Ring Cairn and Stone Circle** confirms that there was life before the ski resort.

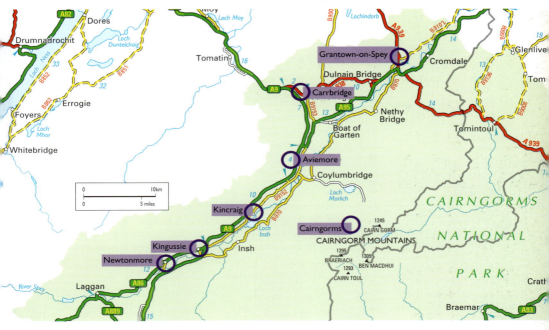

CAIRNGORMS NATIONAL PARK

With four of its peaks topping 4000ft (1219m) (the highest, Ben Macdui, stands at 4296ft (1309.5m)), the Cairngorms comprise some of Scotland's most dramatic mountain scenery. The top of this granite range has been eroded by glaciers to form a plateau covered in rugged tundra, the largest high-altitude region in Britain. A new national park was created here in 2003, at 1400 square miles (3800sq km) the UK's largest, stretching from Grantown-on-Spey to the head of the Angus glens and from Ballater to beyond Dalwhinnie. It contains large tracts of native woodland and natural vegetation, home to rare plants and animals. The Cairngorms are a formidable challenge to experienced mountaineers and hillwalkers. Scotland's top ski area is located here.

CARRBRIDGE

Landmark Forest Theme Park £££
Tel: 0800 731 3446;
www.landmark-centre.co.uk.
Open daily Sep–Mar
1000–1700; Apr–mid-Jul
1000–1800; mid-Jul–Aug
1000–1900.

The picturesque stone **Bridge of Carr** was built over the River Dulnain in 1717 to enable people living on the north side to reach the cemetery when the river was in flood. Carrbridge is Scotland's original ski village and it retains its rustic charm. The **Landmark Forest Theme Park** is one of the area's most popular sites, with a 'Wild Watercoaster', 3-D show, fire tower, forest trails and other themed attractions.

GRANTOWN-ON-SPEY

ⓘ Grantown-on-Spey Tourist Information Centre
54 High Street; tel: 08452 255121; e-mail: info@visitscotland.com. Open Apr–Oct.

Strathspey's capital is one of the first planned towns in Scotland, built in 1765 under the auspices of James Grant of Grant. His vision to develop linen and wool factories, schools and roads earned him the title 'the good Sir James'. The centre of Grantown around the square is now a designated conservation area. Set beneath the 1545-ft (471-m) Beinn Mhór, it is an attractive town and a good base for touring the region.

KINCRAIG

ⓑ Working Sheepdogs £ *Leault Farm, signposted off the B9152 south of Kincraig; tel: 01540 651 310. Open all year, Sun–Fri 1600.*

Highland Wildlife Park ££ *Tel: 01540 651 270; e-mail: wildlife@tzss.org.uk; www.highlandwildlifepark.org. Open all year from 1000, weather permitting.*

The small village of Kincraig is situated beside Loch Insh, formed by a widening in the River Spey. It is a focal point for popular animal attractions. At Leault Farm you can observe a traditional part of Highland life as the **Working Sheepdogs** demonstrate their skills. You can also try your hand at shearing a sheep. Between Kingussie and Kincraig is the **Highland Wildlife Park**, where you can see animals and birds native to the Highlands, including rare species such as wolves, wild cats, pine martens and capercaillie. Join them for the 'Drive-in Breakfast' from 10am as the warden feeds many animals in the reserve, or watch the carnivores feed from 3pm.

Right
Highland deer

KINGUSSIE

Highland Folk Museum £
Duke Street; tel: 01540 673 551; e-mail: highland.folk@highland.gov.uk; www.highlandfolk.com. Open to groups and pre-arranged visits; phone for information.

Pronounced 'Kin-yew-see', this attractive stone-built town grew up in the early 19th century. It has lots of hotels, restaurants and craft shops and makes a more atmospheric base than Aviemore. The **Highland Folk Museum**, founded in 1935, is a social history museum that depicts the life of the Highlander over the past 300 years. There are demonstrations of Highland music, sports and crafts. Creag Bheag, a 1581-ft (482-m) hill, overlooks the town, giving splendid views across the valley to the Cairngorms. Just north of town on the B9152 is the Witches' Hill, where the last witch in Badenoch was burnt.

NEWTONMORE

Tourist Information Centre *Main Street, Newtonmore; tel: 0845 22 55 121; e-mail: info@visitscotland.com. Open all year. Has displays about the natural environment of the Highlands.*

Waltzing Waters £ *On the A86; tel: 01540 673 752. Open Feb–mid-Dec. Shows (45 mins) on the hour 1000–1600 and 2030 Jul–Aug.*

Highland Folk Museum £ *Tel: 01540 661 307; www.highlandfolk.com. Open Apr–Aug daily 1030–1730; Sep–Oct 1100–1630.*

Clan Macpherson Museum *Main Street; tel: 01540 673 332. Open Apr–Oct Mon–Sat 1000–1700, Sun 1200–1700. Free.*

Newtonmore is another pleasant town that is not excessively touristy. **Waltzing Waters** is an aqua theatre, an elaborate production of dancing fountains and lights synchronised to music. On the outskirts of town the **Highland Folk Museum**, an outgrowth of the folk museum in Kingussie, is an ongoing reconstruction of an early 18th-century Highland township, from turf and thatch cottages to a water-powered sawmill. The **Clan Macpherson Museum** provides an interesting look at Highland history through the experiences of clan members down the ages, from Cluny's clever escapes after Culloden to James' fiddling at the gallows.

Accommodation and food

No. 55 Bistro ££ *Ben Mhor Hotel, 53–57 High Street, Grantown-on-Spey; tel: 01479 872 056.* Scottish cuisine such as Speyside salmon, Highland lamb and venison in a relaxed bistro atmosphere.

Muckrach Lodge Hotel & Restaurant ££–£££ *Dulnain Bridge, Grantown-on-Spey; tel: 01479 851 257; fax: 01479 851 325; e-mail: info@muckrach.co.uk; www.muckrach.co.uk.* Built in 1860, this Victorian sporting lodge has been converted into a charming small hotel with country-house comforts, from wood fires and fresh flowers to relaxing sofas and old books. There are ten spacious bedrooms and four family suites, all individually decorated, some with four-poster beds. The highly acclaimed Finlarig Restaurant features the finest local ingredients, from Scotch beef, lamb and game to fresh fish and seafood, accompanied by a fine wine list and rare malt whiskies. There is casual dining in the Conservatory Bistro. Attentive service and beautiful scenery add to a memorable stay.

Sports and activities

For woodland walks, pick up the *Explore Abernethy* leaflet that gives directions for seven waymarked trails, all starting from Nethy Bridge. All are on low-level terrain and are around 3 miles (5km) in length. Available from tourist information centres or the post office at Nethy Bridge.

The Strathspey Steam Railway is a nostalgic journey on a steam train that runs between Aviemore and Boat of Garten. *Open Feb–Jan (incl. over Christmas). Daily service Jun–Sep. Tel: 01479 810 725; www.strathspeyrailway.co.uk*

Monarch of the Glen

BBC Scotland's hit TV series *Monarch of the Glen* was filmed in the Badenoch and Strathspey countryside. A map of the film locations is available from the tourist board.

Right
Silver birches on the banks of the Spey

The Rothiemurchus Highland Estate at Inverdruie, near Aviemore, has a range of outdoor activities from Land-Rover safari tours and 4x4 off-road driving to mountain biking, falconry displays and a fish farm. (*Rothiemurchus Visitor Centre; tel: 01479 812 345; www.rothiemurchus.net*).

The lochs and rivers of Strathspey have some of Scotland's best fishing. (For permits, contact: Rothiemurchus Estate; *tel: 01479 812 345* or the local tourist information centres.) **Loch Insh Watersports** at Kincraig has canoeing, sailing and river trips as well as dry-land activities (*tel: 01540 651 272*). **Loch Morlich Watersports** in Glenmore Forest Park offers fishing, boating and equipment hire and instruction for a number of activities (*tel: 01479 861 221; open May–Sep*).

There are numerous walking and cycling trails of varying lengths to suit all abilities. For information on these and on the many golf courses, pony-trekking and riding centres in the area, contact the tourist information centres. Newtonmore has one of the best inland golf courses in the country.

Shopping

You can take a bit of Highland scenery home to your own back garden. The **Speyside Heather Centre** sells an amazing variety of plants, both on site and by mail order (*Skye of Curr, Dulnain Bridge, Inverness-shire PH26 3PA; tel: 01479 851 359; fax: 01479 851 396; www.heathercentre.com*). **Jack Drake's Nursery** in Aviemore (*tel: 01540 651 287*) also sells alpine and rare plants. *Closed Wed and Nov and Jan–Feb.*

Speyside Horn and Crafts is a small workshop where you can watch a variety of articles being carved from horn and bone, and learn about this old craft of the tinkers. (*On the B9152 beside the Rowantree Hotel by Loch Alvie; tel: 07977 556676; www.speyside-horn.co.uk; open Apr–Oct Mon–Sat 1100–1630.*)

Suggested tour

Total distance: The main route around Strathspey is 69 miles (111km). The Cairngorms detour is a 16-mile (26-km) round-trip from Inverdrurie to the Cairngorm Chairlift.

Time: The main route will take 2.5 hours not counting stops if traffic is light. The drive up through Glenmore Forest Park to the chairlift and back takes about half an hour.

Links: The route parallels the surging A9 trunk road (without having to use it) and it is easily reached from Inverness, Perth or Fort William. It makes a natural link with the Speyside Sampler route (*see page 171*).

Insh Marshes Nature Reserve
On the B970; tel: 01540 661518. Open at all times. Guided tours (£) Apr–Aug.

Glenmore Forest Park Visitor Centre
Tel: 01479 861 220. Open all year.

Cairngorm Reindeer Centre ££ Glenmore; tel: 01479 861 228. Visitor centre open daily Feb–Dec and New Year break; daily guided visits to reindeer.

Cairngorm Mountain Railway
£££ Tel: 01479 861 261; www.cairngormmountain.com. Open daily all year.

Route: Leave Grantown on the A95, passing the Roches Moutonées whose large rocks were smoothed by passing glaciers during the Ice Age. After 2 miles (3km) turn right on the A938 at **Dulnain Bridge ❶**. The **Speyside Heather Centre ❷** has some 300 varieties and an exhibition about the Highlands' prolific plant species. Continue 7 miles (11km) to **CARRBRIDGE ❸**. Follow the B9153/A95 south for 6 miles (9.5km) to **AVIEMORE ❹**. Continue south on the B9152/A86 through **KINCRAIG ❺** and **KINGUSSIE ❻** to **NEWTONMORE ❼**, about 16 miles (26km) on. Backtrack 3 miles (5km) to Kingussie and turn right on the road to Ruthven and Insch Marshes (signposted), the B970. After going over a bridge and under the busy A9, you will see **Ruthven Barracks ❽** standing high on a hill; built in 1719, it was partially destroyed by the Jacobites in 1746. Past the barracks is the **Insh Marshes Reserve ❾**, run by the Royal Society for the Protection of Birds (RSPB), where nearly 200 bird species have been recorded. Large numbers of whooper swans can be seen here in winter, and it is a wildfowl breeding ground in spring. The B970 becomes extremely narrow as it winds its way along dry-stone walls and up along a ridge, with lovely views over the river valley below and large, magnificent fields of heather. After passing Loch Insch, it becomes a forest road through lovely woodland dotted with cottages.

Detour: At the junction at Inverdrurie, near the Rothiemurchus Estate, keep to the right and just beyond Coylumbridge turn right on the minor road leading into **Glenmore Forest Park ❿**. There is a visitor centre with information on the area. There are watersports along the shores of beautiful **Loch Morlich ⓫** and a long sandy beach. The **Cairngorm Reindeer Centre ⓬** harbours Britain's only herd of reindeer; you can wander among them on a guided walk. The drive up to **Cairn Gorm ⓭**, at 4084ft (1245m), has breathtaking views of the big, bald, rounded slopes. For the most spectacular mountain views, take the mountain railway 3600ft (1097m) higher up to the top, where there is a bar, shops, and Scotland's highest restaurant.

Right
Carrbridge

Opposite
Rothiemurchus Woods, near Aviemore

Loch Garten Osprey Centre £
Tel: 01479 821 409. Open Apr–Aug daily 1000–1600.

Revack Estate *On the B970; tel: 01479 872 234. Open Feb–Dec.*

After **Coylumbridge** on the main route the road continues through a landscape of tall grasses, heather and birch trees, with long-horned, shaggy-haired Highland cattle grazing in the pastures. Off to the left (signposted) is **Boat of Garten** ⑭, named after the ferry which once crossed the river here. It is the northern terminus for the Strathspey Steam Railway. Nearby is the **Auchgourish Gardens** botanical gardens and arboretum (*open Easter–Oct*). Nearby at Loch Garten is the RSPB's **Osprey Centre**. **Nethy Bridge** ⑮ was a major centre for timber operations in the 17th–19th centuries, with timber floating down the rivers in a huge commercial operation. Today much of the forest is managed for conservation and there is a network of walking trails starting from the town. On the way into Grantown (4 miles, 6.5km) from Nethy Bridge you pass the **Revack Estate** ⑯, owned by a descendant of 'the good Sir James'. It has beautiful gardens, an orchid house, woodland trails and an adventure playground for children.

Also worth exploring

Left
The Cairngorms

The **Tomatin Distillery** is 7 miles (11km) north of Carrbridge on the A9.

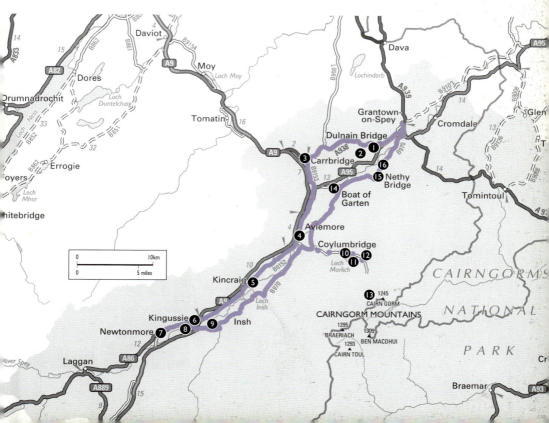

A Speyside Sampler

Ratings

Food and drink	●●●●●
Whisky	●●●●●
Archaeology	●●●○○
Scenery	●●●○○
Architecture	●●○○○
Museums	●●○○○
Shopping	●●○○○
Wildlife	●○○○○

As the River Spey makes its way north from the Grampian Highlands to the Moray coast, it winds through attractive agricultural land that provides the barley, grain and other raw materials for factories in the towns of the region. This is Scotland's Malt Whisky Country, for although the *uisge beatha* ('water of life') is produced throughout the land, more than 40 distilleries, including many top names, are based in Moray. No tour of Speyside – or indeed Scotland – is complete without a visit to at least one distillery, where you can smell the aroma of fermenting malt, peer into the enormous frothing and bubbling vats, have a 'nosing' and sample a wee dram. But whisky is not Moray's only quality product. The region is home to several old family businesses producing woollens, shortbread and fine foods that are known around the world. And dotted between the pagoda-style tops of the distilleries are cathedral and castle ruins, peaceful abbeys and some of the finest carvings of the ancient Picts.

CRAIGELLACHIE

Speyside Cooperage £
Dufftown Road;
tel: 01340 871 108;
www.speysidecooperage.co.uk.
Open Jan–Dec Mon–Fri
0900–1600.

The **Speyside Cooperage** presents an interesting look at another aspect of malt whisky production, the age-old craft of constructing the oak barrels in which the spirits mature. Around 100,000 casks are made and repaired here each year. After an informative audiovisual presentation, you can watch the coopers' skilful handling of the barrel staves from the viewing gallery overlooking the factory floor. There is also a gift shop and a few head of Highland cattle on the grounds.

Right
The house of Glenfiddich

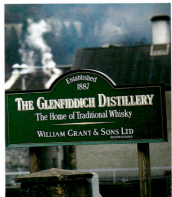

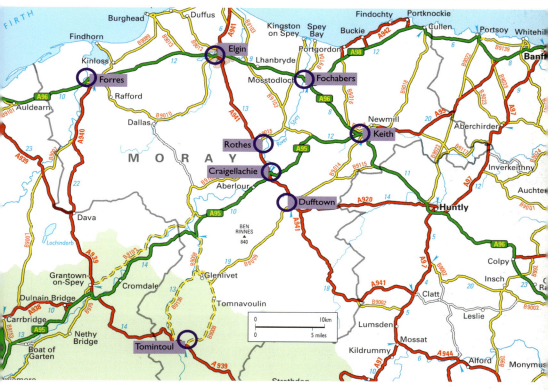

DUFFTOWN

ⓘ Information Centre *In the clock tower on the central square. Tel: 01340 820 501. Open Easter–Oct.*

Ⓖ Glenfiddich Distillery *On the A941; tel: 01340 820 373; www.glenfiddich.com. Open Jan–mid-Dec Mon–Fri 0930–1630; also Easter–mid-Oct Sat 0930–1630, Sun 1200–1630. Free.*

Balvenie Castle (Historic Scotland) £ *Tel: 01340 820 121. Open Apr–Sep, daily 0930–1730.*

Mortlach Church *Open weekdays 1000–1600.*

Dufftown's wide streets, lined with attractive stone-built shops and restaurants, spread out from its clock tower on the central square, which houses a local museum. Numerous distilleries are centred around the town, the largest being the **Glenfiddich Distillery**, which began producing malt whisky here in 1887. Its audiovisual show and tour is among the best, as this is one of the few places where you can see the whisky bottled on site. Behind the distillery are the ruins of **Balvenie Castle**, dating from the late 13th century. **Mortlach Church**, founded in 566, is one of the country's earliest religious sites. It contains the Pictish 'Elephant Stone' and a 'leper's squint' through which the afflicted could worship from outside the church.

Whisky Galore

'Rome was built on seven hills, Dufftown stands on seven stills.' This local rhyming couplet highlights the town's long history as the centre of the malt whisky industry.

ELGIN

Elgin Tourist Information Centre *17 High Street; tel: 01343 542 666. Open all year.*

Elgin Museum £ *1 High Street; tel: 01343 543 675. Open Apr–Oct Mon–Fri 1000–1700, Sat 1100–1600.*

Elgin Cathedral (Historic Scotland) £ *Tel: 01343 547 171; www.historic-scotland.gov.uk. Open Apr–Sep daily 0930–1230 & 1330–1730; Oct–Dec Sat–Wed 0930–1230 & 1330–1630.*

Biblical Gardens *King Street. Open May–Sep daily 1000–1930.*

Gordon and MacPhail *58–60 South Street, is an Aladdin's cave of fine malt whiskies from all over Scotland, including rare bottles. The olde-worlde shop, established in 1895, also sells fine wines, delicatessen and gift items. Tel: 01343 545 110; www.gordonandmacphail. com*

This busy commercial town is set around a medieval centre whose pedestrianised high street with its wynds and pends invites strolling. Look out for Braco's Banking House, the Church of St Giles and the 17th-century tower. The small **Elgin Museum** is one of the best in the north, with dinosaur bones and important Pictish stones such as the Burghead Bulls.

Elgin Cathedral is the town's highlight and one of the loveliest cathedral ruins in Scotland. The original 13th-century building was burned in 1390 by the vengeful earl of Buchan, known as the 'Wolf of Badenoch', after he was excommunicated by the bishop. It was partially rebuilt but fell into decline following the Reformation. Among the towering walls are well-preserved canopied tombs, statues and effigies. Next to the cathedral, the **Biblical Gardens** contain virtually every species – some 104 – mentioned in the Bible. The floral displays are interspersed with sculptures and quotations.

East of the cathedral beside the River Lossie, **Johnstons of Elgin**, established in 1797, occupies a lovely mill. It is the only woollen mill

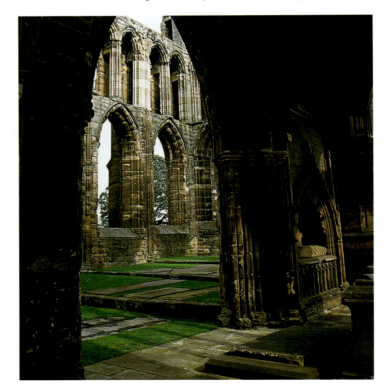

Right
Elgin Cathedral

in the country to process cashmere from fibre to garment, and you can tour the factory to see the various stages.

FOCHABERS

Baxter's Highland Village *Tel: 01343 820 666; www.baxters.com. Open mid-Feb–Dec daily 0900–1730; Jan–mid-Feb 1000–1700.*

Fochabers is the home of **Baxter's of Speyside**, known throughout Britain for its quality tinned soups, preserves and other foodstuffs. Their Highland Village visitor centre is a favourite stop with a re-creation of the original 1868 general store and great gift shops such as Mrs. Baxter's Cookshop. An audiovisual presentation tells the story of this family business, now run by the fourth generation, and there are cooking demonstrations and product tastings. Don't forget to have a pancake in the restaurant. The town, which is known for its antiques shops, has a **folk museum**. A path leads south from the village to the 'Earth Pillars', where red columns of sand and rock formed by river erosion frame a fine view of the River Spey.

FORRES

Brodie Castle (National Trust for Scotland) ££ *Off the A96, tel: 01309 641 371; www.nts.org.uk. Open Apr and Jul–Aug daily 1030–1700; May–Jun and Sep Sun–Thu 1030–1700; grounds open daily all year.*

Forres' narrow wynds and wide main street, centred around its townhouse and mercat cross, reveal its medieval origins, although its stone buildings date from the 19th century. The **Falconer Museum** (*Tolbooth Street; open Mon–Sat in summer, Mon–Thu in winter*) looks at local history and geology. Forres is home to the impressive **Sueno's Stone**, signposted on the eastern edge of town and encased in protective glass. Standing 20ft (6m) high, with rich carvings depicting a battle scene, it is one of the finest examples of Pictish art in Scotland and is thought to date from the 9th century. Battlemented **Nelson Tower** (*open May–Sep Tue–Sun 1400–1600*) in Grant Park was built to commemorate Trafalgar and has great views over the Moray Firth. **Brodie Castle** dates from the 16th century and has fine furniture and paintings. It is particularly delightful in spring when the daffodil collection is at its best. Forres is known for its floral displays and makes a good base for touring the area.

KEITH

Strathisla Distillery ££ *Seafield Avenue; tel: 01542 783 044. Open late Mar–Oct Mon–Sat 1000–1600, Sun 1300–1600.*

A planned town and agricultural centre, Keith is situated in the valley, or strath, of the River Isla. Hence the name of its distillery, which is the oldest in the Highlands, founded in 1786. Housed in picturesque buildings, **Strathisla Distillery**, producers of Chivas Regal, is small enough to allow self-guided tours; the workers are welcoming and happy to explain the craft of brewing. The 'nosing' afterwards is enlightening.

ROTHES

Glen Grant Distillery £ *Tel: 01340 832 118. Open Easter–mid-Dec Mon–Sat 0930–1600, Sun 1200–1600.*

The **Glen Grant Distillery** at Rothes was founded by the two Grant brothers in 1840 and was one of the first to produce single malt whisky. It is surrounded by a beautiful Victorian garden, the creation of the explorer Major James Grant, who inherited the business in 1872. The Major enjoyed taking his guests through the garden to his secret Dram Hut, or whisky safe, for a wee dram, a tradition you can follow.

TOMINTOUL

Tomintoul Museum and Visitor Centre *Town Square; tel: 01807 580 285. Open Easter–Oct Mon–Sat 0930–1700.*

The tourist office has a brochure with a map that details more than a dozen walks, between 1.5 and 7.5 miles (2.5–12km) long, on the Glenlivet Estate.

The 45-mile (72.5-km) long Speyside Way stretches from Tomintoul to the Moray coast.

Tomintoul's **Whisky Castle** contains a huge array of whiskies from around Scotland.

At 1161ft (354m), Tomintoul (pronounced 'Too-min-towel') was the highest village in the highlands until Dalwhinnie was upgraded from a hamlet and usurped the title. A sweet town, it enjoys fresh, invigorating air but is also subject to some of the season's earliest and latest snowfalls. The **Tomintoul Museum**, part of the tourist information centre in the square, contains a reconstruction of a farmhouse kitchen and the village smithy, as well as a display on peat cutting and exhibits on local wildlife and history.

Pictish stones

The Picts inhabited the region stretching from just north of central Scotland to the Northern Isles from about AD 450 to 900. They were descendants of an earlier Iron Age people of whom we have no record. In the 9th century, to protect themselves against Viking raiders, they joined with the Scots and their culture was gradually lost.

The Picts were farmers and hunters and produced fine jewellery and metalwork, but they are best known today for their carved symbol stones. The earlier stones, dating from the 6th to 7th centuries have geometric and animal symbols, while the later cross-slabs bear carved reliefs showing crosses and other motifs that reflect the Picts' conversion to Christianity. There are also ogham stones with notches, thought to be a kind of language. No one can agree on the meaning of the symbols or why the stones were erected. The areas of Grampian and Easter Ross are particularly rich in Pictish sites.

Accommodation and food

The Lodge Guest House £ *20 Duff Avenue, Elgin; tel: 01343 549 981; e-mail: info@thelodge-elgin.com; www.thelodge-elgin.com.* Lovely townhouse set in secluded gardens, well located in a quiet residential neighbourhood, 8 minutes' walk from the town centre. Single, double and family rooms, cheerfully appointed. Comfortable guest lounge, private parking, friendly welcome.

Opposite
The Strathisla Distillery, Speyside

Dallas Dhu Historic Distillery (Historic Scotland) £
Off the A940, tel: 01309 676 548; www.historic-scotland.gov.uk. Open Apr–Sep daily 0930–1730; Oct–Mar 0930–1630, closed Thu–Fri.

Cardhu Distillery £
On the B9102, tel: 01340 872 555; www.discovering-distilleries.com/cardhu. Open Easter–Jun Mon–Fri 1000–1700; Jul–Sep Mon–Sat 1000–1700, Sun 1200–1400; Oct–Easter Mon–Fri 1100–1500, tours at 1100, 1300, 1400.

Pizzeria Toscana £ 20 Thunderton Place, Elgin; tel: 01343 551 066. Authentic Italian pasta dishes made to order using fresh herbs and ingredients. Good selection of pizzas. Takeaway available. Closed Sun lunch. Booking advised.

Sherston House £ Hillhead, Forres; tel: 01309 671 087; fax: 01309 671 087. Delightful countryside B&B, 1 mile (1.6km) past the last roundabout on the A96 heading east towards Elgin; look for the large stone house with pretty flowers, on the right. Large, comfortable rooms, beautifully decorated, and a warm welcome. Good home cooking.

A Taste of Speyside ££ 10 Balvenie Street, Dufftown; tel: 01340 820 860. Home cooking at this pleasant and informal restaurant, which specialises in local foods and Speyside malt whisky. Open for lunch and dinner. Closed Mon.

Ramnee Hotel ££–£££ Victoria Road, Forres; tel: 01309 672 410; fax: 01309 673 392; e-mail: info@ramnee.hotel.com; www.ramneehotel.com. Characterful hotel set in 2 acres (0.8ha) of manicured gardens, with 20 tastefully furnished rooms. Good restaurant serving Scottish and French cuisine and an interesting wine list. The bar here is a popular local spot and serves a wide choice of excellent, high-quality pub meals.

Suggested tour

Total distance: The main route is 76 miles (122km). The detour to Tomintoul will add another 40 miles (64km) to the journey.

Time: The main route will take about 2 hours, not counting stops. Allow another hour for the detour.

Links: This route adjoins two other routes, Strathspey and the Cairngorms (see page 158) and Buchan and the Moray Coast (see page 180). Forres is just 22 miles (35km) from Inverness, about half an hour's drive.

Route: Leave **FORRES ❶** on the B9010 for Dallas, 7 miles (11km) away. The **Dallas Dhu Historic Distillery ❷**, the last to be built in the 19th century and now idle, is a good introduction to the working distilleries. You can wander at will among the facilities, and the audio-visual show presents a good overview of Scotch whisky. Continue on 11 miles (17.5km) to **ELGIN ❸**. Then take the A96 to **FOCHABERS ❹** and **KEITH ❺**.

Now turn off on the pretty B9014 for 11 miles (17.5km) to **DUFFTOWN ❻**. From here it is only 4 miles (6.5km) on the A941 to **CRAIGELLACHIE ❼**. A couple of miles (3km) south of town on A95 is Aberlour, home of **Walker's Shortbread ❽**, founded in 1898 by Joseph Walker and still run by his grandchildren. There are no factory tours,

Left
Bishops and earls lie at rest beneath the roofless ruins of Elgin cathedral

ℹ **Forres Tourist Information Centre**
116 High Street; tel: 01309 672 938. Open Easter–Oct.

🛈 **Glenlivet Distillery**
£ Ballindalloch; tel: 01340 821 720; www.theglenlivet.com. Open Apr–Oct Mon–Sat 0930–1600.

Glenfarclas Distillery £
On the A95; tel: 01807 500 209; www.glenfarclas.co.uk. Open Apr–Sep Mon–Fri 1000–1700; Oct–Mar 1000–1600; Jun–Sep also Sat 1000–1600.

Right
Pluscarden Abbey

but you can visit the factory shop on weekdays. Also nearby is the **Cardow distillery ❾**, 8 miles (13km) west along the B9102 at Knockando, the only malt distillery pioneered by a woman.

Detour: A scenic drive south of Dufftown takes you to the highest village in the Cairngorms. Head south of town on the B9009 for 11 miles (17.5km), and at Auchbreck continue south on the B9008. You are now driving through the **Glenlivet Estate ❿**, part of the Crown Estate, which covers 56,833 acres (23,000ha) in the Grampian Highlands. A network of over 60 miles (96.5km) of waymarked paths and cycling trails gives access to remote landscapes. After another 7 miles (11km) you reach **TOMINTOUL ⓫**. Leave town on the A939 west towards Grantown, and after a mile or so (1.6km) turn right on the B9136. Just past the turning, over the new bridge and on the left, there is a pretty picnic site by the old Bridge of Avon, a good viewpoint for the river. This is a beautiful drive through the rolling hills along the River Avon, with gaggles of grouse and pheasant along the road. Keep an eye out for wildlife – you might be lucky enough to spot a rare Scottish wildcat around here!

After about 9 miles (14.5km), at the Bridgend of Glenlivet junction you will see signs for the **Glenlivet Distillery ⓬** off to the right. Founded in 1824, it is set in open countryside with a magnificent mountain backdrop. Head north on the B9008 for about 3 miles (5km) and at the junction turn right on the A95 (signposted Elgin). Carry on for 9 miles (14.5km), passing the **Glenfarclas Distillery ⓭**, independently run by the Grant family since 1836, to rejoin the main tour at Craigellachie.

As you leave Craigellachie for **ROTHES** ❹, 3 miles (5km) north on the A941, look for the iron bridge across the River Spey, built by Thomas Telford in 1812–15; it is the oldest iron bridge in the country. From Rothes it is 10 miles (16km) further on to Elgin. Return to Forres, 12 miles (19km) away, on the A96.

Also worth exploring

The **Findhorn Foundation**, adjoining the caravan park on Findhorn Bay, is world-famous as a model 'New Age' community. There is a visitor centre where you can learn about the community's lifestyle and tour the village. **Pluscarden Abbey**, founded in 1230, is situated 7 miles (11km) outside of Elgin (signposted from the B9010) in a secluded and beautiful glen. It has 25 resident monks, known as 'white Benedictines' because of their white habits. Visitors are welcome and can attend a Sunday-morning service in the lovely chapel. Set on a rocky promontory above the bay, **Burghead** was the site of a Pictish fort where the Burghead Bulls, some of the finest Pictish carvings, were found. The well is also of interest. Near Elgin on the Laich of Moray are the ruins of **Duffus Castle**, a motte-and-bailey castle with a 14th-century tower and a water-filled moat.

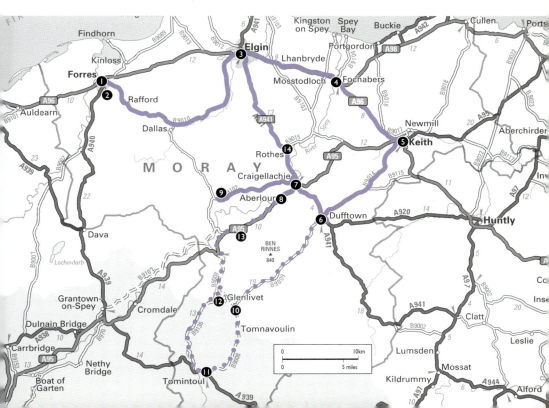

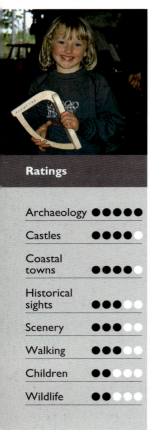

The Grampian Lowlands

Ratings

Archaeology	●●●●●
Castles	●●●●○
Coastal towns	●●●●○
Historical sights	●●●○○
Scenery	●●●○○
Walking	●●●○○
Children	●●○○○
Wildlife	●●○○○

Although geographically north of the Highland line, this part of Scotland is characterised by fertile farmland, a far cry from the empty moorlands north of the Moray Firth. Cut off from central Scotland by the rugged Cairngorms, Grampian has a separate history and rhythm, most noticeable in its distinctive Doric dialect, a throwback to the old Lowland Scots tongue. This land has been farmed since ancient times, and the countryside is full of evidence of these early settlers, including the mysterious recumbent stone circles peculiar to this part of Britain. The Grampian coastline borders the North Sea, and a string of harbour towns – some quaint fishing villages, others booming ports – hug the shore from Cullen to Aberdeen. The North Sea oil industry has also made a major impact. The area also has numerous fine castles and stately homes, many hidden behind the walls and woodlands of their estates. It is perfectly possible to traipse around several archaeological sites in the morning, toss your wellies in the boot and tour a splendid stately home, then pitch up on the coast for a seafood meal at sunset.

ARCHAEOLINK

Archaeolink Prehistory Park ££
Oyne, 8 miles (13km) north of Inverurie and 1 mile (1.6km) off the A96; tel: 01464 851 500; www.archaeolink.co.uk. Open Mar–Oct daily 1000–1700 (last admission 1600).

It would be hard to come up with a more entertaining and informative look at Grampian's ancient past than this excellent prehistory park. The **Archaeodome** is cleverly built under a big mound of turf as if it were an ancient dwelling. Inside, after a film re-enactment of the lives of Scotland's early ancestors, you can wander through the Myths and Legends Gallery with interesting exhibits on sacred stones, wells and other mysteries of the past. Best of all is the **ArchaeoQuest**, an interactive computer station; after browsing through the prehistoric sites in the area, the computer will devise a personal archeo-itinerary based on your interests, available time and even your level of fitness, complete with directions to the sites. On the grounds are a reconstructed Iron Age farm and Roman Marching Camp, and the remains of an Iron Age fort. It's a great place for children, who can dress up in ancient costumes.

BANFF

Banff Tourist Information Centre
Collie Lodge;
tel: 01261 812 419.
Open Apr–Sep.

The Old School
Boyndie *Tel: 01261*
843 249. Visitor centre
Wed–Sun 1000–1600. Free.

This old seacoast town, once a winter retreat for rich landowners, has streets lined with attractive Georgian buildings. Of particular interest is the 18th-century Carmelite House on Low Street, a remnant of the former monastery, and the townhouse next door. Outside is the **mercat cross**, a rare survivor of the Reformation, with religious scenes on the 16th-century finial. The town's finest attraction is Duff House (*see below*). Nearby, **The Old School** at Boyndie has 6 acres (2.5ha) of woodland paths, ponds and natural wildlife surrounding a visitor centre with a four-star restaurant serving local produce. Across the river is the busy fishing port of **Macduff**, where there is a weekday fish market, boat-building yards and a marine aquarium. Nearby at Tarlair there is an open-air swimming pool among the rocks.

DUFF HOUSE

Duff House
(Historic Scotland) £
Tel: 01261 818 181;
www.historic-scotland.gov.uk.
Phone for opening times.

This magnificent baroque mansion with its four corner towers was designed by William Adam in 1735–37 for William Duff of Braco, later Earl Fife. It is now the principal outstation of the National Galleries of Scotland and houses a superb collection of 18th- and 19th-century portraiture, Chippendale and French Empire furniture, tapestries and artefacts. Set in the Deveron Valley between Banff and Macduff, the extensive grounds make for a pleasant country stroll with many points of interest, including the Vinery, the Fishing Temple and the Bridge of Alvah.

EASTER AQUHORTHIES

Easter Aquhorthies Stone Circle

The Easter Aquhorthies Stone Circle is 2 miles (3km) from Inverurie and is signposted. It is an easy 10-minute walk to the site from the car park. Access at all times. Free.

The Easter Aquhorthies Stone Circle is one of the finest and most complete examples of the recumbent stone circles that are unique to northeast Scotland. The name (pronounced 'Ack-war-thees') derives from the Gaelic words for 'field of prayer'. The two tallest stones flank a massive stone laid on its side – the recumbent – forming a frame for the rising and setting of the moon in the southern sky. Sited on the crest of hills with wide southerly views, these stone circles, dating to the 3rd millennium BC, are thought to have been ritual centres for observing the moon, enabling the ancient farmers to establish seasonal calendars. Some 99 stone circles of this type have been found in Grampian, suggesting intense settlement of the area in prehistoric times.

Right
Fordyce Castle

FORDYCE

Fordyce Castle
Note that Fordyce Castle is private and not open to the public.

Joiners' Workshop Visitor Centre *Church Street; tel: 01261 843 322. Open Thu–Mon 1300–2000; Jul–Aug 1000–2000.*

This delightful little village, tucked away beneath Drum Hill off the main coastal road, is a rare undiscovered gem. At its heart is the small pink sandstone **Fordyce Castle**, built in 1592, a charming example of the Scottish baronial style. Nearby is the atmospheric **churchyard** surrounding the ruins of St Tarquin's Kirk, first built in the 13th century and named for St Talorgan, a Pictish saint of the 6th century. Look out for 'Old King Cole', the canopied tomb and effigy of Sir James Ogilvie. The **Joiners' Workshop and Museum**, which has a good audiovisual presentation on the town's history, stands across from the charming **Harp Maker's Workshop**, where you can play a Celtic harp and have a cup of tea.

Right
The Harp Maker's Workshop in Fordyce

FYVIE CASTLE

Fyvie Castle (National Trust for Scotland) ££ *Tel: 01651 891 266. Open Easter–Jun and Sep Sat–Wed 1200–1700; Jul–Aug daily 1100–1700. Grounds open all year, daily 0930–sunset.*

Turrets, sculpted dormers and crow-stepped gables adorn the magnificent façade of the castle. Fyvie means 'Hill of Deer' and the estate was originally a royal hunting ground. Its five towers are testament to the five powerful families who owned it since its beginnings in the 13th century: the Prestons, Meldrums, Setons, Gordons and Forbes-Leiths. Five floors of the castle are connected by the great wheel stair, the finest in Scotland, and there is an outstanding collection of arms and fine paintings, including a dozen Raeburn portraits. Some of the most impressive features were added by Alexander Forbes-Leith, a native son who made his fortune in the American steel industry. This includes the Gallery, or music room, with its self-playing organ.

HADDO HOUSE

Haddo House (National Trust for Scotland) ££ *Off the B999; tel: 01651 851 440, www.nts.org.uk. Open Easter, May–Jun & Sep Sat–Sun 1100–1630; Jul–Aug daily 1100–1630; garden and country park open all year.*

This elegant Palladian mansion house, designed by William Adam in the 18th century, is the ancestral seat of the Gordon Earls of Aberdeen. The interior was redecorated in the 1880s in the Adam Revival style, with coffered ceilings, a panelled library, sumptuous furnishings and family portraits. The grounds contain a terraced garden and a splendid country park with lakes and monuments and walking paths.

PORTSOY

Portsoy is one of the more attractive waterfront towns along this stretch of the coast. The 17th- and 18th-century buildings surrounding its sheltered harbour have been well restored. The village was famous for its vein of pink and green serpentine stone, and Portsoy marble was used to decorate Versailles and other great palaces of Europe. It is still worked today at the Portsoy Marble Workshop by the harbour, where you can purchase a variety of ornaments.

The Seven Wonders of Garioch

The Grampian Lowlands are among the richest areas in Scotland for prehistoric sites. Many lie in the shadow of Bennachie, a landmark hill rising 1733ft (528m) in the farming region of Garioch (pronounced 'gee-rie'). Among the highlights are the Easter Aquhorthies recumbent stone circle and the Brandsbutt Symbol Stone near Inverurie, the Maiden Stone near Pitcaple, the atmospheric Loanhead of Daviot stone circle, the Picardy symbol stone and Dunnideer hillfort near Insch and, atop Bennachie itself, the Iron Age hillfort Mither Tap.

Accommodation and food

Fridayhill Country B&B £ *Kinmuck, Inverurie; tel/fax: 01651 882 252; e-mail: fergusmcgh@aol.com; www.fridayhill.info.* A warm welcome at this lovely, modern Norwegian-style home set in pretty countryside 4 miles (6.5km) outside Inverurie. Large, beautifully decorated bedrooms with cosy extras, such as electric blankets. Guest sitting room and Japanese garden with fish ponds and rockeries. *Open Mar–Oct.*

Fjord Inn ££ *Fisherford, near Inverurie; tel: 01464 841 232; www.thefjordinn.co.uk; Wed–Sat 1800–2100, Sun lunch 1700–2000.* Pleasant country inn serving home-cooked food sourced from fresh local produce.

Opposite
Fordyce churchyard

Above
Duff House, William Adam's
fine baroque mansion

Entertainment

The Doric Festival which takes place in September and October is 'a gran celebration o the tung, music, an traditions o the North East' and features concerts, plays and exhibitions. For details visit *www.thedoricfestival.com* or *tel: 01771 653 320*.

Suggested tour

Total distance: The main route is 86 miles (138km). The detour on the coast to Sandend and Fordyce is only about 7 miles (11km). To return from Fyvie via Haddo House and Tolquhon Castle adds an extra 18 miles (29km).

Leith Hall and Gardens (National Trust for Scotland) ££
On B9002 near Huntly; tel: 01464 831 216, www.nts.org.uk. Open Easter weekend, May–Jun & Sep weekends 1200–1700; Jul–Aug daily 1200–1700; gardens and grounds open all year, daily 0930–sunset.

Time: Allow a half to a full day for the route, depending on how many sites and detours you want to take in.

Links: The route can easily be done as a day-trip from Aberdeen, which is only 17 miles (27km) from Inverurie. It also adjoins the Speyside Sampler route (*see page 171*).

Route: Leave Inverurie on the main road A96 heading west, and follow signs for the **EASTER AQUHORTHIES** ❶ Stone Circle, which is 2 miles (3km) away on minor roads. Return to the A96 and continue west, taking the exit left for Oyne on the B9002. The **ARCHAEOLINK** ❷ is 9 miles (14.5km) from Inverurie. After exploring as many of the nearby ancient sites as your time and interest allow, continue west on B9002 for 9 miles (14.5km) to **Leith Hall and Gardens** ❸ . This grand mansion house displays memorabilia from the Leith family's long history of military service to Crown and country. At the junction with the A97, turn right for **Huntly Castle** ❹ , 9 miles (14.5km) away. Although in ruins, it is impressive for the heraldic sculpture above the doorways and fireplaces. The main building dates from the 15th century. Then take the B9022 north on a pleasant road through woodland and farmland for 17 miles (27km) to **PORTSOY** ❺ on the Moray coast.

Detour: Within a 5-mile (8-km) radius of Portsoy are several atmospheric diversions that, on their own, could make for a leisurely half-day or longer. Set on a bay 2 miles (3km) east of Portsoy, **Sandend** ❻ has one of the best beaches in the area and is backed by

Right
Tolquhon Castle dates from the 15th century

Huntly Tourist Information Centre 9a The Square; tel: 01466 792 255. Open Apr–Oct.

Inverurie Tourist Information Centre 18 High Street; tel: 01467 625 800. Open all year.

Fraserburgh Tourist Information Centre 3 Saltoun Square; tel: 01346 518 315. Open Apr–Oct.

Above
Sir James Ogilvie, known as 'Old King Cole', lies beneath his canopied tomb in Fordyce churchyard

quaint fishermen's cottages. A small single-lane track (signposted) runs from Sandend through countryside to **Findlater Castle** ❼ (the car park is in a farmyard). It's about a half-mile (0.8-km) walk in to the viewpoint overlooking the castle, past the Findlater doocot (dovecot) looking strange and forlorn out in the field. The ruins of this stronghold, dating from 1455, are perched on steep cliffs rising 90ft (27.5m) above the sea, and some 50ft (15m) below the mainland cliffs. It was abandoned in the mid-1600s. There is a path down to the castle and to Sunnyside Beach along the shore. As you leave the farmyard, continue west along the track which winds back to the main road. Turn left and after about a mile (1.6km) take the right-hand turning for **FORDYCE** ❽, 1.5 miles (2km) inland from the main road. Rejoin the main route at Portsoy.

Continue east along the coast 6 miles (9.5km) to **BANFF** ❾ and **DUFF HOUSE** ❿. Take the A947 south for 20 miles (32km) to **FYVIE CASTLE** ⓫. Continue 7 miles (11km) south to Oldmeldrum, then take the B9170 for 5 miles (8km) back to Inverurie.

Detour: From Fyvie, take the B9005 for 8 miles (13km) to Methlick and follow signs from the B999 for **HADDO HOUSE** ⓬. Continue

Tolquhon Castle (Historic Scotland) £ *Tel: 01651 851 286; www.historic-scotland.gov.uk. Open daily Apr–Sep 0930–1730; Oct–Mar 0930–1630.*

Pitmedden House (National Trust for Scotland) ££ *Tel: 01651 842 352; www.nts.org.uk. Open May–Sep daily 1000–1730, grounds open all year.*

south and, just before Pitmedden, follow signs for **Tolquhon Castle** ⑬. These mellow ruins, with an ornamental gatehouse, flagged staircase and 15th-century tower, are pleasingly set among manicured lawns. Also nearby are elaborate formal gardens at **Pitmedden House** ⑭, laid out in the 17th century. The grounds also contain the **Museum of Farming Life** ⑮. From here it is 11 miles (17.5km) back to Inverurie via Oldmeldrum.

Also worth exploring

The coast from Macduff to Fraserburgh is a scenic 44-mile (71-km) stretch. Highlights include the charming seaside villages of **Crovie** and **Pennan**; the latter was the location for the film *Local Hero*. Near the little fishing port of **Rosehearty** are the ruins of Pitsligo Castle and Pittulie Castle, dating from the 15th and 16th centuries respectively. **Fraserburgh**, built on the Kinnaird Head promontory, is one of the east coast's busiest fishing ports. It is home to Scotland's Lighthouse Museum. Inland, at the Aden Country Park at **Mintlaw**, is the highly acclaimed **Aberdeenshire Farming Museum**.

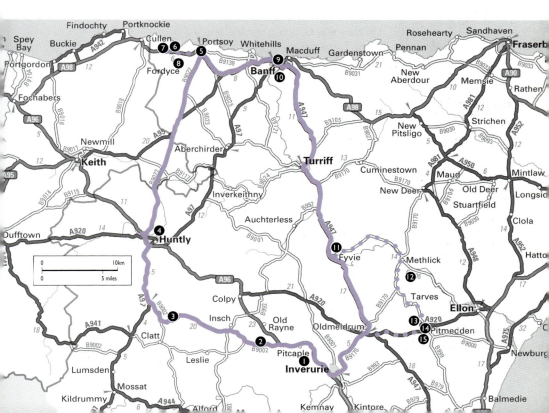

Aberdeen

Ratings

Architecture	●●●●●
Children	●●●●○
Churches	●●●●○
Historical sights	●●●●○
Museums	●●●●○
Art	●●●○○
Food and drink	●●●○○
Shopping	●●●○○

Scotland's third-largest city, Aberdeen, lies between the rivers Don and Dee, a grand merger of two separate fishing villages. The 12th-century burgh of Old Aberdeen was centred around its cathedral and university, while a second trading centre grew up around the old castle (now gone) and port. With the city's expansion in the late 18th and early 19th centuries came the distinctive buildings that gave Aberdeen its sobriquet, 'the Granite City', the silver-grey stone softened by the imaginative addition of round towers, parapets and spires, adding a dignified character to what is now the city centre. The harbour has always been an integral part of Aberdeen's prosperity, from its days as a medieval trading port, a 19th-century shipbuilding centre and a fishing port, to its role today as the offshore oil capital of Europe. Yet there is another side to this surprisingly diverse city. With 2 miles (3km) of beaches and leisure facilities, Aberdeen is a popular holiday resort and hosts an annual surfing competition.

Getting there and getting around

Aberdeen Tourist Information Centre *23 Union Street; tel: 01224 288 828. Open all year.*

By air
Aberdeen Airport is located about 7 miles (11km) northwest of town at Dyce (*tel: 0870 040 0006*). Services to international destinations.

By train
The mainline station is located near the town centre at Guild and College streets (*National Rail Enquiries, tel: 0845 748 4950*).

By sea
NorthLink Ferries sail to Orkney and Shetland from Aberdeen (*tel: 0845 6000 449; www.northlinkferries.co.uk*).

Parking
Most city-centre car parks are limited to 2 hours. There are 4-hour car parks near St Andrew's Cathedral, off King Street north of Castlegate

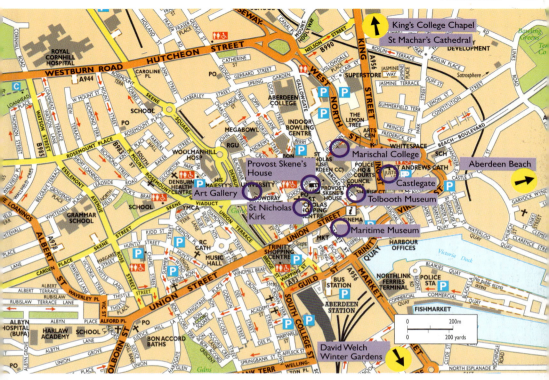

and in Gallowgate, which carries on north from Broad Street. There is a long-term car park in East North Street, off King Street just north of St Andrew's. All-day parking is also available at the shopping centre car parks, but these are more expensive. You may find on-street parking in Old Aberdeen, but you will be lucky to do so.

Sights

Aberdeen Art Gallery *Schoolhill; tel: 01224 523 700. Open Mon–Sat 1000–1700, Sun 1400–1700. Free.*

Aberdeen Art Gallery

The striking pillars in the foyer of the Aberdeen Art Gallery are made of different types and colours of polished local granite. Attractively presented on the ground floor is the gallery's impressive and tasteful collection of 20th-century British art. Upstairs, the Victorian Room features Scottish painters, with some outstanding works by William Dyce, an Aberdeen native, and William McTaggart. There is also a collection of portraiture, works by French Impressionists and contemporary British paintings.

Aberdeen Beach

Aberdeen's 2 miles (3km) of sandy beach have made it the largest resort in Scotland. It is lined with restaurants, cafés, bars and a

Castlegate Market is held year-round, Thu–Sat 0730–1800.

David Welch Winter Gardens
Duthie Park, Polmuir Road. Open daily 0930–1930. Free.

number of attractions, including 10-pin bowling, a golf course, American pool and a cinema complex. Codona's Amusement Park has indoor and outdoor funfair rides and games. The Beach Leisure Centre has a gym, leisure pool and ice-skating arena. Pittodrie Stadium is also located here. At the end of the beach is the picturesque area of Footdee (called Fittie by the locals), a former fishing village designed in 1808 by the city architect, John Smith.

Castlegate

This large square at the head of Union Street was the medieval market place and a market is still held here from Thursday to Saturday. It was the gateway to the old castle, whose former site is now occupied by high-rise blocks behind the Salvation Army Citadel. This building – styled after another castle, Balmoral – was erected in late Victorian times when Castlegate was a degenerate area of the city. The **mercat cross** in the centre of the square dates from 1686; with its unicorn and portraits of the Stuart monarchs it is among Scotland's finest. The Mannie Fountain of 1706 brought the city's first piped water supply.

David Welch Winter Gardens

The magnificent David Welch Winter Gardens at Duthie Park are some of Europe's largest indoor gardens, containing tropical plants,

Below
King's College; the sunken garden

King's College Chapel King's College, Old Aberdeen (1.5 miles (2.5km) north of the city). Open Mon–Sat 0900–1700, Sun 1200–1700. Free.

Marischal Museum Marischal College, Broad Street; tel: 01224 274 301. Open Mon–Fri 1000–1700, Sun 1400–1700. Free.

Aberdeen Maritime Museum ££ Shiprow; tel: 01224 337 700. Open Mon–Sat 1000–1700, Sun 1200–1500.

Provost Skene's House Guestrow (off Flourmill Lane); tel: 01224 641 086. Open Mon–Sat 1000–1700, Sun 1300–1600. Free.

fish and birds and, in summer, a 'talking' cactus. The park is home to the impressive 'Rose Mountain'. Other gardens worth a visit include the Union Terrace Gardens with outstanding floral displays, Johnston Gardens and the rose garden and maze at Hazelhead.

King's College Chapel

Founded by Bishop William Elphinstone in 1495, King's College Chapel is one of the finest examples of a medieval collegiate church in Britain. It was built in the Flamboyant Gothic style, with its landmark Renaissance crown spire restored in the 17th century. Interior highlights include the splendid medieval carvings on the oak rood screen, choir stalls and pulpit and the ribbed wooden ceiling.

Marischal College

The Earl of Marischal founded the Protestant college in 1593 as an alternative to King's College, which was Catholic. They co-existed until 1860, when they joined to form Aberdeen University. The building that stands today was erected between 1837 and 1844; in 1895 the height of the tower was extended to 279ft (85m), while the ornate façade was added in 1906. It is the world's second-largest granite building, after El Escorial near Madrid. Inside, the **Marischal Museum** has ethnographic collections ranging from Egyptian mummies to Inuit kayaks, and a gallery devoted to the heritage of northeast Scotland.

Maritime Museum

The centrepiece of this award-winning museum is its exhibition on the history and lifestyle of the North Sea oil industry, with a model of an oil production platform and computer displays and interactives. There are also exhibits on lighthouses, clipper ships, fishing and shipbuilding, all important facets of Aberdeen's past, as was whaling and herring fishing in the 19th century, and as trawler fishing remains to this day. The complex incorporates Provost Ross's House, built in 1593 in Shiprow, a medieval street leading up from the harbour.

Provost Skene's House

This 16th-century house, swallowed up behind the concrete eyesore of St Nicholas House, is one of the few surviving examples of Aberdeen's early architecture. It was the home of George Skene, a wealthy merchant who served as provost, or town mayor, of the city from 1679–84. It was saved from demolition in the 1930s and has been restored to re-create the style of the house and furnishings in his day. The most outstanding feature is the **Painted Gallery**, with an important cycle of religious panel paintings portraying the life of Christ, rare in Scotland because of their Catholic nature and their survival through the Reformation.

Right
19th-century baronial-style
architecture in Aberdeen's
Union Street

 **St Machar's
Cathedral**

*The Chanonry.
Open daily 0900–1700.*

St Machar's Cathedral

This twin-towered church, the oldest granite cathedral, is one of the best examples of a fortified church in western Europe. It was named after St Machar, a companion of St Columba, who founded the first church here in the 6th century. It became a cathedral church, seat of the bishops of Aberdeen, from 1131. The present building was built between 1320 and 1520. It is now the parish church of Old Aberdeen. Its finest feature is the heraldic ceiling, with 48 shields, which was raised by Bishop Gavin Dunbar around 1520.

Kirk of St Nicholas
*Union Street; tel: 01224
643 494. Open May–Sep
Mon–Fri 1200–1600, Sat
1300–1500; Oct–Apr (entry
through church office)
Mon–Fri 1000–1300.*

The Tolbooth Museum £
*Town House, Castle Street;
tel: 01224 621 167. Open
Jul–Sep Tue–Sat 1000–1600,
Sun 1230–1530.*

Satrosphere ££
*Constitution Street;
tel: 01224 640 340;
www.satrosphere.net.
Open daily 1000–1700.*

Pets' Corner £ *Hazelhead
Park. Open year-round from
1000.*

Doonies Farm *Old Coast
Road, Nigg; tel: 01224 875
879.*

Lochinch Farm
*Redmoss Road (off A90);
tel: 01224 897 400.*

St Nicholas Kirk

St Nicholas is the original parish church of Aberdeen, founded in the 12th century. The huge edifice was divided in two during the Reformation. The West Church, with its pews of dark oak, was reconstructed in 1755 by James Gibbs, an Aberdeen native and the designer of London's St Martin-in-the-Fields. The East Church, restored in 1875, contains the 15th-century St Mary's Chapel.

The medieval transepts, now the vestibule, lead to **St John's Chapel**, which contains the oldest parts of the building and its original stonework. It is now a striking memorial chapel, dedicated in 1990 to those working at sea in the offshore oil industry, with a beautiful stained-glass window by Shona McInnes and a tapestry carpet and chairs of modern design. The church's steeple contains a 48-bell carillon, the largest in the British Isles, on which short recitals are given in summer.

The Tolbooth Museum

The tower of the 17th-century Tolbooth, set behind the 19th-century Town House, was the centre of local government, incorporating the burgh court and the town jail. It is now a museum of city history. The highlight is a trip up the winding stairwell for a re-creation of prison conditions, where model prisoners tell their story. There are also models of Aberdeen in earlier eras.

Entertainment

What's On, available from the tourist information centre, is a guide to arts and entertainment in Aberdeen. The **Aberdeen Arts Centre** (*33 King Street; open Mon–Sat 1000–1600*) is a small gallery devoted to contemporary arts and crafts. It also has a theatre hosting a range of productions.

Performance venues in Aberdeen include His Majesty's Theatre, the Music Hall and the Lemon Tree. You can buy tickets for theatre, dance and live music shows at any of these venues from the ticket offices at His Majesty's Theatre, Rosemount Viaduct, or the Music Hall on Union Street. These box offices are open from 9.30am until 8pm Monday to Saturday (closed at 6pm on non-performance nights). The central telephone number for bookings is *01224 641 122*, and bookings can also be made online at *www.boxofficeaberdeen.com*, which also has full listings of forthcoming events. Top-name concerts and large events are held at the Aberdeen Exhibition and Conference Centre.

Aberdeen has several good attractions for children. **The Satrosphere** is an interactive science and technology discovery centre that will also keep parents entertained. **Hazelhead Park** just west of the centre has a pets' corner and walk-in aviary with a variety of animals. **Doonies Farm**, a rare-breed farm centre with Clydesdale horses, and **Lochinch Farm** provide similar animal experiences on the outskirts of town.

Accommodation and food

 The Gordon Bakery 7 Dee Street, off Union Street, is a good place to try traditional Scottish baked goods such as Eve's Pudding (sponge with apple) or to buy sandwiches and filled rolls.

Cruickshank Botanic Garden St Machar Drive. Open Mon–Fri 0900–1700 and weekends May–Sep, 1400–1700. Free.

Merkland Guest House £ *12 Merkland Road East, Aberdeen; tel/fax: 01224 634 451.* Friendly guesthouse in a great location, 10 minutes' walk from Old Aberdeen and 15 minutes from the town centre, with good bus route between them. Rooms are attractive and comfortable. Cable TV, on-street parking.

Old Blackfriar's £ *52 Castlegate; tel: 01224 581 922.* This atmospheric and friendly pub offers 'centuries of history for the price of a pint'. The back room has a fireplace and low, decorative ceiling. A good range of pub meals, most under £7. Try the huge filled Yorkshire pudding.

The Foyer Restaurant and Gallery ££ *82a Crown Street; tel: 01224 582 277; www.foyerrestaurant.com.* This light and airy restaurant, set in the old Trinity Church, has some of the best food in Aberdeen, from daytime snacks and lunches to a creative dinner menu that mixes contemporary cuisine with old favourites such as rib-eye steak. The changing art exhibitions on the wall add to its style.

Shopping

The main shopping area is Union Street, with its high-street chain stores, and the Trinity Shopping Centre, an indoor mall.

Suggested tour

Begin the walk at **King's College**, which is over 500 years old. It was founded by Bishop Elphinstone under a papal decree in 1495. King's Tower is a university landmark and makes a fitting symbol for the pursuit of knowledge. It is topped by an imperial crown signifying universal dominion. Nearby is another university landmark, which was founded at the same time, **KING'S COLLEGE CHAPEL**. Walk up High Street, the cobbled main street of Old Aberdeen, now bustling with students. The **Old Town House**, now a library, dates from the 18th century and has an older coat of arms above the door. Cross over St Machar Drive and continue along **The Chanonry**, a former walled precinct that contained the homes of the canons, chaplains and university dons. On the left is the entrance to the university's **Cruickshank Botanic Garden**, established in 1898. Among its 11 acres (4.5ha) are a historic rose garden, alpine and water plants and a fabulous sunken garden. At the top of the road is **ST MACHAR'S CATHEDRAL**. Continue along the Chanonry to Don Street, and follow it around the edge of Seton Park and up the hill past the halls of residence. It's a good 10–15 minutes' walk uphill to the **Brig o' Balgownie**. Built in the early 14th century, this lovely bridge spans the wide gorge of the River Don. You may spot wildlife from ducks to deer and even seals along the banks below. At either end of the bridge are the quaint cottages of Cottown of Balgownie. Start back the way you came, but just past the cottages, on your right, take the first entrance gate into **Seton Park** (signposted). Follow the path for a very pretty woodland walk that descends along the river. You may see deer, particularly in the early morning. The path comes out in the middle of Seton Park, at the lower end of the promenade. Follow the promenade, which leads back uphill to St Machar's. From here you can return to the main King's College campus.

The Flower of Scotland

Despite what you might expect from a 'granite city', Aberdeen's townscape is anything but dull. The mica particles in the stone sparkle in the sunlight, while the outstanding gardens and floral displays which form such a colourful contrast have given the city another nickname, the 'Flower of Scotland'. At last count, Aberdeen boasted 12 million daffodils, 3 million crocuses and some 2.5 million roses. More than 25 miles (40km) of rose bushes line the roadsides – which works out to about nine rose bushes per head of population. It's no wonder the city is a multiple winner of the Beautiful Britain in Bloom trophy.

Below
King's College

The Castle Trail

Ratings

Castles	●●●●●
Scenery	●●●●●
Walking	●●●●●
Children	●●●●○
Historical sights	●●●●○
Mountains	●●●●○
Outdoor activities	●●●●○

The ancient Celtic province of Mar included the valleys of the River Don and the River Dee. Today this area is known for its wealth of castles and stately homes, some now in ruins, but many others welcoming visitors. Although Upper Donside is part of an established tourist route, it can remain peaceful even in high summer. The area is a popular centre for outdoor recreation, with walking, rafting, canoeing and skiing on offer. The lower arm of the Castle Trail is called Royal Deeside due to the presence of the Royal Family who spend their summer holidays at Balmoral Castle. In the autumn the heathers and bracken turn the countryside into a regal landscape of purple and gold. The route winds into the mountains at Braemar, home of Scotland's most famous Highland Games, before climbing along Britain's highest main road to 2182ft (665m) and soaring down the 'roader-coaster' through Glen Shee.

ALFORD

ⓘ Alford Tourist Information Centre *Old Station Yard, Main Street; tel: 01975 562 052. Open Easter–Sep.*

🚂 Alford Valley Railway £ *Dunnideer, Kinsford Road; tel: 0787 929 3934. Open Apr–May and Sep weekends; Jun–Aug daily 1300–1630 (also 1030–1430 Jun).*

⛳ There is a golf course at Alford as well as a ski centre with a dry ski slope.

This market town is a popular tourist base and has several attractions. The **Grampian Transport Museum** (*open daily Apr–Oct*) has a collection of vintage automobiles, horse-drawn vehicles and some unusual modes of transport such as the Craigievar Express, a steam tricycle built by a local postman. The **Alford Valley Railway Museum** tells the story of the railroad in Donside and runs narrow-gauge train rides. The **Alford Heritage Centre** (*Mart Road; open daily*) is a museum of rural life housed in the preserved cattle market.

> **The Alford Valley Railway** runs a narrow-gauge train ride (**£**) on steam or diesel locomotives between the restored train station and Haughton Country Park, about a mile (1.6km) away. The trip takes 30 minutes.

BALLATER

ℹ Ballater Tourist Information
Centre *The Old Royal Station, Station Square; tel: 01339 755 306. Open all year.*

Set among mountains and pine forests, this handsome town was a popular Victorian health spa. Today Deeside spring water is bottled at nearby Pannanich Wells. Since the days of Queen Victoria the town has prospered from the proximity of the Royals, and 'By Royal Appointment' signs are displayed in numerous shops. One of Queen Victoria's favourite beauty spots was **Glen Muick** (pronounced 'Mick'), south of town, now a nature reserve and a good place to spot red deer.

BALMORAL CASTLE

🏰 Balmoral Castle ££
Tel: 01339 742 534. Open Apr–Jul daily 1000–1700.

Balmoral is the summer home of the Royal Family. It is open to visitors for a short period each year – usually from April to July, before the royals take up residence in August. During this time you can see the grounds and the ballroom, where there is often an exhibition of paintings from the royal collection. It is important to check the open days and times in advance. There is no access outside these times and the castle is not visible from the gates.

BRAEMAR

ℹ️ **The Braemar tourist information office**, The Mews, Mar Road; tel: 01339 741 600, can advise you on a week's worth of walks around Braemar. Ask for a leaflet.

🏛️ **Braemar Highland Heritage Centre** The Mews, Mar Road; tel: 01339 741 944. Open-year round.

Nestled in the Grampians at the confluence of the rivers Dee and Clunie, the pretty village of Braemar has long been a popular resort, primarily for its magnificent scenery and wealth of walking trails and outdoor activities. The **Braemar Gathering** is perhaps the most famous of Scotland's Highland Games because of its royal patronage. Places of interest include the **Braemar Highland Heritage Centre**. Dress warmly for your visit here – the village sits at 1100ft (335m) and holds the record for the lowest recorded temperature in recent years.

The **Linn of Dee**, 6 miles (9.5km) west of Braemar, is reached by a road into the hills with splendid views over the River Dee. The linn is a waterfall cascading through a narrow chasm, especially dramatic after rain. It is surrounded by woodland and there are walking trails through the National Trust for Scotland's vast Mar Lodge Estate. Further on is the Linn of Quoich.

CASTLE FRASER

🏛️ **Castle Fraser (National Trust for Scotland) ££** Sauchen, off the A944; tel: 01330 833 463; www.nts.org.uk. Open Easter–Jun and Sep–Oct Wed–Sun 1100–1700; Jul–Aug daily 1100–1700 (last admission 45 mins before closing).

Dating from 1575, Castle Fraser is the largest and most sophisticated of Scotland's Z-plan castles. The elaborate decorative detail on the upper towers, the work of master masons of the day, stands out against the bare lower walls, while the two courtyard wings emphasise the height of the towers. The most impressive of the interior rooms is the Great Hall, occupying the entire first floor, with an enormous fireplace measuring 9ft (3m) wide. In the grounds is a lovely walled garden.

CORGARFF CASTLE

🏛️ **Corgarff Castle (Historic Scotland) £** Off the A939; tel: 01975 651 460; www.historic-scotland.gov.uk. Open Easter–Sep daily 0930–1730; Oct–Mar Sat–Sun 0930–1630.

This lonely tower house was built in the mid-16th century and was the hunting lodge of the Earls of Mar. It commands a strategic position at a fording point on the River Don, controlling the route to Speyside over the Lecht Pass. It was torched by the Jacobites in 1689 to prevent it falling to the king's forces, but after Culloden it became a government garrison post and its star-shaped defences were added. It was abandoned in the early 19th century, but troops returned between 1827 and 1831 to help stamp out whisky smuggling.

Drum and Crathes castles

Drum and Crathes castles lie just 5 miles (8km) apart, and their respective lairds, William de Irwyn and Alexander Burnett, were granted the lands in 1323 by King Robert the Bruce for their loyalty to him in battle. A local joke has it that they were given the same land, but instead of fighting over it they just decided to divide it.

The Braemar Gathering is held on the first Saturday in September. If you plan to attend, book early for accommodation (tel: 08452 255121; *www.visitscotland.com*). You can view the games from the hills and terraces within the grounds, but seats generally sell out in advance, so book early by writing to *The Bookings Secretary, BRHS, Society Office, Braemar AB35 5YU; tel: 01339 741 098 for information; e-mail: info@braemargathering.org; www.braemargathering.org*

Right
A test of strength at the Highland Games

CRATHES CASTLE

Crathes Castle £££
On the A193; tel: 01330 844 525; www.nts.org.uk. Open Apr–Sep daily 1030–1730; Oct 1030–1630; Nov–Mar Wed–Sun 1030–1545.

This 16th-century tower house, adorned with turrets and gargoyles, is a superb example of Scottish baronial architecture. Its highlights are the rare painted ceilings in three of the rooms. One of these, the Green Lady's Room, is reputedly haunted. Among the castle's treasures are the ivory Horn of Leys, dated 1323 and given to the first laird by Robert the Bruce who granted him the lands, and the ornate four-poster (1594) carved with the heraldic devices of the Burnett and Gordon families. The splendid **gardens**, with topiary yew hedges planted in 1702, are another highlight and can be visited on their own.

DRUM CASTLE

Drum Castle (National Trust for Scotland) ££ *Off the A93; tel: 01330 811 204; www.nts.org.uk. Open Easter–Jun and Sep–Oct 1230–1700, closed Tue and Fri; Jul–Aug daily 1100–1700. Grounds open all year, daily 0930–sunset.*

Drum means 'ridge' or 'knoll' in Gaelic, and the castle sits on high ground 40ft (12m) above sea level. Its fortified square tower house, one of the three oldest in Scotland, was built in the 13th century, with walls 12ft (3.5m) thick at ground level. It's an altogether eerie place complete with a dungeon. More appealing is the Jacobean mansion with its Victorian additions, made by the Irvine family over 650 years. It is filled with unique pieces of furniture, fine paintings (including a self-portrait by Hugh Irvine, a scion of the family), an impressive library and even a secret tower where the 17th laird hid for two years after Culloden. The grounds contain a lovely chapel and the **Garden of Historic Roses**.

KILDRUMMY CASTLE

Kildrummy Castle Gardens (Historic Scotland) £ *Off the A97; tel: 01975 571 331; www.historic-scotland.gov.uk. Open Easter–Sep daily 0930–1730.*

This 13th-century castle, former stronghold of the Earls of Mar, was once among the most important castles of the north. Its extensive ruins are well preserved and are among the best surviving examples of Scotland's medieval period, displaying both French and English influences. It was built to control the approaches through Donside to the north and was besieged many times. Having served as the headquarters for the Jacobite rising of 1715, it was duly dismantled. **Kildrummy Castle Gardens**, a separate attraction, occupy the quarry where stone for the castle was cut.

Highland Games

Many towns throughout the Highlands hold annual festivities known as the Highland Games or Gatherings. These arose out of contests in the arts of war held by clan chiefs as far back as the 11th century to enable them to choose the best warriors. The games were revived after the repeal of the Proscription Act in 1782, when the survival of Highland music and traditions was at stake. Events include piping, dancing, marching pipe bands and athletic contests such as tossing the caber. Some of the most colourful events take place in this part of Grampian.

Accommodation

Callater Lodge Guest House £ *9 Glenshee Road, Braemar; tel: 01339 741 275; e-mail: bookings@hotel-braemar.co.uk; www.callaterlodge.co.uk.* A warm welcome and comfortable rooms, beautifully decorated, at this family-run guesthouse. Residents' lounge and library.

Opposite
Drum Castle

Suggested tour

Total distance: The main route is a 115-mile (185-km) round-trip from Aberdeen. The detour to Braemar from Crathie Church is 9 miles (14.5km) one way, and the drive up to Linn of Dee from Braemar is 6 miles (9.5km) one way.

Time: Allow a full day for the main route if you want to visit a couple of the castles. If you want to spend time at Braemar and visit the Linn of Dee, it would be best to break your journey halfway.

Links: This tour adjoins the Grampian Lowlands route (*see page 180*). The A93 along Royal Deeside is a popular route to and from Aberdeen. From Braemar, the A93 south through Glenshee is an exciting drive through high mountain moorland, especially on the downhill stretch beyond the ski area – a highly recommended route to Perth. The A939 from Upper Donside connects with Speyside and Inverness.

Route: Leave Aberdeen on the A93. **DRUM CASTLE ❶** is 10 miles (16km) west but is only open in the afternoons, so carry on for 5 more miles (8km) to **CRATHES CASTLE ❷** and return to Drum afterwards. Between Drum and Crathes is the small town of **Drumoak ❸**, so-called because much of the furniture in Drum castle was made from the oak of its woodland. Continue on through **Banchory ❹**, Deeside's largest town. Nearby, you can watch salmon leaping up the river gorge

Below
Crathes Castle and gardens

Banchory Tourist Information Centre *Bridge Street; tel: 01330 822 000. Open Apr–Oct.*

Crathie Tourist Information Centre
The Car Park; tel: 01339 742 414. Open Apr–Oct.

from the **Bridge of Feugh** ❺ . The small village of **Kincardine O'Neil** ❻ is one of the oldest in Deeside and was a rest stop for medieval travellers; its ruined church dates from 1233. About 6 miles (9.5km) beyond Aboyne, budding geologists may enjoy a visit to the **Burn o'Vat** ❼ picnic area, 2 miles (3km) off the main road on the B9119, where marked trails show how the landscape was formed during the Ice Age. It is part of the **Muir of Dinnet Nature Reserve** ❽ , with walks, lochs and a visitor centre. **BALLATER** ❾ is 4 miles (6.5km) ahead on the main road. The road between Ballatar and Braemar is the most scenic stretch of Deeside. In 8 more miles (13km) you come to the car park for **BALMORAL CASTLE** ❿ and **Crathie Church**, where the Royal Family worships when they are at Balmoral. Queen Victoria laid the cornerstone in 1893. You can also visit the small **Royal Lochnagar Distillery** ⓫ at Crathie.

Detour: **BRAEMAR** ⓬ is 9 miles (14.5km) ahead. From here you can head south through **Glenshee** ⓭ along the highest main road in Britain. There is a ski area at the top of the pass, and the chairlift operates in summer to take visitors to the summit of Cairnwell mountain for panoramic views. Or return to Crathie to continue the main route.

From Crathie Church, take the B976 for 5 miles (8km) and then turn left on the A939 through the Grampian Mountains. After 6 miles (9.5km) you reach the A944; **CORGARFF CASTLE** ⓮ is 2.5 miles (4km) west. Head back east for 10.5 miles (16.5km), passing the small village of **Bellabeg** ⓯ , scene of a lively Highland Gathering in August, and the **Candacraig Gardens** at Strathdon (now owned by comedian Billy Connolly and not open to the public). At the junction with A97,

Glenbuchat Castle (Historic Scotland)
Access at all times. Free.

Craigievar Castle (National Trust for Scotland) £££ *On the A980 south of Alford; tel: 01339 883 635; www.nts.org.uk. Reopens in 2009. Grounds open all year.*

turn left and go north for 2 miles (3km) to **Glenbuchat Castle** ⑯, a ruined Z-plan castle built in 1590. In 6 more miles (9.5km) is **KILDRUMMY CASTLE** ⑰. After another mile (1.6km) turn right and go 6 miles (9.5km) on the A944 to **ALFORD** ⑱. With its cupolas, corbels and turrets, **Craigievar Castle** ⑲, 5 miles (8km) south of Alford, is a fairy-tale castle. Its great tower, built in 1626, remains unaltered and the interior boasts original plaster ceilings, fine portraits and period furniture. Continue on the A944 for another 10 miles (16km) to Sauchen and follow signs for **CASTLE FRASER** ⑳. From Sauchen it is 16 miles (26km) back to Aberdeen.

Also worth exploring

Storybook Glen, south of Aberdeen near Maryculter, is amusing for very young children with its models of fairy-tale and cartoon characters. On the coast, **Stonehaven** is a former fishing village with a picturesque harbour. Nearby are the impressive ruins of **Dunnottar Castle**, built in the 12th century and dramatically set on a rocky headland. **Fasque House**, near Fettercairn, was the stately home of former prime minister William Gladstone. **Fettercairn Distillery** is one of the oldest in the country. From here a scenic road, the B974, leads past the **Cairn o' Mount** hilltop cairn, with panoramic views, to Banchory.

Opposite
Dunnottar Castle

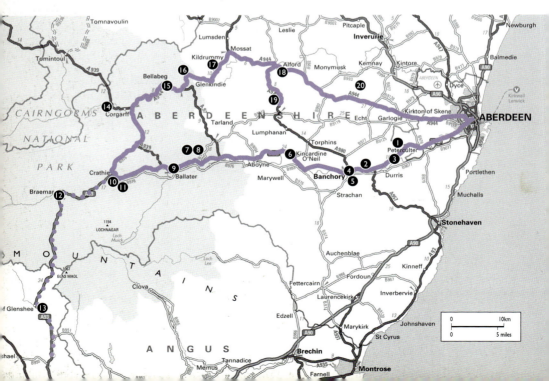

Perth and the Angus Glens

Ratings

Castles	●●●●●
Historical sights	●●●●●
Walking	●●●●●
Museums	●●●●○
Architecture	●●●○○
Children	●●●○○
Scenery	●●●○○
Wildlife	●●○○○

Perth, the 'fair city' of Sir Walter Scott's tale, lies at the centre of a beautiful countryside of green rolling hills. Lying just below the Highland Line that forms the boundary between the Highlands and the Lowlands, it was once the capital of Scotland. Nearby is the charming village of Dunkeld with its cathedral and 'little houses'. This region has two great piles that should be on your list of 'must-see' castles: historic Scone where the early kings of Scotland were crowned, and fairy-tale Glamis, childhood home of the late Queen Mother. The broad valley of Strathmore, which runs from Perth to the coast at Montrose, is the most fertile farming country in Scotland. It is known for its herds of Aberdeen Angus cattle, potatoes and soft fruit, particularly raspberries. Children here have two summer holidays: one for picking raspberries in July/August and a 'tattie holiday' in October. Of course, the picking is now mechanised, but the holiday tradition remains. Forming a scenic backdrop to Strathmore are the Sidlaw Hills to the south and, to the north, the Angus Glens, a walker's paradise.

THE ANGUS GLENS

ⓘ For information on walks in the Angus Glens, visit the tourist information centre in Kirriemuir (see page 206). It is an excellent source of advice and has survey maps of the area. There are no circular routes in the glens and it is important to plan well and keep to the trails, as the heathers and peat bogs make difficult and exhausting terrain.

The Angus Glens run from the towns of Strathmore to Deeside, across a big plateau that is 3000ft (914.5m) high and encompasses 1000 square miles (2590 sq km) between Strathmore, Glen Shee and the sea. There are 22 glens, including the five main ones of Glen Isla, Glen Prosen, Glen Clova, Glen Lethnot and Glen Esk. They are traversed by old cattle droving roads and whisky smugglers' tracks that provide both gentle hill walking and challenging climbs – the area includes ten Munros – through beautiful scenery. The only through-road for cars is along Glen Isla.

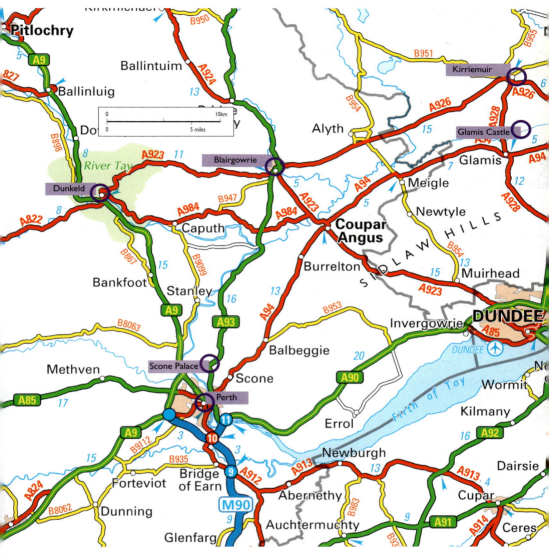

BLAIRGOWRIE

ℹ **Blairgowrie Tourist Information Centre**
26 Wellmeadow;
tel: 01250 872 960;
e-mail: blairgowrietic@ visitscotland.com
Open all year.

Known locally as 'Blair', this former textiles town is a popular outdoor activities centre. It is set along the River Ericht, which is known for its salmon. In winter it is a base for skiers using the Glenshee ski area. Blairgowrie lies at the heart of the region's raspberry fields; watch for signs inviting you to 'pick your own'. Nearby is **Keathbank Mill** (*open daily Easter–Sep*), with an enormous working water wheel, the largest in Scotland, a museum and a large model railway.

DUNKELD

Dunkeld Tourist Information Centre
The Cross; tel: 01350 727 688. Open all year.

Dunkeld Cathedral (Historic Scotland)
High Street; tel: 01350 727 601. Open Apr–Sep 0930–1830; Oct–Mar 0930–1600. Free.

Ell Shop (National Trust for Scotland)
Tel: 01350 727 460; www.nts.org.uk. Open Apr–Oct Mon–Sat 1000–1730, Sun 1230–1730; Nov–23 Dec Mon–Sat 1000–1630, Sun 1230–1630.

Set along the banks of the River Tay, this charming, compact village is surrounded by scenic wooded crags. Its situation on the Highland Line at the southern boundary of the Grampian Mountains gave it an historical importance that surpassed its small size as a strategic meeting place for Highlanders and Lowlanders. Kenneth MacAlpine, Scotland's first king, made Dunkeld the country's religious capital in the ninth century, and **Dunkeld Cathedral** recalls that legacy. The present building dates from 1318 but was ruined during the Reformation. Part of it has been restored as a beautiful parish church, which contains the tomb of the infamous Wolf of Badenoch. The Cathedral is surrounded by green lawns stretching down to the river, where a path leads to a splendid view of the seven-arched **Dunkeld Bridge**, built in 1809 and one of Thomas Telford's best. Between the cathedral and the ornamental cross in the town square are Dunkeld's famous **Little Houses**, built after the town's destruction by the Cameronians in 1689 and restored by the National Trust for Scotland in the 1950s as homes for local residents. On the square is the Trust's **Ell Shop**, with an original Scottish ell, or weaver's measure, fixed to the wall outside; based on the length of the 'average' arm and slightly over a yard (0.9m) long, it was used for measuring cloth. The town is a centre for traditional Scottish music.

GLAMIS CASTLE

Glamis Castle ££
A494, 6 miles (9.5km) west of Forfar; tel: 01307 840 393; www.glamis-castle.co.uk. Open mid-Mar–Oct daily 1000–1800; Nov–Dec 1100–1700; guided tours only.

Glamis (pronounced 'Glahms') is a favourite among castle-goers, not only for its fairy-tale façade but also for its collection of resident ghosts. It is renowned as the family home of Elizabeth Bowes-Lyon, the late Queen Mother, and the castle contains an exhibition about her life and much memorabilia. It is also associated with Shakespeare's *Macbeth*. Glamis has been the seat of the Earls of Strathmore and Kinghorne since 1372. Among the highlights are the crypt, the drawing room with its splendid vaulted ceiling and the Royal Apartments, where the late Princess Margaret was born.

The Dunkeld Larches

Perthshire is known for its 'planting lairds' who pioneered commercial forestry in the 18th century. In 1738 the second Duke of Atholl planted five European larches which were the parents of millions of larches now beautifying the area; one of the originals still stands near the Cathedral. In the 19th century Japanese larches were also planted, and the two cross-pollinated to produce a heartier variety, called the Dunkeld Hybrid, now common throughout Britain. Unusually for conifers, larches shed their needles in autumn. The dukes planted larches by firing cannonballs loaded with seed at the cliff face above Dunkeld, allowing otherwise inaccessible places to be planted.

Dunkeld is the home of one of Scotland's most famous folk musicians, Dougie MacLean. The live music in the Taybank Hotel is a lively spot where local musicians gather for impromptu sessions at the weekend.

In summer, Sunday-evening concerts are held at Dunkeld Cathedral, which also serves as a venue during the Dunkeld and Birnam Arts Festival in June. The Duchess Anne, a Victorian school in the square, holds the Cathedral Art Exhibition each summer.

There are excellent walks from Dunkeld and Birnam, including trails to see the Hermitage, the Dunkeld Larches and to the summit of Birnam Hill. A leaflet outlining the trails is available from the tourist office.

Right
Dunkeld Cathedral

KIRRIEMUIR

Barrie's Birthplace (National Trust for Scotland) ££ *9 Brechin Road; tel: 01575 572 646. Open Easter–Jun and Sep–Oct Sat–Wed 1200–1700, Sun 1300–1700; Jul–Aug daily 1100–1700, Sun 1300–1700.*

Kirriemuir is an attractive town of red sandstone buildings lining narrow, winding streets, and is the starting point for walks into several of the Angus glens. J M Barrie, the playwright and author of *Peter Pan*, was born here in 1860 and you can visit **Barrie's Birthplace** in a humble weaver's cottage. The delightful exhibition about his life includes the wash house outside, where the budding dramatist staged his first plays. You can also visit Barrie's grave at the cemetery, with good views over Strathmore, the Camera Obscura he deeded to the town, and the Aviation Museum.

PERTH

Perth Tourist Information Centre *Lower City Mills, West Mill Street; tel: 01738 450 600; e-mail: perthtic@ visitscotland.com. Open daily.*

Perth Museum and Art Gallery *78 George Street; tel: 01738 632 488. Open Mon–Sat 1000–1700, Sun 1300–1630. Free.*

Lower City Mills £ *West Mill Street. Mill shop open all year.*

Bell's Cherrybank Gardens £ *Cherrybank, Perth. Tel: 01738 472 800. Open Mar–Dec Mon–Sat 1000–1700, Sun 1200–1700 (Nov–Dec till 1600).*

Branklyn Garden ££ (National Trust for Scotland) *116 Dundee Road; tel: 01738 625 535. Open Easter–Oct daily 1000–1700.*

Fairways Heavy Horse Centre ££ *Newton Farm, Glencarse, on the A90; tel: 01738 632 561. Open all year Mon–Fri 0900–1700.*

Scotland's former capital on the banks of the River Tay was a great ecclesiastical centre with four monasteries until rioting mobs destroyed them, fired by John Knox's Reformation sermons in **St John's Kirk** in 1559. The river was the source of the city's prosperity, with dyeing and bleaching of cloth once a major industry. Although Perth is Scotland's fifth-largest city, its agricultural roots still hold

Black Watch Regimental Museum *Balhousie Castle, Hay Street; tel: 0131 310 8530. Open May–Sep Mon–Sat 1000–1630; Oct–Apr Mon–Fri 1000–1530. Closed last Sat in Jun. Free.*

sway, with important agricultural shows and societies based here. Walter Scott's 'Fair City' lost most of its historic buildings long ago (although a few remnants remain if you wander down the side streets), but its inner ring is a handsome centre of early 19th-century buildings and a pedestrianised shopping area. One survivor is the **Lower City Mills**, a traditional oatmeal mill powered by a water wheel. The **Museum and Art Gallery** is well worth a visit to see the fine Pictish symbol stone, decorative arts and natural history displays. One room of the art gallery is geared towards children. Other attractions in and around town include **Bell's Cherrybank Gardens**, with the National Heather Collection, the rare plants at **Branklyn Garden**, **Fairways Heavy Horse Centre and Horse Sanctuary** with the magnificent Clydesdales and the **Black Watch Regimental Museum**. The North Inch, scene of the Battle of the clans in 1396, is today public parkland with walks, golf and other outdoor activities. Fine woodland and burnside walks can be had just north of town off the A93 at the Quarrymill Woodland Park.

SCONE PALACE

Scone Palace ££
Tel: 01738 552 300; www.scone-palace.co.uk. Open late Mar–Oct daily 0930–1645 (closes 1730). Note that visitors are not permitted to take photographs in Scone Palace.

Scone (pronounced 'Skoon') commands an important place at the centre of Scotland, both geographically and historically. Kenneth MacAlpin brought the Stone of Destiny here in the 9th century when he made Scone the centre of his Scots-Pictish kingdom, and **Moot Hill**, on the palace grounds, became the crowning place of Scottish kings until 1651. The palace, built in the early 19th century, is the home of the Earls of Mansfield. It contains a fabulous collection of ivories, the unique Vernis Martin collection of papier mâché objets d'art, fine porcelain, furniture and memorabilia. The grounds contain a chapel on Moot Hill, a replica of the Stone of Scone and the Murray Star Maze. There are lovely walks through the Pinetum, which contains towering conifers over 150 years old, and magnificent trees raised from seed brought back from North America in 1827 by David Douglas, who worked as a gardener at the palace.

Left
Scone Palace

Right
The Ambassador's bed, Scone Palace

The Stone of Destiny

Said by some to be the biblical Jacob's pillow, the Stone of Destiny is believed to hold mystical powers of sovereignty. It is thought to have been brought to Dunadd (*see page 108*) from Ireland and was used in the inaugural rites of the early Scots kings. It was later moved to Dunstaffnage until Kenneth MacAlpin brought it to Scone. There it became the coronation throne of the united kingdom of the Scots and Picts. In his drive to crush the power of the Scots, Edward I of England grabbed the sacred stone and installed it in the coronation chair at Westminster Abbey in 1296, where it remained until 1950, when it was stolen by Scottish nationalists on Christmas Eve and hidden at Arbroath. The stone was returned in time for the coronation of Queen Elizabeth II in 1953. In 1997, the Stone of Scone was officially returned to Scottish soil and is now on display in Edinburgh Castle. However, many say the real stone never left. They believe the monks of Scone Abbey substituted a fake stone all those centuries ago, and that when the time is right the real Stone of Destiny will be revealed.

Below
Replica of the ancient Stone of Scone at Scone Palace

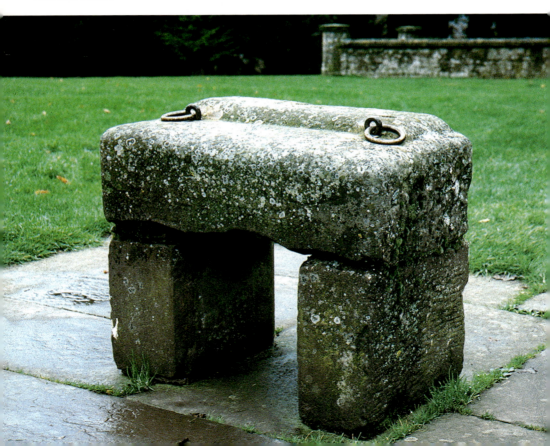

Accommodation and food

The Pend ££ *5 Brae Street, Dunkeld; tel: 01350 727 586; fax: 01350 727 173; e-mail: Molly@thepend.sol.co.uk; www.thepend.com.* A little bit of luxury awaits at this beautiful Georgian guesthouse. Rooms are spacious and handsomely decorated with antiques and thoughtful amenities. Top-floor rooms are cosy with great views over the town. There are two large bathrooms (not en suite). The table d'hôte menu reflects a rich variety of local fare and good home cooking. And this is one place where you can sleep late and not miss out on breakfast.

Ramada Jarvis Hotel ££ *West Mill Street, Perth; tel: 01738 628 281 or 0844 815 9105; fax: 01738 643 423; e-mail: sales.perth@ramadajarvis. co.uk; www.jarvis.co.uk.* This well-appointed hotel is set within a lovely historic building, a water mill built in the 15th century. You can still see fresh running water through port holes in the reception and lounge areas. It sits in a quiet but central area of the city, close to many attractions. The 76 rooms are spacious and comfortable. The Arts Bar & Grill serves good food and there is a comfortable lounge bar. Located in the town centre, free parking.

Suggested tour

Total distance: The main tour is 72 miles (116km). The detour through Glen Isla is 30 miles (48km).

Time: You could easily drive this route in under 2 hours, but with visits to the castles you should allow a full day. The detour through Glen Isla will add another 45 minutes. For those with little time, try to see one or both of the castles and the town of Dunkeld.

Links: With Perth's central location at the junction of several main roads, it is easily reached from other main city centres. This tour adjoins Breadalbane and the Central Highlands (*see page 151*); The Mill Trail (*see page 96*); The Kingdom of Fife (*see page 220*); and is linked to the Castle Trail (*see page 198*) through Glen Shee.

Route: Leave **PERTH** ❶ on the A93 to visit **SCONE PALACE** ❷, 2 miles (3km) northeast of the city. Continue north for 10 miles (16km) to Meikleour, passing the **Meikleour Beech Hedge** ❸ on the main road. It was planted in 1746 and is now over 98ft (30m) high; it is listed in *Guinness World Records* as the highest of its kind in the world. Turn right on the A984 and head east for 4 miles (6.5km) through the market town of Coupar Angus, where you take the A94 east towards Forfar. About 5 miles (8km) on, the little town of **Meigle** ❹ has an outstanding museum of 25 carved Pictish stones found around its old churchyard. From here it is 7 miles (11km) to **GLAMIS CASTLE** ❺. The A928 leads north 5 miles (8km) to **KIRRIEMUIR** ❻.

 **Perthshire Visitor Centre** *Bankfoot, off the A9, 6 miles (9.5km) north of Perth; tel: 01738 787 696. Open Apr–Sep daily 0900–2000; Oct–Mar Mon–Thu 0900–1900, Fri–Sun 0900–2000.*

Beatrix Potter Exhibition *Station Road, Birnam; tel: 01350 727 674. Open daily 1000–1630. Free.*

Detour: The B951 from Kirriemuir runs 19 miles (30.5km) through Glen Isla, the only one of the Angus glens you can drive all the way through. The highlight of this very scenic drive is the Reekie Linn waterfall, the highest in Angus. At the junction with A93, turn left, through the lower part of Glen Shee and Strathardle, to return to the main route at Blairgowrie.

From Kirriemuir, take the A926 west for 14 miles (22.5km) passing the pretty town of **Alyth** ❼, to **BLAIRGOWRIE** ❽. A pack bridge crosses the burn running through the centre of town, which is overlooked by 13th-century church ruins. Continue west on A923 to **DUNKELD** ❾. Between Blairgowrie and Dunkeld are the 'Five Lochs', popular with birdwatchers and fishermen. The Loch of the Lowes Wildlife Centre has numerous observation hides where you can see many bird species, including breeding ospreys. Nest-cams in the centre provide close-up views. The Victorian village of **Birnam** ❿, where you can visit the **Beatrix Potter Garden** ⓫, lies across the river from Dunkeld. The author drew her inspiration for *Peter Rabbit* and other tales from her holidays in this area. The town's other literary connection is Birnam Oak, which features in Shakespeare's *Macbeth*. It's a quick trip back to Perth, 14 miles (22.5km) on the A9. On the way you will pass the **Perthshire Visitor Centre** ⓬, which is in fact a private enterprise geared around a large shop and restaurant.

Right
Dunkeld's 'Little Houses'

Also worth exploring

The **Angus Folk Museum** (NTS) has many curious artefacts and is housed in six charming 18th-century cottages at Kirkwynd, near Glamis. The Angus coast has a long beach and famous golf course at **Carnoustie**. **Arbroath** is a busy fishing town known throughout the country for Arbroath smokies, smoked haddock cured using oak chips. **Montrose** is another town with a good beach backed by sand dunes. Nearby is the **House of Dun** (NTS), a fine William Adam building with exquisite plaster work; in the courtyard you can watch linen weaving on a traditional hand loom. A re-creation of Dundee's jute industry can be seen at the **Verdant Works**; the *Discovery*, which took Captain Scott to the Antarctic, is also berthed in the town.

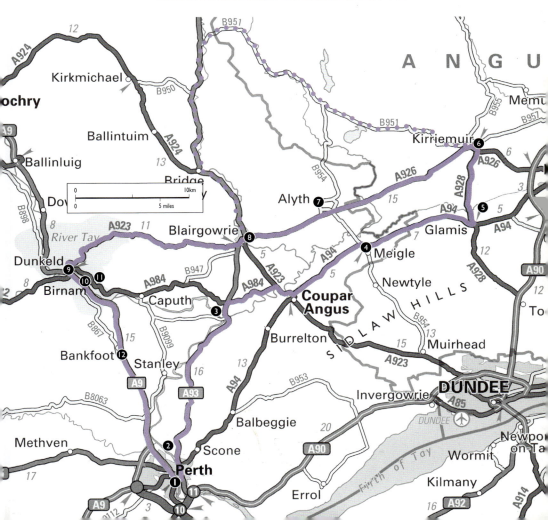

The Kingdom of Fife

Ratings

Golf	●●●●●
Historical sights	●●●●●
Villages	●●●●●
Walking	●●●●○
Architecture	●●●○○
Coastline	●●●○○
Museums	●●●○○
Scenery	●●●○○

The Kingdom of Fife lies between the Firth of Forth and the Firth of Tay. It is the only one of seven ancient Celtic kingdoms to retain its princely title. Although small in area, it is rich in attractions. The medieval Scottish capital of Dunfermline; St Andrews, university centre and home of golf; the splendid Falkland Palace; the charming fishing villages of the East Neuk and the restored 17th-century burgh of Culross are shiny jewels in a rolling agricultural landscape. Fife is just a few miles from Edinburgh and less than an hour's drive from Glasgow, yet it feels distinctly set apart, perhaps because it is approached on three sides by bridges: the Forth Road and Rail bridges to the south, Kincardine to the west, and the Tay Bridge to the north. For those who prefer a more basic form of transport, the Fife Coastal Path runs for 78 miles (125.5km) between the great bridges of the Forth and the Tay.

CULROSS

Culross Palace, Study and Town House (National Trust for Scotland) ££ *Culross; tel: 01383 880 359; www.nts.org.uk. Open mid-Mar–May and Sep Thu–Mon 1200–1700, Jun–Aug daily 1200–1700, Oct Thu–Mon 1200–1600; garden open all year 1000–1800 or sunset if earlier.*

A visit to Culross (pronounced Coo-ross) is a step back in time. The National Trust for Scotland has restored the old royal burgh as it was in the 16th and 17th centuries, when it was a prosperous trading centre on the Forth, dealing in coal and salt. Much of its trade was with Veere in the Netherlands, and Dutch influence can be seen in the architecture. You can easily spend a couple of hours exploring the narrow cobbled streets lined with whitewashed houses with pantile roofs. The ochre **Palace**, built by Sir George Bruce (a descendant of King Robert) in 1597–1611, has much of its original wood panelling and superb painted ceilings, as well as a fine period garden. The **Town House** contains an exhibition on the town's history. The **Study**, in a corbelled tower near the **Mercat Cross**, is also worth a visit for its painted ceiling and panelling. At the top of the hill are the ruins of the 13th-century Cistercian **abbey**. Many of the gravestones in the churchyard are carved with tradesmen's symbols.

DUNFERMLINE

ℹ **Dunfermline Tourist Information Centre**
1 High Street; tel: 01383 720 999; e-mail: dunfermline@visitfife.com. Open all year.

🏛 **Dunfermline Abbey and Palace £**
St Margaret Street; tel: 01383 739 026; www.historic-scotland.gov.uk. Open Apr–Sep daily 0930–1730; Oct–Mar Mon–Wed and Sat 0930–1630, Thu 0930–1230, Sun 1400–1630.

Scotland's capital during the reign of Malcolm Canmore in the 11th century, Dunfermline holds a wealth of history. **Dunfermline Abbey** was built by David I in the 12th century, although an earlier church was established by Malcolm's queen, who later became St Margaret. Although much altered over the years, it contains some of the finest Norman architecture in Scotland. The abbey church preceded the island of Iona as the burial place of Scottish kings and queens, including Robert the Bruce whose tomb is marked with a brass memorial. **Abbot House** (*Maygate; open daily*) houses a heritage centre with interesting displays on the town's history. Across from the abbey is **Pittencrieff Park**, where the remains of the royal palace sit opposite the monastery ruins. Within the park, there are good views from the steep hill topped by the ruins of **Malcolm Canmore's Tower**, and a museum at **Pittencrieff House** (*open daily*). The **Andrew Carnegie Birthplace Museum** (*Moodie Street; tel: 01383 724 302; open Apr–Oct daily*) incorporates the humble weaver's cottage where the multi-millionaire industrialist was born and contains exhibits about his life and philanthropic work. The ornate **Town House**, the displays on linen weaving and damask in the **Dunfermline Museum**, and **Queen Margaret's Cave** are also worth a look.

East Neuk of Fife

When driving in the **East Neuk**, look for the quaint 19th-century milestones and wayside markers.

Crail Museum and Heritage Centre
Marketgate; tel: 01333 450 869. Open Easter & May Sat–Sun 1400–1700; Jun–Sep Mon–Sat 1000–1300, 1400–1700, Sun 1400–1700. Free.

Anstruther Tourist Information Centre *Harbourhead; tel: 01333 311 073. Open Apr–Oct.*

Scottish Fisheries Museum £
Harbourhead, Anstruther; tel: 01333 310 628; www. scotfishmuseum.org. Open Apr–Sep Mon–Sat 1000–1730, Sun 1100–1700; Oct–Mar Mon–Sat 1000–1630, Sun 1200–1630.

Anstruther Pleasure Trips £££ *Tel: 01333 310 103; www.isleofmayferry.com sails from Anstruther Harbour to the Isle of May, Apr–Sep.*

A feature of the Fife landscape, particularly in the East Neuk, is the circular *doocots* (dovecots), built between the 16th and 18th centuries. They housed pigeons that provided fresh meat in winter.

The East Neuk (corner) of Fife, stretching along the coast from St Andrews to Largo, is famous for its string of picturesque fishing villages. Although they appear somewhat isolated today, they were once part of the North Sea trading routes, exporting coal, salt, potatoes and grain. Their large stone buildings with crow-stepped gables and pantile roofs were signs of prosperity, as well as Dutch influence. When the sea trade declined, fishing became the dominant industry and, along with tourism, remains so today.

The East Neuk villages are best explored on foot in order to appreciate the atmosphere and details of the old streets and houses. There are also fine walks along the beaches at Elie and Lower Largo, and on the Fife Coastal Path between Elie, St Monans and Pittenweem.

Crail is the oldest of the East Neuk burghs and arguably the most popular, due to its much-photographed harbour. The squat tower of the tolbooth is topped with a weathervane in the shape of a 'Crail capon', a dried haddock that was once the town's main export. The town museum is nearby.

Anstruther is more touristy than the other villages. It is home to the highly acclaimed **Scottish Fisheries Museum**, which portrays life in the old fishing villages and at sea. There are historic boats in the harbour, ship models and an aquarium. The harbour is also the departure point for boat trips to the **Isle of May**, a nature reserve for seals and sea birds, with remains of a 12th-century monastery and Scotland's first lighthouse. In Anstruther Wester High Street, look out for Buckie House, decorated with seashells.

Pittenweem is Fife's main fishing port, with an attractive harbour and lively morning fish market. Its name is Pictish for 'place of the cave', and

Right
Pittenweem harbour

St Fillan's Cave
Pittenweem; tel: 01333
311 495. Open daily
1000–1800. Free.

**Kellie Castle (National
Trust for Scotland) ££**
Near Pittenweem; tel: 01333
720 271. Castle open
Easter–Oct daily
1300–1700;
gardens open daily year-
round 0930–1730.

St Fillan's cave near the harbour, with a well and altar used by the 7th-century missionary, can be visited. Three miles (5km) north of town is **Kellie Castle**, dating from the 14th century with wonderful plaster ceilings, painted panelling and furniture.

St Monans, or St Monance, has no High Street, as the focus of this village has always been the shore. Even the fine medieval church contains a hanging ship's model. Many of the old houses around the harbour have forestairs leading to living quarters on the first floor, the ground floor being used for storage, while the garret windows have hoists for lifting fishing gear to storage areas on the roof. On the outskirts of town are the ruins of Newark Castle and an 18th-century windmill used to pump seawater up to a row of salt pans.

Elie, along with neighbouring **Earlsferry**, is a popular seaside resort with a sandy beach, but the village retains its historic houses. **Lower Largo**, also a resort, was the home of Alexander Selkirk, the real-life Robinson Crusoe. In the main street there is a statue of the castaway in a niche above his birthplace. The 13th-century church at **Upper Largo** had its spire added in the 17th century to serve as a landmark for ships at sea, a common practice in the East Neuk.

FALKLAND

**Falkland Palace
(National Trust for
Scotland) ££** Falkland;
tel: 01337 857 397;
www.nts.org.uk. Open
Mar–Oct Mon–Sat
1000–1700, Sun
1300–1700.

The charming medieval village of Falkland, nestled beneath the Lomond Hills, would be worthy of a visit even without its splendid palace. The **Royal Palace of Falkland**, built between 1501 and 1541, was the country retreat of the Stuart monarchs who enjoyed hunting in the then forests of the Howe of Fife. The Renaissance architecture has been beautifully restored, particularly the magnificent Chapel Royal with its decorated timbered ceiling. The bedroom contains an impressive carved four-poster reputed to have belonged to James VI. In the grounds are fine gardens and the Royal Tennis Court, said to be the world's oldest (1539).

KIRKCALDY

**Kirkcaldy Tourist
Information Centre**
339 High Street;
tel: 01592 267 775.
Open all year.

**Kirkcaldy Museum
and Art Gallery**
War Memorial Gardens;
tel: 01592 583 213. Open
Mon–Sat 1030–1700, Sun
1400–1700. Free.

Kirkcaldy (pronounced Kir-coddy) lives up to its nickname 'the lang toun' (long town). It is the main shopping centre for the district, and its 1-mile (1.6-km) long promenade is the venue for the April Links Market (now a funfair), an event dating back to the 14th century. Industrial development, mainly linoleum works, wiped out most other traces of its past. It has a good **Museum and Art Gallery** with outstanding works by the Scottish artists William McTaggart and S J Peploe, along with a fine collection of locally made Wemyss pottery. Nearby are **Ravenscraig Castle** and the restored 17th-century houses at **Dysart**.

Golf Links

As far back as 1457, Scotsmen were forgoing their archery practice for the pastimes of 'futeball and golfe'. James II, anxious to maintain his military defences against the English, tried to ban the games, but instead they flourished.

The land around St Andrews, with its grass-covered coastal sand dunes known as links, was perfect for golf, providing natural fairways and bunkers. From here the sport spread round the world. Mary Queen of Scots played the occasional round, and her son James VI was a keen player. In 1754, the Society of St Andrews Golfers was founded to establish a yearly competition. It was later given the title Royal and Ancient Golf Club, and today it is recognised as the governing body for the rules of the game in most countries. St Andrews hosts prestigious international tournaments each year, including the British Open.

ST ANDREWS

St Andrews Tourist Information Centre 70 Market Street; tel: 01334 472 021; e-mail: standrews@visitfife.com; www.standrews.co.uk. Leaflets are available outlining self-guided walks around the town, and interpretive panels and plaques commemorate famous people and events.

St Andrews gets very busy and street parking can be difficult. Car parks are located outside the town centre – on the Bruce Embankment, at East Sands beach, and to the west off Double Dykes Road and Argyle Street. If you do find a spot on the central streets, you will need to buy a parking voucher from nearby retailers.

St Andrews is an attractive city with many claims to fame. Its **university** is the oldest in Scotland, founded in 1410–11, and it remains very much the heart and soul of the town. Thousands of students milling about give it a busy, vibrant atmosphere. You can visit the quads of two colleges, St Mary's in South Street (1537) and St Salvator's (1450) in North Street, as well as the chapel of the old St Leonard's (1512), reached from The Pends.

St Andrews was founded as a religious settlement by Celtic monks; the ruins of their first church, **St Mary on the Rock**, stand near the harbour. Pilgrims flocked to a shrine holding the relics of St Andrew; he became the country's patron saint and his saltire cross flies on Scotland's flag. The town was a great ecclesiastical centre in the Middle Ages. You can climb to the top of **St Rule's Tower**, the remnant of the first Augustinian priory, for sweeping views over the town and sea. The **Cathedral**, founded in 1160, was the largest religious edifice ever built in Scotland. It was ravaged by the Reformers in the 16th century, and only the towering ruins and museum attest to its former splendour.

The **Castle**, the stronghold of the bishops from the 13th century, was an infamous place of imprisonment and execution, best seen in the bottle dungeon and the mine and countermine dug during the 16th-century siege.

St Andrews enjoys a happier reputation as the home of golf, and the Royal and Ancient Golf Club here is the governing body for the game worldwide. The famous Old Course clubhouse is not open to visitors, but you can indulge in golf history and trivia at the **British Golf Museum**.

Open-top bus tours run from between Jun and mid-Sep from Church Street.

St Andrews Cathedral £
Tel: 01334 472 563;
www.historic-scotland.gov.uk.
Open daily Apr–Sep
0930–1830; Oct–Mar
Sat–Wed 0930–1630.
Charge for museum and St Rule's Tower.

St Andrews Castle and Visitor Centre £
Tel: 01334 477 196;
www.historic-scotland.gov.uk.
Open daily 0930–1730 (until 1630 Oct–Mar Sat–Wed).

British Golf Museum ££
Bruce Embankment;
tel: 01334 460 046;
www.britishgolfmuseum.co.uk.
Open mid-Mar–Oct
Mon–Sat 0930–1730, Sun
1000–1700; Nov–Mar
Mon–Sat 1000–1600.

St Andrews Museum
Kinburn Park; tel: 01334 659
380. Open daily Apr–Sep
1000–1700; Oct–Mar
1030–1600. Free.

St Andrews Aquarium
££ The Scores; tel: 01334
474 786;
www.standrewsaquarium.co.uk.
Open daily in summer
1000–1800, phone for
winter hours.

St Andrews Botanic Gardens £ Cannongate;
tel: 01334 476 452;
www.st-andrews-botanic.org.
Open daily May–Sep
1000–1900; Oct–Apr
1000–1600.

Right
The famous Royal and Ancient
Golf Club, St Andrews

The town centre still has the appearance of the market town it always was, with medieval wynds and closes to explore and Edwardian and Victorian buildings. Noteworthy features include the Mill Port and West Port gateways, the vaulted gatehouse called The Pends and Louden's Close. The **St Andrews Museum**, the **Aquarium** and the **Botanic Garden** are also of interest. In July and August, from Thursday to Sunday, street performers re-enact the town's history at the Castle, Bow Butts and Church Square. St Andrews Week is a week-long festival at the end of November.

Accommodation and food

The Inn at Lathones £££-£££ *By Largoward, St Andrews; tel: 01334 840 494; fax: 01334 840 694; e-mail: lathones@theinn.co.uk; www.theinn.co.uk.* Just 5 miles (8km) south of St Andrews city centre, this superb country inn dates back to the late 17th century and has a colourful history complete with resident ghost. The 14 rooms are characterful and well appointed, two with wood-burning stove and whirlpool. The old stables is now an atmospheric bar, while an excellent range of local seafood and gourmet Scottish fare is served in the restaurant.

The Peat Inn £££-£££ *Near St Andrews; tel: 01334 840 206; fax: 01334 840 530; e-mail: stay@thepeatinn.co.uk; www.thepeatinn.co.uk.* This 5-star restaurant with rooms, one of Scotland's best, is just 6 miles (10 km) outside St Andrews. Chef-proprietor Geoffrey Smeddle's menu is based on classic French cuisine, featuring fresh produce from local artisan suppliers, backed by a superb 400-bin wine list. Small, intimate dining rooms, with a cosy lounge and gardens for coffee and aperitifs. Set menus are excellent value. Eight luxury suites, set around a garden, make it perfect for a romantic stay. *Open Tue–Sat for lunch and dinner.*

Above
Culross Palace, Fife

Sport and beaches

For more information on golfing in Fife, including golf passes and discount cards, ask for the *Golf* brochure from the tourist board or visit *www.fifegolf.com*. More golfing information is available on *www.standrews.com*, or ask for the Golf in Scotland brochure from tourist information centres; also available from *www.visitscotland.com*.

St Andrews has six golf courses, which host many international events. To book a round, contact the Reservations Office; *tel: 01334 466 666; e-mail: reservations@standrews.org.uk; www.standrews.org.uk*

Fife boasts four 'Blue Flag' beaches – the coveted EU rating of cleanliness and quality – at St Andrews, Burntisland, Elie and Aberdour. St Andrews West Sands beach was the backdrop for scenes from *Chariots of Fire*, while the East Sands Leisure Centre has pools, a water slide and fitness equipment. The best beaches on the East Neuk are at Elie and Kingsbarns.

The **Fife Coastal Path** extends for 78 miles (125.5km) from the Forth Bridge in the south to the Tay Bridge in the north. The tourist office publishes leaflets on circular walks covering several sections of the route. A fine stretch in the East Neuk runs between Pittenweem and St Monans (1 mile, 1.6km) and continues to Elie (2.5 miles, 4km). There are bus stops at either end for the return journey, and there are shorter walks as well.

Below
Culross Town House, or Tolbooth

Suggested tour

Total distance: 65 miles (104.5km).

Time: The main roads can be driven in about 2 hours, although you could easily devote a day to the East Neuk alone if you want to explore all the villages, for although they are fairly small and close together, parking and walking to the harbourfronts takes time. Those with limited time should concentrate on St Andrews, one or two villages in the East Neuk and Falkland Palace.

Links: Dunfermline and Culross could be visited on a day-trip from Edinburgh. The Fife tour is also easily joined with the suggested routes for Perthshire (*see page 209*) and Stirling (*see page 96*).

Route: Leave **ST ANDREWS** ❶ on the A917 heading east to Crail. Continue down the coast, visiting the **EAST NEUK** ❷ villages. After Lower Largo, continue on the A915 through the busy town of Leven, then follow the A911 to Glenrothes. Take the A92 north, exiting left

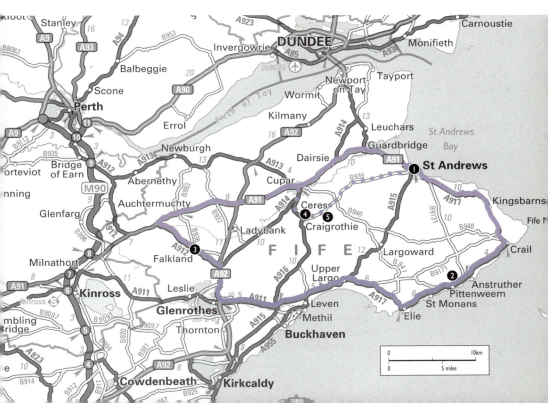

Hill of Tarvit Mansion House (National Trust for Scotland) ££ Tel: 01334 653 127; www.nts.org.uk. Open May–Oct Thu–Mon 1300–1700, Jun–Aug daily 1300–1700.

Fife Folk Museum £ Ceres; tel: 01334 828 180. Open Easter and mid-Apr–Sep daily 1130–1630.

Scotland's Secret Bunker ££ Troywood, near St Andrews; tel: 01333 310 301; www.secretbunker.co.uk. Open Apr–Oct daily 1000–1700.

on the A912 to **FALKLAND** ❸. After a visit to the palace, continue on the A912 to Strathmiglo. Turn right (east) on the A91 to return to St Andrews through the pretty fields and woodlands that make up the agricultural district known as the Howe of Fife.

Detour: At the busy market town of Cupar, turn off on the A916 and follow signs to the **Hill of Tarvit** ❹, 2.5 miles (4km) south. This mansion house was rebuilt in 1906 by the Scottish architect Robert Lorimer, and contains fine furniture and Chinese porcelain as well as paintings by Raeburn and Ramsay. There is a restored Edwardian laundry in the garden. Follow signs to **Ceres** ❺, on the B939, with its attractive village green. The **Fife Folk Museum**, with a collection of farming tools and costumes, is housed in the 17th-century Weigh House alongside the humped-back stone bridge. A memorial commemorates the townsmen who fought with Robert the Bruce at Bannockburn. The B939 continues east to St Andrews.

Also worth exploring

Scotland's Secret Bunker, disguised as a farm building 10 miles (16km) southeast of St Andrews on the B940, is a former nuclear war headquarters that provides a sinister reminder of the Cold War era.

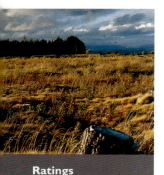

The Great Glen

Ratings

Historical sights	●●●●●
Outdoor activities	●●●●○
Walking	●●●●○
Scenery	●●●○○
Wildlife	●●●○○
Castles	●●○○○
Children	●●○○○
Villages	●●○○○

The Great Glen, a geological fault running from the Moray Firth to Fort William along a series of freshwater lochs, bisects the Highlands. It was a natural inland route for missionaries and militias and, with the building of the Caledonian Canal, an important avenue of trade. Today it is one of Scotland's busiest tourist corridors. At its northern end lies Inverness, the largest city in the north of Scotland. This Highland capital enjoys a scenic position spanning the River Ness, with historic castles and battlegrounds nearby and it is an important centre for traditional Highland music. It is situated on the inner banks of the Moray Firth, and one of the great pleasures of a visit here is the chance to see seals along the shore and dolphins leaping beneath the Kessock Bridge without ever leaving town. But the city borders another more famous body of water, Loch Ness, with its legendary monster. Whether or not you're lucky enough to get a glimpse of Nessie, a drive along the shores of this scenic waterway is not to be missed. To the west, past the villages of Beauly and Cannich, are the beautiful glens of Affric, Cannich and Strathfarrar.

BEAULY

Campbells of Beauly on the main square, is known around the world for its high-quality tartans, tweeds, woollens and Highland accessories, and their bespoke tailoring service.

Beauly Priory (Historic Scotland)
£ On the A862;
tel: 01663 783 444;
www.historic-scotland.gov.uk.
Open all year. Contact key keepers.

There are several tales of how the town got its name. Whether the words *beau lieu*, which means 'beautiful place', were uttered by Mary Queen of Scots on her visit in 1564 or by the French-born lairds, the Lovats, the pretty village with its large market square still deserves its title today. More likely it was thus christened by Burgundian monks who established **Beauly Priory** in 1230. The roofless church is all that remains; note the fine trefoil windows in the south wall. South of town is Beaufort Castle, formerly the Lovat clan seat (now private). Nearby at Muir of Ord you can visit the **Glen Ord Distillery** to watch the distillers at work making their sweet, dry malt whisky (*tel: 01463 872 004; open Mon–Fri year-round and weekends Jul–Sep*).

The **Beauly Centre** (*High Street; tel: 01463 783 444*) was set up by the Beauly Firth and Glens Trust and presents a wealth of information on the area's history and culture, including a clan room. From Beauly there is a lovely drive south through the delightful river valley known

as Strathglass to the village of Cannich, and a few miles further to Glen Affric, said by many to be Scotland's most beautiful glen. There are picnic spots and viewpoints here.

CALEDONIAN CANAL

ⓘ Fort Augustus Tourist Information Centre
Car park; tel: 0845 22 55 121; e-mail: info@visitscotland.com. Open Apr–Oct.

ⓝ Caledonian Canal Heritage Centre
Canal Side, Fort Augustus; tel: 01320 366 493; www.waterscape.com. Open Apr–Oct 1000–1730. Free. A history of the canal, its uses and renovation.

The Clansman Centre
Fort Augustus; tel: 01320 366 444. Open 1030–1800.

Built in the early 19th century primarily by Thomas Telford, the Caledonian Canal was one of the greatest engineering feats of its time. Over 60 miles (96.5km) long, it connects the North Sea and the Atlantic Ocean via three lochs – Loch Ness, Loch Oich and Loch Lochy – creating a waterway between Inverness and Corpath, near Fort William, that saved trading vessels the long journey around the northern coast. There are 29 locks along the route, and you can watch boats passing through the system at Fort Augustus and at Banavie. Today the canal is used mainly by pleasure boats.

Straddling the canal at the southern end of Loch Ness is the busy little town of **Fort Augustus**. Its beautiful abbey, built on the site of the original 18th-century fort, is still a landmark in the town, although its future is uncertain (cloisters and gardens open to visitors in summer, but development plans may change this). Other attractions include the **Caledonian Canal Heritage Centre** and the **Clansman Centre**.

CAWDOR CASTLE

ⓝ Cawdor Castle ££
On the B9090; tel: 01667 404 401; e-mail: info@cawdorcastle.com; www.cawdorcastle.com. Open May–mid-Oct daily 1000–1730.

Although reputedly the place of Duncan's murder in Shakespeare's *Macbeth*, the origins of Cawdor Castle post-date Macbeth by around 300 years. According to legend, the founder, Thane William of Cawdor, was told in a dream to load a donkey with gold and to build a fortress on the spot where the donkey stopped. It paused for a rest under a holly tree, where William built the central tower. A fragment of this ancient tree has been carbon-dated to the late 14th century. With its drawbridge and turrets, Cawdor is a romantic castle, still inhabited by the Cawdors. To enhance your enjoyment of the many heirlooms on show, buy a copy of the castle guide with humorous captions written by a previous Lord Cawdor. There are also lovely gardens.

CULLODEN

In 1746, the Jacobite dream was crushed forever on the bleak fields of Culloden Moor. Here the Highland forces of Bonnie Prince Charlie were greatly outnumbered by the government forces of the Duke of Cumberland, who became known as 'Butcher Cumberland' for his

Culloden (National Trust for Scotland) £
Culloden Moor, on the B9006; tel: 01463 790 607; www.culloden.org.uk. Battlesite open all year.

brutal slaughter of innocent bystanders and wounded soldiers in the aftermath of the battle. A new visitor centre, which opened in September 2007, features an exhibition overlooking the battlefield that tells the story of events leading up to the battle and its aftermath.

Cruises on Loch Ness aboard the *Royal Scot* are available Mar–Jan from Fort Augustus. The boat features high-tech sonar on the loch, bar and light snacks. Cruises on the hour from 1000 daily. *Tel: 01320 366 277; www.cruiselochness.com*

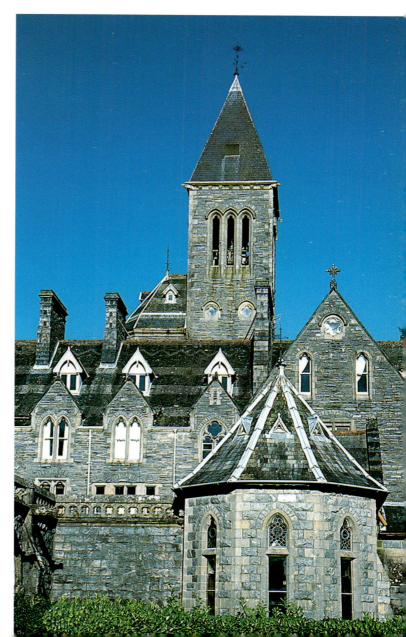

Right
A Fort Augustus landmark, the Abbey

FORT GEORGE

Fort George (Historic Scotland)
££ *Off the A96; tel: 01667 460 232; www.historic-scotland.gov.uk. Easter–Sep daily 0930–1730; Oct–Mar daily 0930–1630.*

Opposite
St Andrew's Cathedral, Inverness

Standing on a peninsula jutting out into the Moray Firth, this formidable military stronghold was built between 1748 and 1769 to deter any further rebellion by the Highlanders after the Jacobite Rising. It is the finest example of an artillery fortress in Europe. The Jacobite threat had died out by the time the fort was completed, and it has never seen armed conflict. It remains an army barracks, but visitors can walk along the pentagon-shaped walls, each with their bastions and sentry posts. The guardrooms, period barracks, chapel and grand magazine can be seen, and the **Highlanders Regimental Museum** is housed here.

INVERNESS

Inverness Tourist Information *Castle Wynd; tel: 0845 22 55 121; e-mail: info@visitscotland.com. Open all year.*

St Andrew's Cathedral
Ardross Street. Open daily 0830–1800 (later in summer).

Inverness Castle
Castle Street; tel: 01463 243 363. Open daily during the tourist season 1030–1730.

Riverside Gallery *11 Bank Street; tel: 01463 224 781. Open Mon–Fri 0900–1700, Sat 0900–1600.*

Castle Gallery *43 Castle Street, Open Mon–Sat 0900–1700.*

Art-TM Gallery
14A Seafield Road; tel: 01463 718999. Open Tue–Sat 1200–1600 (until 1800 Thu).

Scottish Kiltmaker Visitor Centre *4–9 Huntley Street; tel: 01463 222 781.*

Inverness is an important gateway to the Highlands. The mainline railway station is located in the town centre. Central information and reservations tel: 0845 748 4950.

A strategic Highlands crossroads, Inverness has been settled since ancient times. The city centre along the banks of the River Ness has an attractive charm, especially on a sunny day. Two features of the town are the suspension foot bridges that span the river, and the wooded islands downstream that are a favourite haunt of local fishermen. You can reach them in about 10 minutes on the Ness Walk walking trail, signboarded near the cathedral. **St Andrew's Cathedral**, built between 1866 and 1869 in neo-Gothic style, has beautiful stained glass over the entrance. **Inverness Castle**, built in the 19th century, overlooks the river and houses law courts and offices. Below the castle is the **Inverness Museum and Art Gallery** (*Castle Wynd; tel: 01463 237 114; open Mon–Sat*), with exhibits about the history of the Great Glen and Highland life. Scottish art is represented in a number of galleries. The **Riverside Gallery** shows paintings, prints and etchings of Highland landscapes and contemporary images by Highland artists; the **Castle Gallery** sells paintings, sculpture and crafts by Scottish and British artists, the **Art-TM Gallery** promotes visual arts and crafts of the Highlands. The **Scottish Kiltmaker Visitor Centre** is worth a visit to learn about the production of Scotland's national dress. **James Pringle Weavers** (*Holm Mills, Dores Road; tel: 01463 223 311*) also has a free exhibition that tells the story of tartan.

The Loch Ness Monster

Nessie has become such a favourite figure in Scotland's folklore that the word 'monster' hardly seems appropriate. Does a prehistoric creature with a humped back and snake-like neck really inhabit the depths of Loch Ness? The first sighting was reputedly made by a monk in the 8th century. Since that time, countless expeditions to discover the truth have been made by everyone from obsessed trainspotters to serious scientists equipped with high-tech gear. Hoaxers aside, enough viable 'evidence' exists to keep the quest alive, while somewhere in the dark waters Nessie guards her secret well.

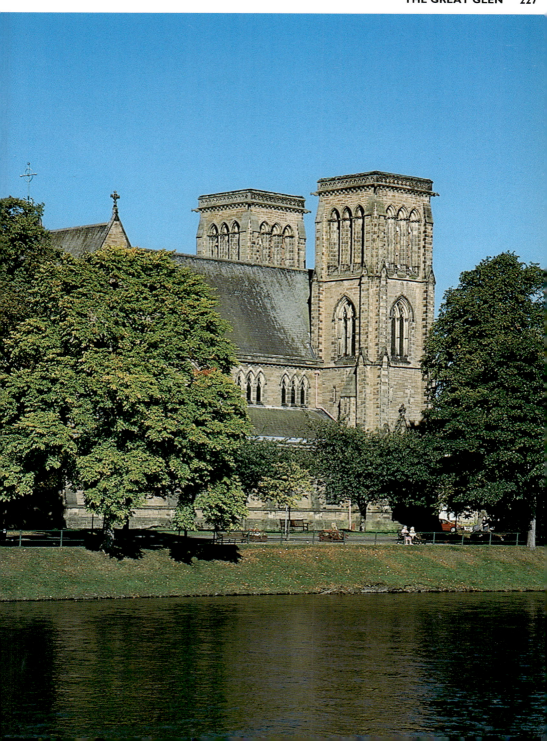

Accommodation and food

Castle Tavern ££ *1–2 View Place (top of Castle Street), Inverness; tel: 01463 718 178; www.castletavern.net.* Opposite Inverness Castle, this popular bar and restaurant serves a casual menu along with award-winning real ales and quality malt whiskies from around Scotland. The beer garden overlooks the castle and river.

Moyness House Hotel ££ *6 Bruce Gardens, Inverness; tel/fax: 01463 233 836; e-mail: info@moyness.co.uk; www.moyness.co.uk.* This elegant Victorian villa, in a quiet residential area 5 minutes' walk from the town centre, was once the home of the Scottish author Neil M Gunn. The de luxe bedrooms are furnished with attentive extras. There is a spacious sitting room and walled garden.

The Mustard Seed Restaurant ££ *16 Fraser Street, Inverness; tel: 01463 220220; www.themustardseedrestaurant.co.uk.* On the banks of the River Ness and set in a former church with high vaulted ceiling and arched windows, this informal restaurant combines traditional French and Scottish cuisine with international accents.

Below
Inverness Castle

The Original Loch Ness Monster Visitor Centre
Drumnadrochit; tel: 01456 450 342; e-mail: info@lochness-centre.com; www.lochness-centre.com. Exhibitions, cinema, cruises, gift shop, restaurant. Nearby is the **Loch Ness Exhibition Centre £** *tel: 01456 450 573; www.loch-ness-scotland.com,* with themed, multimedia presentations.

Right
Fort George

Suggested tour

Total distance: 70 miles (112.5km) for the main route, 94 miles (151km) taking the detour.

Time: Depending on traffic, the main route will take 2.5 to 3 hours, not counting stops. Add an extra 40 minutes for the detour.

Links: The trip from Inverness to Fort William on the busy A82 is 65 miles (104.5km) and takes about an hour and a half. The Black Isle is just over the Kessock Bridge and makes a pleasant day-trip from Inverness. The A9 continues up the northeast coast. Ullapool, on the west coast, is an hour away via the A835.

Route: The route circles legendary **Loch Ness ❶**. This narrow loch runs for 23 miles (37km) along the Great Glen, reaching depths of over 750ft (228.5m). It is largely surrounded by forest land that obscures the view for much of the way, particularly on the lower end of the A82. The eastern (southern) side has better access to the shore. Although it is a

Dolphin cruises ££ around the Moray Firth operate from Inverness and Cromarty on the Black Isle. *Contact Moray Firth Cruises, Shore Street Quay, Inverness; tel/fax: 01463 717 900; e-mail: info@inverness-dolphin-cruises.co.uk; www.inverness-dolphin-cruises.co.uk*

The Great Glen Cycle Route features woodland trails for cyclists and walkers. Ask at the tourist information centres.

A good day out for children is the **Inverness Aquadome**, with a swimming pool, water flumes and other attractions. Parents can relax in the spa pool, sauna and steam rooms. *Bught Park; tel: 01463 667 500; www.invernessleisure.com. Open all year.*

There are several riding and pony-trekking centres in the area. Try the **Highland Riding Centre**, *Borlum Farm, Drumnadrochit; tel: 01456 450 220. Open daily all year, closed Sun in Jul–Aug.*

The Kyle Line is a scenic train trip from Inverness to the Kyle of Lochalsh, operating during the summer season. *Tel: 01599 534 824; www.kylerailway.co.uk*

Left
Urquhart Castle overlooking Loch Ness

narrow, single-track road for much of the way, it is less travelled than the busy A82 on the opposite side, which can often be clogged with traffic.

Leave Inverness along the B862, signposted the Loch Ness Trail. After about 9 miles (14.5km), at Dores, keep to the right-hand fork which becomes the single-track B852 (again signposted Loch Ness Trail). There are beautiful views of the loch at this point. The road meanders right along the loch, and there are places to pull off and walk down to the water, as well as scenic picnic spots.

After about 18 miles (29km) you enter the **Farigaig Forest ❷**. There is a visitor centre off to the left with parking and toilets, and the Forestry Commission has set up a good display about the geology and wildlife of the area. It's a beautiful area and there are several walks, most taking an hour or less, along the river and to the Farigaig Gorge. Leaflets are available here or at Fort Augustus. Another beautiful spot for walks is at Foyers, 3 miles (5km) further on, where a forest trail leads to the rushing **Falls of Foyers ❸**.

The road now veers away from Loch Ness, and reconnects with the B862. Around Whitebridge there are fine views of the rounded Monadhliath mountains on the left. The little town is centred around a fine specimen of General Wade's 18th-century military bridges. The road continues to **FORT AUGUSTUS ❹**, 32 miles (51.5km) from Inverness.

Returning up the western (northern) side of the loch on the A82 is a totally different experience. This major trunk road is winding and fast, that is, unless you find yourself behind a logging truck, tour coach, caravan, etc. Clear views of Loch Ness are few until you get to **Urquhart Castle ❺**. Set against the backdrop of the loch, these impressive ruins, dating from the 12th century, were once one of Scotland's largest castles. Government troops blew it up in 1692 to prevent it from falling to the Jacobites. There is a somewhat steep path down to the castle, or you can admire it from a parking area and viewpoint farther above. Just north of the castle at **Drumnadrochit ❻** there are two exhibitions on the Loch Ness Monster. From here it is 14 miles (22.5km) back to Inverness on the main road.

Detour: A more attractive route back to Inverness can be explored by heading west from Drumnadrochit on the A831. After about a mile (1.6km) you can turn right on the A833, heading north through forest and wild moorland, or continue west along Glen Urquhart to **Cannich ❼**, 12 miles (19km) away. It marks the meeting point of three beautiful Highland glens to the west. From Cannich you can follow minor roads to explore **Glen Affric ❽**, the most impressive and most popular, where you will find one of the best examples of Scotland's old Caledonian pine forest, and **Glen Cannich ❾**, which leads to the huge Mullardoch Dam. The A831 turns north along the River Glass for 15 miles (24km) of scenic countryside to Beauly.

Above
Inverness on the River Ness

Strathglass ❿ has a poignant beauty, however, for its entire population was evicted during the Clearances of the early 19th century (*see page 259*). At Struy you can head west into **Glen Strathfarrar** ⓫ along several hiking paths; the road is private, so ask the gatekeeper for permission to take your car (*tel: 01463 761 260*). There are ruins of two Iron Age forts at **Kilmorack** ⓬, 2 miles (3km) from **BEAULY** ⓭. From there it is 11 miles (17.5km) back to Inverness on the A862.

Also worth exploring

The **Clava Cairns**, signposted one mile (1.6km) east of Culloden, is an impressive Neolithic burial site consisting of three cairns, each surrounded by stone circles, with some stones bearing cup and ring marks. **Nairn** is a holiday resort on the Moray Firth with sandy beaches, golf courses and other recreational activities.

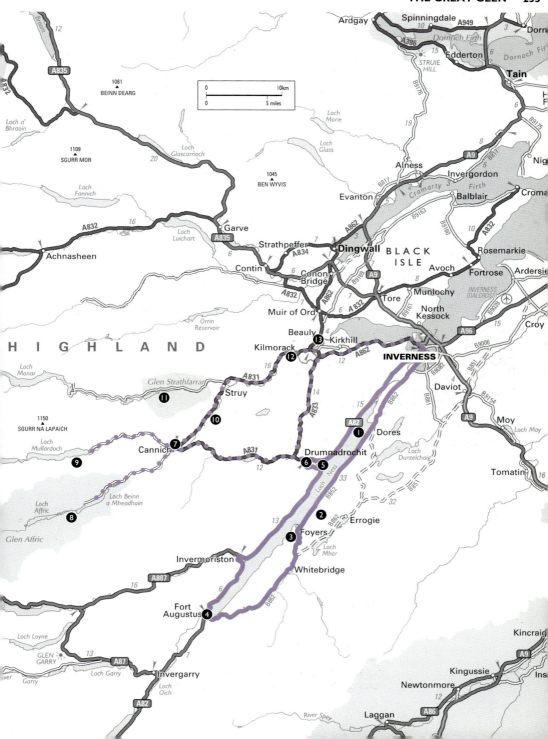

Easter Ross and Sutherland

Ratings

Archaeology	●●●●●
Golf	●●●●●
Museums	●●●●●
Wildlife	●●●●●
Historical sights	●●●●○
Castles	●●●○○
Scenery	●●●○○
Walking	●●●○○

Just over the Kessock Bridge from Inverness lie the fertile farmlands of the Black Isle and eastern Ross-shire, or Easter Ross. Slicing into the landscape are four sea estuaries – the Moray, Beauly, Cromarty and Dornoch Firths. Along this coastline are picturesque fishing villages, bird reserves and places to spot dolphins and seals. The Black Isle, not an island at all but a peninsula, has seen 5000 years of settlement and is a repository of Pictish stones and ancient remains. Inland, as you head north into the Highlands, roads become fewer and the landscape higher and more remote. From the Struie viewpoint on the B9176, you can look across the firth to the glens of Sutherland, where the Highland Clearances began in 1807. Inland towards Lairg, salmon leap up the tempestuous Falls of Shin, while on the coast at Dornoch is one of Scotland's finest golf courses. Further north, the area upriver from Helmsdale saw the Great Sutherland Gold Rush of 1869.

BLACK ROCK GORGE

Black Rock Gorge is located on private land and there is no parking. Because it is potentially dangerous for unattended children and dogs, you won't find any signposts encouraging a visit. Those who are keen enough to explore will discover a phenomenal 2-mile (3-km) long narrow chasm cut by the River Glass, with sheer sides dropping as far as 200ft (61m) deep. As there is only enough space for one car at the start of the footpath, it is best to park in Evanton and walk in. Proceed through town past the caravan park and over the bridge, taking the first turning to the left signposted Glenglass and Assynt. Continue for about 1 mile (1.6km), passing five lay-by signs and passing the entrance to Balavoulin on the right. After another 328ft (100m), take the wide track on the left which passes in front of a white cottage. Pass a left-hand track and after a further 328ft (100m), look for a small footpath to the left. This leads to the first of two bridges. The second bridge is upstream and can be reached from either side of the gorge.

Above
Dunrobin Castle

The Great Gold Rush

Like many other countries in the mid-19th century, Scotland too had its gold rush. In 1869 Robert Gilchrist, a native of Sutherland, returned home after years in the Australian gold fields and discovered gold in the Strath of Kildonan, inland from Helmsdale. A shanty town soon sprang up as hundreds of prospectors rushed here to pan for the precious metal. Within a year it was all over, but small pieces of gold are still found today. If you want to try your luck, ask at the Helmsdale tourist information centre.

CROMARTY

Cromarty Courthouse £
Church Street; tel: 01381 600 418; www.cromarty-courthouse.org.uk. Open Apr–Oct daily 1000–1700.

Hugh Miller's Cottage (National Trust for Scotland) £ Church Street; tel: 01381 600 245; www.nts.org.uk. Open Easter–Sep daily 1300–1700; Oct Sun–Wed 1300–1700.

Set on one of Scotland's finest natural harbours, this picture-postcard town is a delightful place to wander. Thanks to clever restoration of its historic buildings, it retains the atmosphere of the prosperous 18th-century port and fishing village it once was. The town is largely the creation of George Ross, who bought the estate in the 1760s and built the hempworks, one of Scotland's first factories, as well as a brewery, the Gaelic chapel and the **Cromarty Courthouse**. This now houses an award-winning town museum, where you can put on a 'law suit' and join in a re-creation of a trial with animated mannequins. You can take an audio tour of Cromarty that will take you around the places of interest. **Hugh Miller's Cottage** contains the writing, fossils and personal effects of the Cromarty stonemason who became a renowned geologist, journalist and author.

DORNOCH

Dornoch Tourist Information Centre The Square; tel: 0845 22 55 121; e-mail: info@visitscotland.com. Open Jul–Aug.

Dornoch Cathedral
Open during daylight hours. Guided tours in summer after evening service.

Dornoch is a pleasant town of sandstone buildings 2 miles (3km) east of the A9. It is a popular holiday resort thanks to its sweeping sandy beaches and championship golf courses, which rank among the best in Scotland. Dornoch Cathedral, built between 1224 and 1239, is small and lovely with beautiful stained-glass windows, those in the north wall a gift of Andrew Carnegie. The last witch to be burned in Scotland was executed at Dornoch in 1722, accused of turning her daughter, who had a deformed hand, into a pony. In fact, poor Janet Horne was so senile that she warmed her hands at the fire lit for her execution. A Witch's Stone in a private garden in Carnaig Street marks the spot.

DUNROBIN CASTLE

Dunrobin Castle ££
Golspie; tel: 01408 633 177; e-mail: info@dunrobincastle.net; www.dunrobincastle.co.uk. Open Mar–May, Sep & Oct Mon–Sat 1030–1630, Sun 1200–1630; Jun–Aug daily 1030–1730.

In its first incarnation in 1275, Dunrobin Castle, seat of the dukes and earls of Sutherland, was built as a huge square keep. It was given its French Gothic makeover in the mid-19th century by Sir Charles Barry, designer of the Houses of Parliament. From its high terrace it looks out across gorgeous formal gardens to the sea. The castle has some fine paintings as well as furniture, tapestries, robes and mementoes belonging to one of the country's wealthiest families.

South of Dunrobin Castle, at the top of Ben Vraggie near Golspie, is a gigantic **statue** 100ft (30.5m) high of the first Duke of Sutherland, who was primarily responsible for the Highland Clearances. A couple of miles (3km) north of the castle is **Cairn Liath**, a fine example of a Pictish *broch* (stone tower). The car park is on the opposite (left) side of the road, but it is worth climbing down the bank to reach the site for a close-up look.

HELMSDALE

Timespan
Heritage Centre £
Dunrobin Street; tel: 01431
821 327;
www.timespan.org.uk.
Open Easter–Oct Mon–Sat
1000–1700, Sun 1200–1700.

Below
Helmsdale's bridge, built by
Thomas Telford in 1815

Helmsdale had its beginnings as a resettlement town for crofters following the Highland Clearances. It prospered during the herring boom, and still maintains a fishing fleet, although the town's main industry is processing shellfish. Don't miss the excellent **Timespan Heritage Centre**, with clever tableaux re-creating local history, from the Vikings to the Clearances to the great Gold Rush. A visit here will enhance your travels through the Highlands by revealing the poignant story behind the magnificent landscape. The museum is housed in the former toll house for the Helmsdale bridge, which was constructed by Thomas Telford.

LAIRG

ⓘ **Falls of Shin Visitor Centre** *Tel: 01549 402 231; e-mail: info@fallsofshin.co.uk; www.fallsofshin.com. Open daily.*

ⓗ **Ferrycroft Countryside Centre** *Lairg; tel: 01549 402 160. Open Apr–Oct.*

Below
The remains of Cairn Liath, a Pictish *broch*, or defensive tower, near Dunrobin Castle

Lairg is a useful, rather than attractive, town at the crossroads of several Highland roads. Set beside the River Shin, it is a popular base for fishing holidays. Until the Highland Clearances it was the centre of a well-populated farming district. The **Ferrycroft Countryside Centre**, which also serves as the tourist office, has displays on Sutherland's landscape, wildlife and history. Down river are the **Falls of Shin**, a fresh scenic spot where you can see salmon leaping up the falls on their return journey to their spawning grounds. There is a large visitor centre and cafeteria, and forest walks.

The Brahan Seer

Còinneach Odhar, or Brown Kenneth, a 17th-century soothsayer, came to work at the Brahan estate near Dingwall. He made an eerie number of accurate predictions about the Highlands, some of which have not yet been fulfilled. Among these were the Highland Clearances, the arrival of railroads and the building of the Caledonian Canal. When the Countess of Seaforth pressed him to divine what her husband was doing on a visit to Paris, he angered her by reporting the earl's unfaithfulness. She ordered him to be burned in tar at Chanonry Point. Before he died he made one last, accurate prediction – the downfall of the Seaforth Mackenzies.

STRATHPEFFER

ⓘ **Strathpeffer Tourist Information Centre**
Village square; tel: 0845 22 55 121. Open Easter–late Oct.

🏛 **Highland Museum of Childhood £**
Old Railway Station; tel: 01997 421 031; www. highlandmuseumofchildhood. org.uk. Open Apr–Jun and Sep–Oct Mon–Sat 1000–1700, Sun 1400–1700; Jul–Aug Mon–Fri 1000–1900, Sat 1000–1700, Sun 1400–1700.

♿ Nestled below Ben Wyvis, **Strathpeffer** has many scenic walks in the nearby Blackmuir Wood.

Strathpeffer was just a small hamlet with mineral springs in 1819 when the first pump room was built. With the coming of the railroad it became a grand Victorian spa town visited by royalty. The splendid architecture of this era remains and you can still sample the water at a pavilion in the village square. The old Victorian railway station now houses the **Highland Museum of Childhood**. On a hill to the east of town is the **Eagle Stone**, a 3ft- (0.9m-) tall Pictish symbol stone engraved with an eagle and a horseshoe.

Accommodation and food

The Eagle Hotel £–££ *Castle Street, Dornoch; tel: 01862 810 008; fax: 01862 811 355; e-mail: info@eagledornoch.co.uk; www.eagledornoch.co.uk.* Friendly pub atmosphere and good home-cooked food. Satellite TV.

2Quail Restaurant ££ *Castle Street, Dornoch; tel: 01862 811 811; e-mail: info@2quail.com; www.2quail.com. Open Apr–Oct Tue–Sat 1930–2130; Nov–Mar Fri–Sat only, booking essential.* Top-quality cuisine served in an intimate atmosphere, featuring such dishes as Scotch beef with wild mushroom and sherry gravy.

Dornoch Castle Hotel ££ *Castle Street, Dornoch; tel: 01862 810 216; fax: 01862 810 981; e-mail: enquiries@dornochcastlehotel.com; www. dornochcastlehotel.com. Open all year.* A former bishop's palace, this hotel offers 17 large, comfortable rooms in the old castle and a new wing. Atmospheric bar, supper room, gardens, and restaurant in the former castle kitchens.

Suggested tour

Total distance: 78 miles (125.5km) for the main route to Dornoch, 110 miles (177km) via the detour route.

ⓘ North Kessock Tourist Information Centre
*On the A9 near the Kessock Bridge; tel: 0845 22 55 121; e-mail: info@visitscotland.com. Open daily Easter–Oct. It overlooks the Moray Firth and has the **Red Kite Viewing Centre** and the **Dolphin and Seal Centre** in the grounds.*

ⓡ A good outing for children is the **Black Isle Wildlife and Country Park**,
near North Kessock; tel: 01463 721 656. Open daily Apr–Oct 1000–1700; Nov–Mar 1000–1600. You can feed and stroke many animals.

Groam House Museum
High Street, Rosemarkie; tel: 01381 620 961; www.groamhouse.org.uk. Open May–Oct Mon–Sat 1000–1700, Sun 1400–1630; Nov–mid-Dec and Mar–Apr weekends 1400–1600; Easter 1400–1630. Free.

Time: The main route will take about 1 hour and 45 minutes, not counting stops. The detour will add another 45 minutes to the journey.

Links: The Black Isle and Strathpeffer make an easy day-trip from Inverness over the Kessock bridge. For those who want to carry on to the tip of the mainland, see the Coast of Caithness tour (*see page 251*). From Lairg you can also cross the Highlands to the northwest coast via the scenic A838.

Route: Start in **STRATHPEFFER ❶**. Go east 7 miles (11km) to **Dingwall ❷** on the A834. This attractive market town was an important centre during Viking times. Go south towards Maryburgh, turning left on the A835 which takes you onto the Black Isle. At Tore, continue on the A832 which takes you through **Munlochy ❸**, where there is a nature reserve, to the pleasant fishing village of **Avoch ❹** (pronounced 'Och', as in loch), 9 miles (14.5km) away. About 2 miles (3km) beyond you can turn right for a 1-mile (1.6-km) detour (through a golf course!) to **Chanonry Point ❺**. There is a lighthouse here and a memorial to the Brahan Seer, who was said to have been burnt to death in a tar barrel (*see page 240*). This is a good spot from which to watch for dolphins and seals. Return to the main road at **Fortrose ❻**, with its red sandstone cathedral. At the nearby village of **Rosemarkie ❼**, equally attractive, visit the small but splendid **Groam House Museum ❽**. Among its fine exhibits of Pictish carved stones, pride of place goes to the Rosemarkie Stone, a cross slab standing nearly 10ft (3m) tall and carved with early Christian symbols. Also nearby is the pretty Fairy Glen, said to be the home of a black witch, with waterfalls and rapids beneath the red boulder cliffs.

From here the road heads inland through rolling farmland for the next 9 miles (14.5km) to **CROMARTY ❾** on the tip of the peninsula. Take the B9163 along the Cromarty Firth, through a peaceful rural landscape. After 15 miles (24km) turn right on the A9 to cross

Right
Avoch village sits on the edge of a small harbour

There are cruises to see dolphins, seals and other marine creatures from **Cromarty**.

the mile- (1.6km-) long bridge over the Cromarty Firth, which has sweeping views. Three miles (5km) on, take the exit for **Evanton** ❿ if you want to walk into the **BLACK ROCK GORGE** ⓫ . On the outskirts of Evanton is **Seal Point** ⓬ , where there are beautiful views over the Cromarty Firth. The A9 carries on 26 miles (42km) to Dornoch via **Tain** ⓭ , a place of pilgrimage in medieval times. You can visit the remains of St Duthac's Chapel and St Duthus church.

Detour: For a longer, scenic route to Dornoch, take the B9176 (2 miles (3km) beyond Evanton), signposted Moray Firth Tourist Route. It climbs over dramatic heather-covered moors and winds down to the Dornoch Firth. Stop at the **Struie viewpoint** ⓮ for a splendid panorama over the Kyle of Sutherland. After 19 miles (30.5km) you come to the junction with A836. Turn left, pass through Kincardine and Bonar Bridge, following signs to Lairg. About 4 miles (6.5km) past Bonar Bridge, follow signs to the **Falls of Shin** ⓯ on the B864. Continue north to **LAIRG** ⓰ . Take the A839 along the River Fleet through high rolling hills and heather for 14 miles (22.5km) to where it meets the A9 at Mound. Turn right. **DORNOCH** ⓱ is 10 miles (16km) south via the A9 and A949.

Also worth exploring

The **Dolphin and Seal Centre**, at the tourist information centre on the A9, just over the Kessock Bridge from Inverness, has information on the marine life of the Moray and Beauly firths. The centre has high-tech sound equipment that enables you to listen to the mating roars of the seals and the high-pitched sounds of the bottlenose dolphins. The **Falls of Rogie**, west of Contin on the A832, is a popular picnic spot. There is a suspension bridge over the river where you can watch salmon leaping the falls. Between Invergordon and Tain are the **Seaboard Villages** of Nigg, Shandwick, Hilton and Tarbat, part of the Easter Ross Pictish Trail. Pick up a leaflet at the tourist office for information on the ancient sites.

Right
Dornoch Castle, now a comfortable hotel

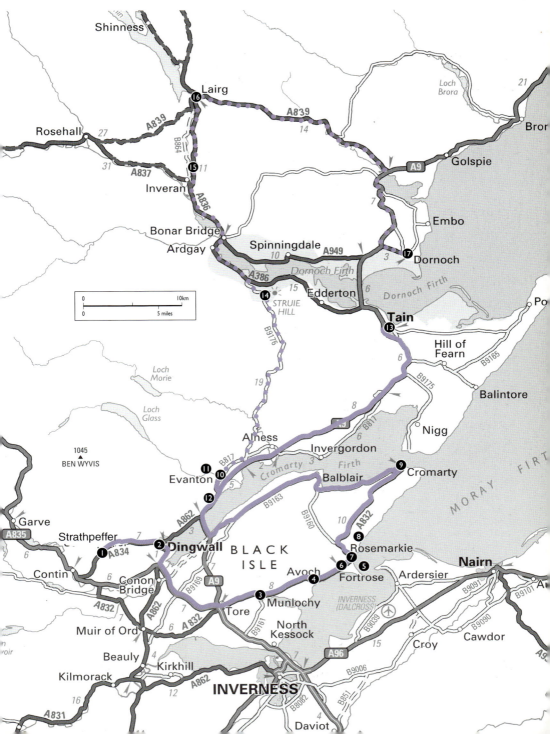

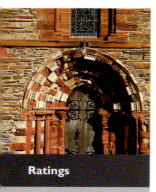

Caithness and Orkney

Ratings

Archaeology	●●●●●
Coastal views	●●●●○
Scenery	●●●●○
Beaches	●●●○○
Museums	●●●○○
Wildlife	●●●○○
Children	●●○○○
Walking	●●○○○

Caithness includes the most northerly point on the mainland, at Dunnet Head, and indeed this northeast corner of Scotland has a distinct, end-of-the-road feel. The scenery is often windswept and sparse, lacking the high mountains of the west but with sweeping views over field and sea across to the islands of Orkney. The region is unique, with a strong Viking influence most evident in its place names and its strong ties to the sea. The harbours, though much changed since the heyday of the herring industry when they were jammed with fishing boats, are peaceful and attractive. Inland lies the Flow Country, a vast blanket peat bog covering nearly a million acres (404,700ha) in Caithness and Sutherland, forming a rich and rare ecological environment. Another feature of the landscape is the outcrops of hard sandstone known as Caithness flagstone. Used for building in ancient times, it has been quarried since 1825 and exported for pavements; thus, every day, people around the world walk across a little piece of this remote corner of Scotland.

DUNBEATH

Dunbeath Heritage Centre £ *Old School; tel: 01593 731 233; www. dunbeath-heritage.org.uk. Open Easter–Oct daily 1000–1700, winter by arrangement.*

Laidhay Croft Museum £ *Tel: 01593 731 244. Open Easter–Oct daily 1000–1700.*

The author Neil M Gunn was born in Dunbeath and for most of his life he lived and worked in the Highlands. His novels, which include *The Silver Darlings* and *Highland River*, draw on the history and culture of the region. There is a memorial sculpture of one of his central characters at the harbour. The **Dunbeath Heritage Centre**, situated in Gunn's old school, has interesting exhibits on the history, people and geology of the area. Pick up a leaflet on the Dunbeath Strath Heritage Trail which will point the way to the **Dunbeath Broch**, one of the best preserved in the region, and other points of interest. Nearby is the **Laidhay Croft Museum**, housed in a traditional longhouse and barn, filled with local artefacts.

Strathy Point
Scrabster
Tórshavn (Summer Only)
Stromness
Dunnet Head
Stroma
Duncansby Head
John O'Groats

Portskerra
Thurso
Dunnet
Gills
A836
15
A836
Strathy
Melvich
Reay
A836
16
Castletown
Freswick
A99
17

Dalhalvaig
A897
21
Loch Calder
Loch Shurrery
B874
Halkirk
B870
B876
B874
Keiss

Kinbrace
Loch nan Clàr
B871
Loch Badanloch
16
A897
17
Loch More
Spittal
Watten
A882
A9
23
B874
B870
21
WICK
Wick

Thrumster

Latheron
Lybster
A9
A99
17

Dunbeath
20

Berriedale
A9

Helmsdale
A897
17

Loch Brora
21
Brora
A9

Golspie
Embo
Dornoch
A9
3
6
Loch Brora

Portmahomack
Tain
Hill of Fearn
B9165
8

0   10km
0   5 miles

Orkney Islands

Mull Head
Papa Westray
North Ronaldsay
Pierowall
Westray
Rapness
Sanday
Midbea
B9066
Braeswick
Calfsound
Eday
Stronsay
Wasbister
Rousay
A986
Brinyan
Backaland
Brough Head
ORKNEY
Hackland
Shapinsay
Dounby
MAINLAND
Finstown
Balfour
A967
Kirkwall
Stromness
ISLANDS
Aberdeen
Rora Head
Houton
St Mary's
A964
A960
Scapa Flow
Burray
HOY
Lyness
Flotta
St Margaret's Hope
A961
South Ronaldsay
Scrabster
Burwick
PENTLAND FIRTH
Gills
Lerwick

JOHN O'GROATS

John O'Groats Tourist Information Centre
County Road; tel: 0845 22 55 121. Open Apr–Oct.

Wear wellies if you have them for the walk to the viewpoint at **Duncansby Stacks**. The land is very boggy especially after rain, and without proper footwear you're likely to spend the rest of the day in wet trainers.

A 6-mile (9.5km) (one-way) walk from Freswick on the A99 to John O'Groats takes a scenic route along the coast and passes the Stacks of Duncansby. Ask at the tourist information office for directions.

John O'Groats is Britain's most northerly village – although not its most northerly point; Dunnet Head, a few miles to the west, holds that title. The town was named after Jan de Groot, a Dutchman who was granted a charter to run a ferry to the Orkneys in the 15th century. That legacy lives on, as the harbour here is the terminal for the daily passenger ferry to the islands. Contrary to the romantic 'end-of-the-line' expectations of visitors, John O'Groats itself is unimpressive, a rather bleak village sprawled across a flat landscape with little besides the ferry terminal, tourist shops and a large car park. A couple of miles (3km) east of the town is **Duncansby Head**, with high cliffs and a lighthouse. From here you can follow a boggy path to see the striking sandstone pinnacles rising offshore, the **Stacks of Duncansby**.

Right
Duncansby Stacks

Above
The Last House in Scotland, at John O'Groats

ORKNEY ISLANDS

For information and bookings on the **Orkney Islands** Day Tours, contact John O'Groats Ferries, Ferry Office, John O'Groats, Caithness KW1 4YR; tel: 01955 611 353; e-mail: office@jogferry.co.uk; www.jogferry.co.uk. Tours operate May–Sep from John O'Groats, Jun–early Sep from Inverness. Prices are reasonable and are very good value.

Mysterious and alluring, the Orkneys are an archipelago of 70 islands, 20 of which are inhabited, stretching northwards across the Pentland Firth from mainland Scotland. People have lived here since the 4th millennium BC, and the islands have the greatest concentration of prehistoric sites in Western Europe. The Vikings arrived in the 8th century, and the Scandinavian influence is stronger here than anywhere on the mainland. There is a car ferry from Scrabster to Stromness, but this is expensive and few people feel that a short visit justifies the trip. The best way to see the Orkneys is on one of the excellent day-trips run by John O'Groats Ferries, which takes in the highlights on a well-run and entertaining excursion.

The sea crossing takes 45 minutes, and you may well spot seals or dolphins in the firth. Coaches meet the ferry at Burwick and take you

ⓘ Kirkwall Tourist Information Centre *6 Broad Street; tel: 01856 872 856; e-mail: info@visitorkney.com; www.visitorkney.com. Open all year.*

ⓗ St Magnus Cathedral *Broad Street; tel: 01856 874 894. Open daily 0900–1700 summer, Mon–Fri only winter.*

Bishop's and Earl's Palaces (Historic Scotland) £ *Tel: 01856 871 918; www.historic-scotland.gov.uk. Open Apr–Sep daily 0930–1730.*

Skara Brae (Historic Scotland) ££ *On the B9056; tel: 01856 841 815; www.historic-scotland.gov.uk. Open Apr–Sep 0930–1730; Oct–Mar 0930–1630.*

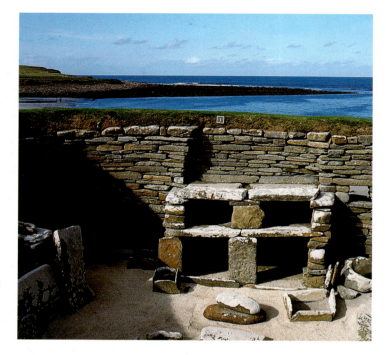

across the **Churchill Barriers** which connect five islands to form the eastern boundary of the huge natural harbour, **Scapa Flow**. This was of great strategic importance during both World Wars and many warships are sunk beneath its surface. **Kirkwall**, the capital of Orkney on the island called Mainland, is an attractive town dominated by the splendid **St Magnus Cathedral**, the most northerly cathedral in Britain. Built of red sandstone, it dates from the 12th century and has an impressive, ornate interior. Other sights of interest include the **Earl's Palace** and **Bishop's Palace**.

The drive across Mainland shows Orkney's green, pristine and largely treeless landscape in all its glory. The islands are largely agricultural, with oats, barley and herds of beef and dairy cattle. **Stromness**, Orkney's second city and ferry port, was a staging post for the Hudson Bay Company in the 18th century and saw traders from around the world. Its pretty stone houses with crow-stepped gables give it a 19th-century appearance.

The Orkneys' most famous attraction, and deservedly so, is **Skara Brae**. This 5000-year-old Neolithic village lay buried under the sand dunes at Skaille Bay and was only discovered 100 years ago, the dwellings perfectly preserved with stone beds, dressers and wall cupboards. The tour also takes in the **Ring of Brodgar** stone circle, the **Standing Stones of Stenness** and the **Italian chapel**.

Above
Skara Brae prehistoric village

THURSO

ℹ **Thurso Tourist Information Centre** *Riverside;* tel: 0845 22 55 121 or 01847 892 371; e-mail: info@visitscotland.com. Open Apr–Oct.

🏛 **Thurso Heritage Museum £**
Town Hall, High Street. Currently closed for renovation; check website: www.caithnesshorizons.co.uk

Thurso, the largest town north of Inverness, was founded by the Vikings and was an important trading centre. Subsequently it has twice undergone a change of fortunes leading to rapid development. First, in the 19th century, it became a major centre for the export of Caithness flagstone, then, in the 20th century, it witnessed an influx of scientists and engineers with the building of the Dounreay nuclear reactor nearby. It retains much of its earlier architecture, with lovely 18th-century sandstone houses around the central square. The River Thurso is one of Scotland's best salmon rivers, while Thurso's patch of the Pentland Firth is considered to be one of the best surfing waters in Europe, and championships are hosted here. Among the sights are **St Peter's Church**, dating from the 12th century, **Thurso Heritage Museum** – housing the Ulbster Pictish Stone – and the ruins of the Victorian **Thurso Castle**.

WICK

ℹ **Wick Tourist Information Centre**
Norseman Hotel, Riverside; tel: 0845 22 55 121; e-mail: info@visitscotland.com. Open all year.

🏛 **Wick Heritage Museum £** *20 Bank Row;* tel: 01955 605393; www.wickheritage.org. Open Easter–Oct Mon–Sat 1000–1545.

Wick was founded in Viking times, its name stemming from the Norse word for 'a bay'. During the 19th century it was one of the largest herring fishing ports in the world, with more than 1100 boats crowded into its harbour. The **Heritage Museum** near the harbour tells the story. Wick is now the county seat, and fishing remains an important industry. Just 17 miles (27km) from John O'Groats, the town is a good base for touring Caithness and the Orkneys. Wick was the original home of the famous **Caithness Glass** factory. Although it has closed and is now based in Crieff, a collection of glassware through the years is on display at the museum.

Accommodation and food

The Clachan B&B £ *13 Randolph Place, South Road, Wick; tel: 01955 605 384; e-mail: enquiry@theclachan.co.uk; www.theclachan.co.uk.* Lovely B&B with en-suite rooms, residents' lounge, parking.

No. 1 Bistro £–££ *Adjacent to Mackay's Hotel, Union Street, Wick; tel: 01955 602 323.* This friendly restaurant is a favourite local spot. The menu features local produce such as Highland venison, freshwater loch trout and fish fresh from the boats at Scrabster. *Open daily 1030–2100.*

Mackay's Hotel ££ *Union Street, Wick; tel: 01955 602 323; fax: 01955 605 930; e-mail: info@mackayshotel.co.uk; www.mackayshotel.co.uk.* Attractive, stone-built hotel in the centre of town by the River Wick. Rooms are smartly appointed and extremely comfortable. Restaurant, plus residents' lounge serving connoisseur malt whiskies and an adjacent pub. Free golfing for residents on local courses.

Above
The sculpted cliffs of the
northeast Scottish coastline

Cairns and Castles

The first Highlanders settled northern Scotland as long ago as 8000 BC, and some of the best prehistoric sites can be found in Caithness. These include burial cairns, standing stones and *brochs,* which were defensive stone towers that developed around circular forts, or duns. *Brochs* are only found within a small area; they were in use before the Pictish period and radio-carbon dating proves they are much older than first thought. Of the many prehistoric sites, some of the best and most easily reached are Cairn Liath near Brora (see *page 237*), the Dunbeath Broch, Hill O'Many Stanes and the Grey Cairns of Camster. Caithness also has several clifftop castle ruins, including Sinclair, Girnigoe and Old Wick castles around Wick.

The main roads in **Caithness** are very good. But remember that in the Highlands, people are generally not in a hurry. Slower vehicles, bicycles, and other obstructions mean that a given distance may take a bit longer than it would elsewhere.

The more significant cairns and *brochs* are usually signposted, but the signs are small and the turn-offs onto the minor roads narrow, so they are easy to miss if you're driving fast.

P Many of the prehistoric sites stand in fields on private land and there are no special parking places for visitors. Do respect local residents and do not block farm gates and drives, or park in passing places on single-track roads.

Northlands Viking Centre £
Auckengill, on the A99; tel: 01955 603 761. Open Jun–Sep daily 1000–1600.

Castle of Mey ££
Tel: 01847 851 473; www.castleofmey.org.uk. Open mid-May–Sep Sat–Thu 1030–1600; closed first 2 weeks of Aug (dates vary slightly each year, phone to confirm).

RSPB Forsinard Flows Visitor Centre *On the A897; tel: 01641 571 225; www.rspb.org.uk. Open Easter–Oct daily 0900–1730. Free.*

Suggested tour

Total distance: 83 miles (133.5km) for the main route, 125 miles (76km) for the detour route.

Time: The main route will take under 2 hours, not counting stops. The longer detour route will take between 3 and 3.5 hours. Those with little time should try and take in the Duncansby Stacks and Dunnet Head. If you have time to spare, explore the sidetracks off the A836 leading to the clifftops, bays and beaches of the Pentland Firth.

Links: The route is a natural link with the tours on *pages 240 and 260* for those driving around the coast of the mainland.

Route: Begin at **WICK ❶**, a good central touring base. Head north along the A99 coastal road, passing the crumbling castles of Sinclair, Girnigoe and Keiss on the shores of Sinclair's Bay. At Auckengill, 10 miles (16km) further on, visit the **Northlands Viking Centre ❷** for a look at the area before and during Norse times. Continue on to **JOHN O'GROATS ❸**, 17 miles (27km) from Wick. It's worth taking an extra half hour or so to make a 2-mile (3-km) detour to Duncansby Head to view the striking **Duncansby Stacks ❹**.

Head west on the A836, the main road along the north coast. After 7 miles (11km) you may spot the turrets of the **Castle of Mey ❺**, summer home of the late Queen Elizabeth, the Queen Mother. The castle and gardens are open in summer and offer fine views over the bay. At the village of Dunnet, turn right for the 5-mile (8-km) detour on a single-track road across the wild, windswept promontory to **Dunnet Head ❻**, the most northerly point on the mainland. There is a lighthouse here and a colony of puffins, as well as spectacular views across the Pentland Firth to the Orkneys and their landmark rock, the Old Man of Hoy. Back at the outskirts of Dunnet, you can visit **Mary-Ann's Cottage ❼** for a first-hand look at traditional crofting life. **Castletown ❽**, 3 miles (5km) further on, has remnants of the old flagstone industry; stones were shipped from its harbour to pave the Strand in London.

Continue another 5 miles (8km) to **THURSO ❾**. A mile (1.6km) outside town, take the right-hand turning signposted to **Scrabster ❿**. This pretty harbour is the car ferry port for crossings to Stromness in the Orkneys, and is backed by the strange, sculpted cliffs of Holborn Head.

Detour: To extend the tour, continue west along the A836. After about 7 miles (11km) the ominous shape of the Dounreay Nuclear Power Station looms into view on the shoreline. It was closed in 1994 and is being decommissioned; there is a visitor exhibition in summer. About 5 miles (8km) past the village of Reay, turn left on the A897, a single-track road through Strath Halladale and Strath of Kildonan. There's a good chance of seeing stags along this route. The **RSPB Forsinard Flows Visitor Centre ⓫** is a good place to discover the peatland environment of the Flow Country. The road continues

Clan Gunn Museum and Heritage Centre £
Latheron, tel: 01593 741 700. Open Jun–Sep Mon–Sat 1100–1300, 1400–1600.

Grey Cairns of Camster (Historic Scotland) *Access at all times. Free.*

Wildlife cruises to see puffins, grey seals, a variety of breeding birds and rugged cliff scenery operate daily mid-Jun–Aug from John O'Groats. *Contact John O'Groats Ferries (see page 247).*

Below
The coast near John O'Groats

through bleak moorland to the crofting village of **Kinbrace** ⑫ . The countryside is littered with prehistoric remains, and you can see several chambered cairns near Kinbrace Burn. The road then follows the **Strath of Kildonan** ⑬ , site of the great Gold Rush before reaching the coast at Helmsdale. Rejoin the main route at Dunbeath.

For the main route, take the A9 south for 24 miles (38.5km) to the coast at Latheron (or, for a quicker route back to Wick, take the turning for the A882). Along the way (about 18 miles, 29km along) you will pass the **Achavanich Standing Stone Circle** ⑭ , which may have contained up to 60 stones at one time. The **Rangag Broch** ⑮ , dating from 150 BC, is less than a mile (1.6km) to the west. Turn right on the A9 and go 3 miles (5km) south to **DUNBEATH** ⑯ . Then turn around and head north to Wick on the A99. At Latheron, the **Clan Gunn Museum and Heritage Centre** ⑰ tells the story of this ancient family whose origins stretch back to Norse times. **Lybster** ⑱ is the largest of the fishing villages along this beautiful stretch of coastline with its high cliffs and rocky ledges. During the herring heyday it was the third-largest fishing station in the country, and the harbour remains attractive, if reduced in scale.

A mile (1.6km) east of town, a minor road to the left leads to the **Grey Cairns of Camster** ⑲ , 5 miles (8km) over the moor. These Neolithic burial sites are superbly restored, and you can even crawl inside. A couple of miles (3km) further up the main road, a short side road leads to the mysterious Bronze Age site, the **Hill o' Many Stanes** ⑳ , with 22 rows of stones that once numbered nearly 200, set out in a fan-shaped pattern on the hillside. It may have had astronomical significance. On the main road, between Bruan and Ulbster, is the hamlet of **Whaligoe** ㉑ , where a flight of 350 flagstone steps winds precariously down the steep cliff. They were built in the 18th century for fishermen to reach the harbour.

Also worth exploring

After the junction for the A897, the A836 abruptly becomes single-track through the high moorland. About 4 miles (6.5km) beyond, **Strathy** is a pretty village folded into the hills, with a lovely beach. A detour onto the headland to the lighthouse at **Strathy Point** (3 miles, 5km) leads through sand dunes and grasslands with rare plant species, and is a good spot for birdwatching.

The Northwest Highlands

Ratings

Mountains	●●●●●
Outdoor activities	●●●●◐
Scenery	●●●●●
Walking	●●●●●
Wildlife	●●●●○
Beaches	●●●○○
Coastal scenery	●●●○○
Children	●●○○○

No matter how many photographs you see or how many superlatives you read about the Northwest Highlands, nothing can dull the wonder of seeing them for the first time. This remote, majestic landscape pierces the soul with its lonely beauty, a land of solitary mountains and shimmering lochs, the rocky moorland softened by undulating blankets of plum-coloured heathers and leafy bracken that turns red and gold in autumn. Along the coast on a sunny day you will gaze out across the sea to the distant islands through an azure sky whose intensity is like no other. There are deserted beaches, boat trips and walking routes to enjoy, but you will find no towns of any size except Ullapool, with its ferry port to the Western Isles. It's worth remembering as you marvel at this sparse, spacious landscape, that it wasn't always so. Until the Highland Clearances, the glens were home to hundreds of clanspeople and the bald hills were covered in timber. The sheep you see grazing among the outcrops are the interlopers.

ACHILTIBUIE

Achiltibuie Hydroponicum ££
Tel: 01854 622 202;
www.thehydroponicum.com.
Reopening in 2009.

The **Lilypond Café** at the Hydroponicum features home-baking, meals and snacks.

Summer Isles Cruises £££
Tel: 01854 622 200; www. summer-isles-cruises.co.uk. May–Sep Mon–Sat from Badentarbet Pier. Cruises at 1030 and 1415.

Pronounced 'Ach-il-tee-boo-ee', this idyllic hamlet strung along the western shore of the Coigach peninsula has become a favourite holiday spot and makes a good day-trip from Lochinver and Ullapool. Amid such beautiful scenery and with plenty of walking, boating, beaches and outdoor pursuits it hardly needs any man-made attractions, yet a visit to the **Hydroponicum** is a unique experience; an abundance of tropical plants, flowers and exotic fruit grown hydroponically in a soil-less, water-fed environment. You can also visit the **Achiltibuie Smokehouse** and buy cured meat and fish. From the pier there are cruises to the **Summer Isles** which beckon offshore.

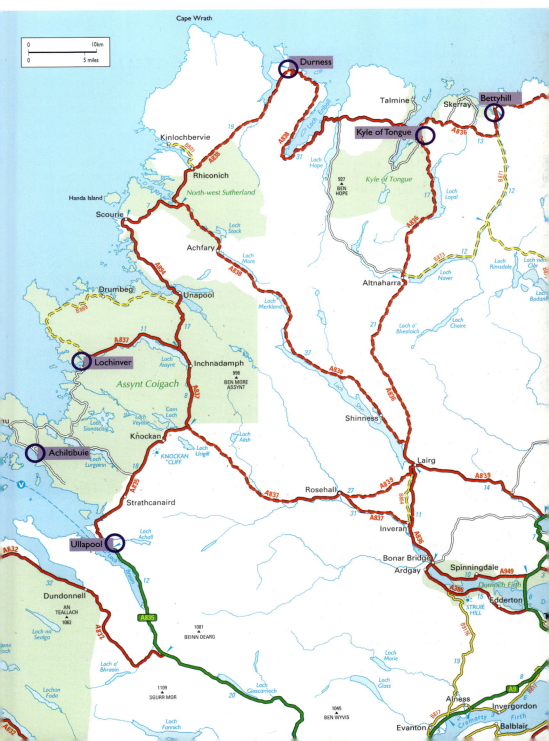

BETTYHILL

ⓘ Bettyhill Tourist Information
Centre *Clachan; tel: 0845 22 55 121; e-mail: info@visitscotland.com. Open Apr–Oct.*

ⓘ Strathnaver Museum £
Tel: 01641 521 418; www.strathnavermuseum.org. uk. Open Apr–Oct Mon–Sat 1000–1300, 1400–1700. There is a helpful tourist information office next to the Strathnaver Museum, where several books and publications giving a background to the area are for sale.

This village had its sad beginnings in 1819 when the people of Strathnaver (the valley of the River Strath) were 'cleared' here to start new lives on the coast. It was named after Elizabeth, Countess of Sutherland, who with her husband was the instigator of the Highland Clearances. It is said that this vain woman wanted the town to be called Mount Elizabeth in her honour, but the contemptuous Highlanders shortened it to Bettyhill. The **Strathnaver Museum**, housed in the old parish church, gives a poignant account of the tragic events and tells the story of the clan Mackay.

Right
Roadside burn, near Bettyhill

DURNESS

ⓘ Durness Tourist Information
Centre *Durine; tel: 01971 511259; e-mail: info@visitscotland.com. Open all year.*

ⓒ Cape Wrath Ferry Service ££
Tel: 01971 511 376. Sailings May–Sep, daily weather permitting. All sailings connect with minibus.

Somewhat scattered and not particularly attractive in its own right, Durness is a popular tourist stop for its beautiful coastal scenery and wide sandy beaches. A favourite attraction is **Smoo Cave**, a series of limestone caverns the largest of which is some 200ft (61m) long. There is also an excursion by ferry and bus (you cannot take your car) to **Cape Wrath**, the most northwesterly tip of the mainland, where there are spectacular sea cliffs, including Clo Mor, the highest in Britain. Nearby at Balnakeil are the ruins of a church on a site founded by St Maelrubha, one of the first Highlands missionaries, and the **Balnakeil Craft Village** with a variety of workshops where you can buy local handiwork.

KYLE OF TONGUE

This famous beauty spot is one of the most celebrated views in the Highlands. The broad sea inlet, or kyle, is spanned by a causeway that gives a magnificent vista of Ben Loyal in the distance. A parking area halfway across allows you to get out and admire the view. The village of **Tongue** was the stronghold of the Mackays, whose mansion, the House of Tongue, stands on the eastern shore near the causeway. On a hill to the west of the village are the ruins of Castle Varrich, thought to be the site of an 11th-century Norse fortress.

LOCHINVER

ⓘ Lochinver Tourist Information Centre *Assynt Visitor Centre, Kirk Lane, tel: 0845 22 55 121; e-mail: info@visitscotland.com. Open Apr–Oct.*

Below
Lochinver sunset

Founded during the Clearances of 1812, the pleasant village of Lochinver is the main town of Assynt. Its pretty harbour is a major European fishing port specialising in shellfish and whitefish. The town is a popular base for anglers in pursuit of brown trout and salmon, and for walkers, the most intrepid of whom make the long trek to the top of Suilven, a distinctive and solitary mountain rising nearly 2400ft (731.5m). Visitor attractions include the Assynt Visitor Centre and the Highland Stoneware factory.

ULLAPOOL

Ullapool Tourist Information Centre *20 Argyle Street; tel: 0845 22 55 121; e-mail: info@visitscotland.com. Open Apr–Nov.*

Ullapool Museum *£ 7–8 West Argyle Street; tel: 01854 612 987; www.ullapoolmuseum.co.uk. Open Apr–Oct Mon–Sat 1000–1700.*

The *Summer Queen* *runs 4-hour cruises to the Summer Islands, Apr–Oct Mon–Sat 1000–1400, Sun 1100–1400 and a 2-hour Nature Cruise to see a variety of wildlife, Mon–Sat 1415–1615. There are also Sunset Sails. Booking office at Ullapool Pier; tel: 01854 612 472; www.summerqueen.co.uk*

For information on ferries to the Western Isles, contact **Caledonian MacBrayne Ferries** *Tel: 01854 612 358 (Ullapool); or 01475 650 000; www.calmac.co.uk*

A delightful seaport on the shores of Loch Broom, Ullapool is the gateway to the Western Isles. Ferries cross The Minch – the sea between the mainland and the Outer Hebrides – to Stornoway on the Isle of Lewis, and there are day cruises in summer. Ullapool has a lovely waterfront and several pleasant pubs and restaurants. The **Ullapool Museum** has a good audiovisual presentation, 'The People of the Loch', and other exhibits.

Accommodation and food

Ardvreck Guest House £ *Morefield Brae, Ullapool; tel: 01854 612 028; fax: 01854 613 000; e-mail: ardvreck@btconnect.com; www.smoothhound. co.uk/hotels. 1.5 miles (2.5km) north of Ullapool off the main A835.* This bright, attractive guesthouse takes its name from the romantic castle on Loch Assynt. Surrounded by crofting land, with scenic views overlooking Loch Broom, it is a peaceful base for exploring the area. Evening meals are available if requested in advance. Residents' lounge with panoramic views, children's play area.

The Seaforth Inn £ *Quay Street, Ullapool; tel: 01854 612122; www.theseaforth.com.* Right by the pier, this wonderful pub is renowned for its music nights (early in summer), the bistro serves food all day and 'The Chippy' is a past winner of a BBC award for Best UK Takeaway.

The Highland Clearances

With the clan system broken after Culloden, Highland crofters were powerless against new landowners who squeezed as much profit as possible out of their holdings at the expense of their tenants. When the market for Highland produce collapsed following the Napoleonic Wars in the early 19th century, the landlords evicted the people from their homes and burned vast tracts of land to create grazing land for sheep. One of the worst instigators was the Duke of Sutherland who, with his wife Elizabeth, cleared more than 5000 Highlanders in a programme of 'estate improvements'. Great atrocities were committed on their behalf by estate agents, such as Patrick Sellar, who burned homes with elderly people still inside. Amazingly, the duke and many like him actually believed they were improving the people's lot by resettling them on marginal coastal land where they were forced to turn to fishing for a living. As a result, many emigrated to Nova Scotia and beyond.

Left
Ullapool's fishing fleet

The Ceilidh Place ££ *14 West Argyle Street, Ullapool; tel: 01854 612 103; www.theceilidhplace.com.* Small, intimate dining room serving good nouvelle cuisine-style dishes.

Inver Lodge Hotel £££ *Lochinver; tel: 01571 844 496; fax: 01571 844 395; e-mail: info@inverlodge.com; www.inverlodge.com.* This is the place to spoil yourself with a bit of luxury amid the unspoiled wilderness. Set on a hillside above the village, all 20 rooms enjoy a spectacular view over Loch Inver. Rooms – named after a loch or mountain – are large and well appointed with writing desk, comfy chairs and amenities. The dining room has panoramic views, a superb table d'hôte menu featuring fresh seafood and imaginative Scottish fare and fine wines, and a Sunday buffet in summer. The hotel offers salmon and trout fishing. Gentlemen are requested to wear collar and tie for dinner.

Suggested tour

Total distance: The main coastal route is 118 miles (190km) from Bettyhill to Ullapool. The Strathnaver detour is 40 miles (64km). The detour around the Assynt peninsula is 33 miles (53km), with an extra 8 miles (13km) for the return trip to Stoer lighthouse.

Time: The majority of the route is on single-track roads, and if you're used to this type of driving, which can be demanding, you can cover the main route in 2.5 hours, though it would be a shame to rush through this spectacular landscape. If you have the time, take it and pull off frequently at the viewpoints and side tracks to admire the views. The detours are best done when you can spend more than a day in the region, perhaps breaking your journey halfway, because the roads are single-track, narrow and winding and cannot be travelled quickly. The Strathnaver detour will take about 1 hour and 10 minutes. The Assynt peninsula can take between 1 and 3 hours, depending on traffic.

Links: The A835 between Ullapool and Inverness takes about 1 hour. For scenic routes between Lochinver and Ullapool, and between the Northwest Highlands and the east coast, see *Also worth exploring.*

Route: Most first-time visitors to this region want to 'do' the main coastal roads that comprise the Northwest and Highlands Tourist Route between Ullapool and John O'Groats. This is highly recommended, but for those who have the time to venture off the beaten track, the detours suggested here will prove extremely rewarding.

Begin at **BETTYHILL** ❶ and drive west on the A836 for 12 miles (19km) to the.**KYLE OF TONGUE** ❷. If you are moved by the story of the Highland Clearances, a **detour** can be made on B871 south through **Strathnaver** ❸, where you will see the ruins of abandoned crofts and villages. At the Rossal Pre-Clearance Village there is an interpretive trail.

Boat trip to Eas Coul Aulin £££
Kylesku Bridge; tel: 01971 502 345. May–Oct Sun, Tue, Thu 1500, call for additional times; also a garden tour at 1300, Sun, Tue & Thu to Kerrachar Gardens, tel: 01571 833 288.

Handa Island Ferry Trips *Tel: 01971 502 252. Open Apr–mid-Sep Mon–Sat 0930–1400.*

This is an idyllic riverside road through wooded glens with an almost cosy feeling that suggests that the spirit of Strathnaver was never cowed. When the road forks at Syre, bear right on the B873 which runs along Loch Naver. At the junction turn right on the scenic A836 heading north past Loch Loyal to rejoin the main route at Tongue.

From the Kyle of Tongue the A838 leads across empty moors to **Loch Eriboll ❹**, the deepest sea loch in Britain. Convoys assembled here during World War II, when it was nicknamed 'Loch 'orrible'. The view from the hill overlooking the loch on the eastern side is stupendous. The road winds down one side of the loch and up the other through gorgeous scenery that changes from mountain-backed moorland to sandy coves and breakwater as you reach the coast. **DURNESS ❺** lies 27 miles (43.5km) from Tongue. From here the route turns south down the west coast and there are 19 more miles (30.5km) of single-track road, passing lovely stretches of sand along the Kyle of Durness and sweeping mountain views inland, until the road widens to two lanes at Rhiconich.

Further south, go round the sharp, narrow curve at Laxford Bridge and bear right on the A894 to the pretty village of **Scourie ❻**, a crofting community and small resort. Halfway along, you'll pass the turn-off to the right for Tarbet, the departure point for boat trips to the bird sanctuary at **Handa Island ❼**.

From Scourie, a beautiful 9-mile (14.5-km) stretch runs south over **Duartmore Bridge ❽** – its reed-filled waters best admired from the roadside parking area/viewpoint on the north side – and on to **Kylesku Bridge ❾**. From the jetty beneath the bridge's south side, boat trips sail up scenic Loch Glencoul to see Britain's highest waterfall, **Eas Coul Aulin ❿**, which plunges 600ft (183m), and to Kerrachar Gardens.

Detour: Seven miles (11km) south of Kylesku, turn right on the A837 to circle the beautiful **Assynt Peninsula ⓫**. The road winds along the loch, strewn with pine-covered islands, for 10 miles (16km) to **LOCHINVER ⓬**, a good base for the area. From here take the single-track B869 for 7 miles (11km) to Stoer, near the pretty little beach of **Clachtoll ⓭**; just beyond the village you can take a left-hand track (signposted) to **Stoer lighthouse ⓮**, a further 4 miles (6.5km) on. Here woodland quickly gives way to bleak, open moorland; the road is very narrow and slow-going, not suitable for caravans. From the lighthouse you can walk along the cliffs to the point (about an hour away) and the rock stack called the Old Man of Stoer. Back on the main road, a few miles on from Stoer you'll pass a broad, beautiful beach at **Clashnessie ⓯** with reddish sand. Further on at **Drumbeg ⓰** there is a viewpoint with magnificent views north to Handa Island. The B869 rejoins the main road after 8 more miles (13km).

From the turn-off for Lochinver, the main road, now the A837, passes the romantic ruins of **Ardvreck Castle ⓱** on the shores of Loch

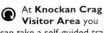

At **Knockan Crag Visitor Area** you can take a self-guided trail up the crag for a good introduction to the geology of the area. From the top you will have a superb panoramic view of the mountains of the Inverpolly Reserve: Stac Pollaidh, Cul Mor and Cul Beag and, to the south, Ben Mor Coigach, which towers over Ullapool.

The **Inverpolly National Nature Reserve** covers some 24,700 acres (10,000ha) of wild landscape including mountain peaks, heathland, bogs, lochs and marine islands along the shore. There are superb hiking trails, but most should only be attempted by experienced walkers with proper outdoor gear. The Knockan Crag visitor centre has information.

There is a campsite near the marvellous beach at **Enard Bay**, on the Coigach peninsula near Achiltibuie. **£**

Assynt – thought to date from around 1597 – and the **Inchnadamph National Nature Reserve** ⑱, with the Bone Caves used by some of Scotland's earliest Stone Age settlers. After 8 miles (13km), at **Ledmore Junction** ⑲, turn right on the A835 for **ULLAPOOL**, 18 miles (29km) southwest. Along the way you'll pass the entrances to **Knockan Crag** ⑳ and the **Inverpolly National Nature Reserve** ㉑ which give access to scenic hiking trails and fantastic views. From here it's an easy drive south along the A835 back to Ullapool.

Detour: There is one more drive that is highly recommended, although it is best undertaken as a separate day-trip. It is the route to Achiltibuie along the unclassified roads of the Coigach peninsula. The round-trip from Ullapool via Lochinver is 95 miles (153km) and will take about 3 hours, not counting stops.

Leave Ullapool on the A835 north and after 9.5 miles (15km) take the turn-off (signposted) for Achiltibuie. After 5 miles (8km), stop at the Inverpolly Nature Reserve car park to admire the views of Stac Pollaidh. Continue on for 10 miles (16km) to **ACHILTIBUIE** ㉒. From here, the 5-mile (8-km) journey north on the headland to **Rieff** ㉓ is very worthwhile for the fine views over a rocky beach (note that the road ends abruptly at a private home, so park off the road above the hamlet if you want to walk down to the shore). Return towards Achiltibuie and turn left at the sign for Ullapool. Near Achnahaird, turn left at the sign for the **beach** ㉔ at Enard Bay. This is a fabulous spot, with a path leading down to the broad sandy crescent sweeping round the bay. Continue on, turning left at the signpost for Lochinver (12 miles, 19km). The road takes you through magnificent countryside with Suilven towering ahead. Shortly before Lochinver, cross the Kirkaig Bridge where there is a car park. Stop to admire the river or take the footpath to the Kirkaig Falls. From Lochinver, return to Ullapool on the main A837/A835 roads.

Also worth exploring

The **A838** from Laxford Bridge to Lairg is a spectacular inland route that follows a chain of lochs through the heart of the Highlands. The granite mountains, wooded slopes and abandoned crofts give you a sense of the wild grandeur of the Highlands, and what they must have looked like when they were covered in forest. A couple of miles (3km) before Lairg, you can turn north on the **A836** which leads to the Kyle of Tongue, another splendid route that passes through great tracts of conifers planted for timber cutting (note the difference!) and drops suddenly into barren, overgrazed moorland.

At Rhiconich, on the main road south from Durness, the B801 leads to the busy fishing port of **Kinlochbervie** about 5 miles (8km) away, and beyond there is marvellous coastal scenery and beaches on the minor road to Sheigra.

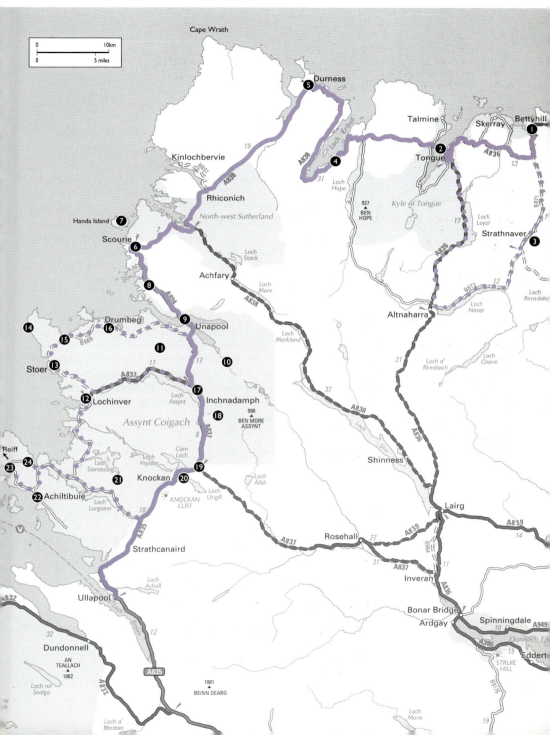

The Celtic Fringe

Ratings

Mountains	●●●●●
Outdoor activities	●●●●●
Scenery	●●●●●
Walking	●●●●●
Wildlife	●●●●●
Coastal scenery	●●●●○
Beaches	●●●○○
Gardens	●●○○○

The peninsular region of Wester Ross is often called the Celtic Fringe. Families here can trace their roots back to their early Celtic and Viking ancestors, and over the years there have been few 'incomers'. In many of the isolated coastal villages, religious fundamentalism and Sabbatarianism still runs deep. Often bypassed by visitors speeding along to Ullapool and Inverness, this area contains some of the most unspoiled and least visited corners of the mainland. With the dramatic mountains and awesome landscapes of the Torridons, these Highlands are one of the great wilderness destinations in Europe. The national nature reserve at Beinn Eighe has remnants of the old Caledonian pine forest, while further inland are the natural wonders of Corrieshalloch Gorge and the Falls of Measach. Along the coast are broad, sandy beaches, often deserted, and Inverewe Gardens, arguably the finest in the country. And, for those who dare, there is the dramatic drive over the Bealach na Bà pass.

APPLECROSS

There are no apple orchards on Applecross, but it is nonetheless a leafy and idyllic spot on a peninsula that is otherwise fairly bleak. The sweet little village consists of a few quaint cottages backed against the hillside facing the bay. Some do B&B, and there's an inviting bar and hotel where you can hire bicycles or just sit and watch the shorebirds on the beach. The Irish monk Maelrubha founded a monastery here in 673, making Applecross one of the earliest centres of Christianity in Scotland. Only a few fragments of crosses have survived from that era, but the atmosphere of peace and tranquillity remains.

GAIRLOCH

Excellent sandy beaches, some of the best in western Scotland, make the fishing and farming community of Gairloch a popular tourist

ⓘ Gairloch Tourist Information Centre
Achtercairn; tel: 01445 712 071; e-mail: info@visitscotland.com. Open May–Sep.

ⓘ Gairloch Heritage Museum £ *Achtercairn, tel: 01445 712 287; www.gairlochheritagemuseum. org.uk. Open late Mar–Sep Mon–Sat 1000–1700; Oct Mon–Fri 1000–1330.*

centre. Two of the best are at Big Sand, 3 miles (5km) north of town, and Redpoint to the southwest. The harbour is a base for landing catches of prawns, lobsters and crabs. The history of the crofting community is well told at the **Gairloch Heritage Museum**; its reconstructed croft-house is cleverly done and worth a visit.

North of Gairloch the coastal road peters out at the Rubha Reidh headland, where there are cliffs and deserted beaches and fine views over the Minch to the Outer Hebrides.

LOCHCARRON

Strung prettily along the shores of Loch Carron, the town has several guesthouses, hotels and shops and is a popular base for hill walkers and climbers exploring the southern mountains of Wester Ross. From here you can drive up the glaciated valley of Glen Carron along its corridor of magnificent Munros. Between Achintee and Attadale, there is a car park with a plaque explaining various features of the Lochcarron landscape. South of town on the shores of the loch are the 15th-century ruins of **Strome Castle**, which was blown up in 1602 during clan warfare between the Macdonalds and the Mackenzies.

LOCH MAREE

Set between the backdrops of Beinn Eighe and Ben Slioch and studded with pine-covered islands, this 12-mile (19-km) long loch is one of the most beautiful in Scotland. It is also a place of legend. In the 7th century, St Maelrubha set up his hermit cell on Isle Maree, a site sacred to the Druids, and it is one of his reputed burial sites. It became a place of pilgrimage and the loch, formerly called Loch Ewe, was renamed Maree (a corruption of the saint's name). The island is also the legendary burial place of a Viking Romeo and Juliet who died tragically in the 9th century. Queen Victoria made a famous visit here in 1877.

POOLEWE

Below
Loch Torridon

The River Ewe runs between Loch Maree and its sea loch, Loch Ewe, and to many minds this pretty, laid-back village set along its banks is a happy alternative base to touristy Gairloch down the road. It is also home to the outstanding **Inverewe Gardens**, among the finest in Europe. The gardens were planted by Osgood Mackenzie on barren

Inverewe Gardens (National Trust for Scotland) *££ Poolewe, on the A832; tel: 01445 781 200; www.nts.org.uk. Open daily Apr–Oct 0930–2000; Nov–Mar 0930–1500.*

ground in 1862 and have grown to encompass 60 acres (24ha) of woodland and flowering plants that cover the peninsula. Although on the same latitude as Siberia, the warm currents of the North Atlantic Drift have created an oasis for exotic tropical species. The views over the loch from among the pines are fabulous.

TORRIDON

Torridon Countryside Centre (National Trust for Scotland) *£ Off the A896; tel: 01445 791 368; www.nts.org.uk. Open Easter–Sep daily 1000–1700.*

This small village has a stunning situation on the shores of Loch Torridon at the base of lofty Liathach. The National Trust for Scotland's **Countryside Centre**, off the main A896, has information about the Torridon mountains and its wildlife, and there is a small deer museum and deer park, with ranger-led walks in season. The narrow piece of land jutting into the loch by the jetty is **Am Ploc**, which means 'the lump'; there was once an open-air church here with a pulpit rock. The minor road along the north side of the loch through Inveralligin and Diabaig is also worth exploring.

Accommodation and food

Loch Maree Hotel ££ *Loch Maree; tel: 01445 760 288; fax: 01445 760 241; e-mail: info@lochmareehotel.co.uk.* Five years after it opened in 1872, this lovely lochside hotel played host to its most famous guest, Queen Victoria. There are beautiful views of the islands from the dining room, which features such local fare as venison, grouse and fresh seafood. Fishing from boat or bank available. Self-catering accommodation also available. *Open Mar–Nov.*

Pool House Hotel £££ *Poolewe; tel: 01445 781 272; fax: 01445 781 403; e-mail: enquiries@poolhousehotel.com; www.poolhousehotel.com.* A truly splendid, small family-run hotel right on the water's edge; you can watch seals and sea birds in the loch over breakfast or from the comfortable residents' lounge (a great spot from which to watch the sunset). It was formerly the home of Osgood Mackenzie, who founded Inverewe Gardens, just up the road. The well-appointed bedroom suites have every amenity and are designed to evoke the age of the great steam liners of the early 20th century. The highly acclaimed North by Northwest dining room serves superb Highlands cuisine amidst views of stunning sunsets, birds and sea life, while the Rowallan Room features billiards and a large selection of single malt whiskies.

Below
The Pool House Hotel enjoys fine views over Loch Broom

Suggested tour

The Munros

A Munro is a mountain over 3000ft (914.5m). The name comes from Sir Hugh Munro who, in 1891, was the first to survey Scotland's peaks and published a list of 277 surpassing that height. The number sometimes varies as new surveys add or eliminate particular peaks, but the official figure remains the same. Munro-bagging is a favourite sport among Scottish climbers.

Total distance: The main route is 140 miles (225km). The Applecross detour adds another 37 miles (59.5km).

Time: The main route will take between 3 and 3.5 hours. Allow 2 hours to drive the 37-mile (59.5-km) detour route on the minor roads over Bealach na Bà and around the Applecross peninsula. Those with little time should concentrate on seeing Inverewe Gardens, Loch Maree and the Torridons.

Links: Many people approach this route from Kyle of Lochalsh, and the road up through Plockton, Stromferry and Strathcarron is a little gem. Alternatively, it can be approached from the A832 and A890 through Achnasheen and Glen Carron. From Braemore Junction on the A835, you are just 11 miles (17.5km) from Ullapool and less than 1 hour from Inverness.

Route: Start the tour at **LOCHCARRON** ❶ and, for the most direct route, take the A896 to Shieldaig. At Kishorn, 6 miles (9.5km) on, North Sea oil platforms were built out in its deep sheltered loch. For an insight into the effects of grazing on the natural landscape of the Highlands, stop by the **Rassal Nature Reserve** ❷, where fenced areas of protected woodland thrive in stark contrast to the overgrazed moors surrounding them. **Shieldaig** ❸ is a picturesque village with a row of whitewashed houses along the shore. Out in the loch, Shieldaig Island, covered with native Scots pine, has a heronry.

Detour: The alternative route to Shieldaig via Applecross, on the western shore of the peninsula, is one of the most exciting drives in Scotland. It follows the **Bealach na Bà** ❹, which means 'Pass of the Cattle' in Gaelic, and it is indeed an old drover's trail for taking cattle to market. The road is truly stunning and rises to a height of 2053ft (626m), punctuated by hair-raising hairpin bends. It is not suitable for caravans or learner drivers, and is closed if there is snow in winter. At the top there is a viewpoint with spectacular views across to the Isle of Skye. If the day is clear it will be one of your most memorable vistas. If the day is foggy and the clouds are low, it will also be memorable – as the scariest drive of your life!

Beyond the pass, the road drops down into the idyllic village of **APPLECROSS** ❺, 12 miles (19km) from the foot of the pass. Continue around the peninsula on the coastal road, which gives splendid views of the islands of Raasay and Rona in the Inner Sound, and Skye beyond. Largely barren of trees, the land here is lonely and abandoned, with a string of tumble-down stone croft-houses and empty villages along the shore. Amazingly, nearly 3000 people still lived here in 1850, until they fell victim to the Clearances. As you drive the winding road along Loch Torridon there are stupendous views of the mountains. After 25 miles (40km), rejoin the main route at Shieldaig.

ℹ Nature trails starting at the **Beinn Eighe Nature Reserve** visitor centre pass through ancient stands of the old Caledonian forest.

From Shieldaig it is 7 miles (11km) to **TORRIDON** **⑥** on the A896. Continue up the broad glacial valley of Glen Torridon, with the lofty 3456-ft (1053-m) Munro, Liathach (the name means 'grey one'), on your left. Like the ridges of the towering Beinn Eighe range to the north, four of its seven peaks are capped with white quartzite, giving the appearance of snow. After 10 miles (16km) you reach **Kinlochewe** **⑦**, at the base of Loch Maree (formerly called Loch Ewe, hence the town's name). The Aultroy Visitor Centre near the village provides an introduction to the flora and fauna of the **Beinn Eighe National Nature Reserve** **⑧**, the first land set aside for preservation in Britain. Turn left on the A832 for 19 miles (30.5km) of magnificent scenery en route to Gairloch. To the right are the romantic shores of **LOCH MAREE** **⑨**. Further on, **GAIRLOCH** **⑩** and **POOLEWE** **⑪**, 6 miles (9.5km) away, are good bases for the area.

It is 38 miles (61km) from Poolewe to Braemore Junction on the A832 through a remote and often sombre landscape. Military buffs should stop by the pier at **Aultbea** **⑫**, 5 miles (8km) along, where there is information on the area's role as a convoy station in World War II. The road curves around the wide Gruinard Bay. **Little Gruinard Beach** **⑬** is a splendid place to stop for a walk across the sands; the picturesque island offshore was contaminated with anthrax during military experiments in 1942. A few miles on, as you round a hill above Loch Broom, the almost surreal dome of Beinn Ghobhlach looms across the water.

Scotland, like Ireland, suffered a potato famine in the 1840s, and the stretch from Dundonnell to Braemore Junction is one of the so-called 'Destitution Roads' built to provide employment. After passing the Dundonnell Timber, keep an eye out for a crumbling ruin with the chimney hearth still standing, set back from the road in a bare field on the right-hand side. It has a grim story: the crofter went mad (possibly from living in this lonely spot), killed his wife and chopped her into tiny pieces.

The landscape here is devastated, a result not only of the Clearances but from clearing the land for iron extraction. Reforested stands of Scandinavian pine are an odd contrast to the natural scenery just a few miles back. Just before the junction, stop at the **Strathmore-Loch Broom viewpoint** **⑭** to survey the 'Valley of the Broom' where three rivers and their valleys meet,

Below
Glen Torridon

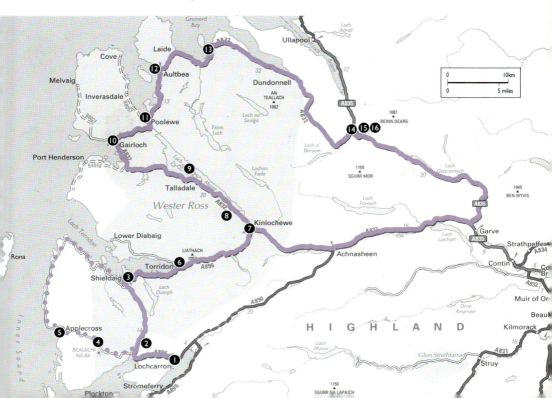

Plockton is the second-to-last stop on the **Kyle Line** from Inverness, and day-trippers may find it more rewarding than the Kyle itself.

Corrieshalloch Gorge £ (National Trust for Scotland) *On the A835. Open all year.*

Stop in at the **West Highland Dairy** at Achmore (between Plockton and Loch Carron) for a variety of speciality cheeses made from cow's, sheep's and goat's milk, as well as ice cream and yoghurt. *Tel: 01599 577 203; www.westhighlanddairy.co.uk. Open Mar–Oct 1000–1700. Closed Sun & Tue.*

particularly colourful in autumn. To the left off the A835 is the mile- (1.6km-) long **Corrieshalloch Gorge** ⓯, sculpted by Ice Age glaciers, with the **Falls of Measach** ⓰ plunging 150ft (46m). You can see them from an observation platform or from a knee-knocking suspension bridge across the gorge.

To complete the circuit back to Kinlochewe, turn right on the A835 for 19 miles (30.5km) to Gorstan and the junction for the A832 (signposted Gairloch).

Also worth exploring

The B8057 north from Poolewe is a scenic 8-mile (13-km) road along Loch Ewe that ends at **Cove**, where there is a deep, sheltered cave once used by the 'Wee Frees' to hold church services. You can glimpse the continuing influence of this fundamentalist Scottish sect in the small communities you pass, such as Inverasdale, where you can see signs regarding the observance of the Lord's Day.

If you're driving up from Kyle of Lochalsh, the picturesque village of **Plockton** is a favourite stop, though it has let tourism go to its head. The BBC series *Hamish MacBeth* was filmed here. **Attadale Gardens**, on the south shores of Loch Carron, has lush gardens and woodland dating from 1890.

The Isle of Skye

Ratings

Mountains	●●●●●
Outdoor activities	●●●●●
Scenery	●●●●●
Walking	●●●●●
Beaches	●●●○○
Castles	●●●○○
Children	●●●○○
Museums	●●●○○

Its very name makes the Isle of Skye one of the most romantic destinations in Scotland. It is derived from the Gaelic for 'Winged Island', a reference to the shape of its northern promontories. Skye's distinctive mountains, the Cuillens, are a mecca for climbers, while in the north are the bizarre upthrusts of the Quirang. The coastal views, across the islands of the Inner Sound and out to the Hebrides, are stunning. Sunsets are truly spectacular here. Skye is called the Isle of Mist, and even on a sunny day the distant peaks and crumbling castles may appear in soft-focus as if seen through a veil. The island is a standard-bearer of the Gaelic revival, with language and music courses at Sabhal Mor Ostaig, the Gaelic college, enjoying huge popularity. You should stay a minimum of two nights if you can, and even then you will be pressed to see all of the island. But it doesn't matter; it's very likely you'll be back.

THE CUILLIN HILLS

The word 'hills' doesn't do justice to these magnificent mountains, especially as 20 of them are Munros. The name (pronounced 'Cool-ins') derives from the Celtic hero Cú Chulainn. The dark gabbro peaks of the Black Cuillins form an arc around Loch Coruisk in the southwest; the highest peak is Sgurr Alasdair, at 3310ft (1009m). They are a mecca for serious climbers. Across Glen Sligachan are the rounded domes of the Red Cuillins, whose pink granite surface does indeed glow red in the sunset.

DUNTULM CASTLE

This castle's fine situation on a coastal precipice was its strength in the 16th century but is its nemesis today as it sadly tumbles into the sea. It is, however, an atmospheric spot, with views across the Minch to the isle of Harris. It was the stronghold of the Macdonalds of Sleat,

who abandoned the castle after a nurse accidentally dropped the chief's baby son into the sea while holding him out of a window to see the boats.

DUNVEGAN CASTLE

Dunvegan Castle
££ *On the A850;*
tel: 01470 521 206;
www.dunvegancastle.com.
Open Mar–Oct daily
1000–1730; Nov–Feb
1100–1600.

The ancestral seat of the MacLeods has been occupied for more than seven centuries, making it the oldest inhabited castle in the north of Scotland. Among Dunvegan's treasures are the Fairy Flag, said to have been given to the 4th clan chief by his fairy wife; the ancient scrap of silk reputedly holds the power to save the clan from destruction three times and has been used twice. Also on show is the drinking horn of Rory Mor; it holds nearly two bottles of claret, which must be drunk in one go by the MacLeod heir as an initiation rite.

ELGOL

Many claim that the finest view of the Cuillins is seen from Elgol, and indeed the vista inspired some of J M W Turner's landscapes. Out to sea are more wonderful views of the small islands of Rum, Eigg and Canna. Elgol is set on the shores of Loch Scavaig, and boat trips are available across to Loch Coruisk.

KILMUIR

Skye Museum of
Island Life £
On the A855; tel: 01470
552 206;
www.skyemuseum.co.uk.
Open Easter–Oct Mon–Sat
0930–1700.

The **Skye Museum of Island Life** displays the way of life on the island a century ago and is housed in a group of traditional thatched 'black houses', few of which survive. Nearby in the churchyard is the grave of **Flora MacDonald**, Skye's most famous hero. She is revered throughout Scotland for helping Bonnie Prince Charlie to escape after Culloden by disguising him as her maidservant. The towering Celtic cross is a replacement for the original, pieces of which were carried off by tourists until there was nothing left. The monument bears an inscription by Dr Johnson, who visited her in 1773.

KYLE OF LOCHALSH

Kyle of Lochalsh
Tourist Information
Centre *Car park; tel: 0845*
22 55 121; e-mail:
info@visitscotland.com.
Open Apr–Oct.

This mainland town is the gateway to Skye and the terminus for the railway line from Inverness. Since the opening of the Skye Bridge in 1995, which replaced the ferry across the Kyle, few people have reason to hang about here. The bridge, with a main span of 780ft (238m), is

The **Black Cuillins** should only be ascended by skilled climbers who are experienced and well equipped; they have claimed many lives and are not for amateurs. The Red Cuillins are gentler, with hidden valleys and corries, but both ranges are prone to sudden mists that can be deadly. Always seek local advice before exploring either range.

Boat cruises run between Easter and October from the jetty below the castle to a seal colony in **Loch Dunvegan** where you can see them at close quarters.

Boat trips on the *Bella Jane* to **Loch Coruisk** run between April and October. Bookings, which are essential, are taken 1930–2200 the night before or 0730–1000 on day of departure. *Tel: 0800 731 3089; www.bellajane.co.uk*

Lochalsh Woodland Gardens (National Trust for Scotland) £ *Kyle of Lochalsh; tel: 01599 566 325; www.nts.org.uk. Open daily 0900–sunset.*

Right
Luib, on the eastern side of Skye

the longest cantilever bridge in Europe. Nearby, on the A87, is the National Trust's **Balmacara Estate** and **Lochalsh Woodland Gardens**, with pleasant lochside walks.

KYLEAKIN

When the Skye Bridge opened, the car ferry that had plied its way back and forth across the Kyle for so many years ceased to operate, depriving visitors of this more romantic approach and leaving Kyleakin something of a backwater below the bridge. It's worth a stop, however, to see the proud ruins of **Castle Moil** still standing sentry on its knoll beside the abandoned ferry port. It served as a lookout post and stronghold against Viking raiders and was held by the Mackinnons of Strath.

PORTREE

ⓘ Portree Tourist Information Centre
Bayfield Road; tel: 0845 22 55 121; e-mail: info@visitscotland.com. Open all year.

ⓗ Aros ££ *Viewfield Road, on the A850; tel: 01478 613 649; www.aros.co.uk. Open daily 1000–1700.*

Skye's capital is a pretty little town which somehow manages to accommodate all the tourists who pass through here and make it their touring base. Its most beautiful part is the harbour, nestled in a sheltered bay, where you can watch Skye's tremendous sunsets. To the south of town is **Aros**, Skye's heritage centre. It has an excellent exhibition and an audiovisual show that traces the history of the people of the island and nest-cams with live pictures of sea eagles, owls and other birds. It also stages evenings of traditional music and cultural events.

THE QUIRANG

The Quirang is one of Scotland's most bizarre natural features, a twisted, tortured escarpment formed by a massive landslip. The stone stacks and pinnacles have been given names such as The Needle, The Table and The Prison. You can hike up through a narrow gorge to a large grassy amphitheatre, where cattle were once driven to protect them from raiders. The views are fabulous. There are two small lay-bys at the top, though many prefer to park at the cemetery and hike in across the moor.

Over the Sea to Skye

Flora MacDonald, born in 1722, became a Scottish hero when she helped Bonnie Prince Charlie escape after Culloden. She disguised him as her maidservant, Betty Burke, and brought him from North Uist, in the words of a popular song, 'over the sea to Skye', keeping him safe until his departure from Portree. Her bravery won her a brief spell in prison. In 1751 she married Captain Allan Macdonald of Kingsburgh and moved to Flodigarry, where six of her seven children were born. The family later moved to North Carolina, but she returned to spend the last ten years of her life on Skye, where she died at the age of 68.

SLIGACHAN

The hard-to-pronounce name of this hamlet – some say 'Slig-a-chan' (accent on the first syllable and 'ch' as in 'loch'), most give up and corrupt it to 'Slee-gan' – means 'place of the shells'. This reflects its position on the sea loch of the same name. From here there are beautiful views of the Cuillins, black and red, especially from the old bridge over the river near the Sligachan Hotel. A path through Glen Sligachan leads to scenic Loch Coruisk.

Above
The Quirang

Accommodation and food

You can also reach Skye on a ferry from Mallaig, north of Fort William. The trip takes 30 minutes. In summer there is also a short crossing from Glenelg to Kylerhea. There is also a service to the Western Isles from Uig. Contact Caledonian MacBrayne (see page 18).

Sligachan Hotel ££ *tel: 01478 650 204; fax: 01478 650 207; e-mail: reservations@sligachan.co.uk; www.sligachan.co.uk.* At the head of a sea loch, surrounded by the stunning scenery of the Cuillins, this hotel is a wonderful base at the centre of the island. It is popular with climbers and sportspeople, who lend an easy-going, energetic atmosphere to the characterful building and friendly service. Rooms are comfortable and cosy. There is fine dining in the Cairidh Seafood Restaurant, and excellent pub meals in the large, bustling Seumas's Bar, with big-screen TV, snooker and table tennis. The special winter rates are a bargain.

Flodigarry Country House Hotel ££–£££ *Flodigarry; tel: 01470 552 203; fax: 01470 552 301; e-mail: info@flodigarry.co.uk; www.flodigarry.co.uk.* Flora MacDonald's cottage lies in the grounds of this beautiful country-house hotel, and has been renovated into seven period-style bedrooms (named after her seven children). The hotel, built in 1895 as a private house, is set amid gardens and woodland with panoramic views across the sea. Charming bedrooms, lovely conservatory and public rooms. Table d'hôte menu of fresh Scottish fare in the Water-Horse Restaurant (open to non-residents). Lively bar, popular with the locals, serves home-made dishes.

Suggested tour

Total distance: 69 miles (11km) for the main route around the Trotternish peninsula, 98 miles (157.5km) to take the detour route to Dunvegan Castle.

Time: Allow half a day for the main route and, for those with more time, a full day for the longer detour route.

Links: The main road to Skye is the A87 through Glen Shiel to Kyle of Lochalsh, a beautiful scenic drive in itself. It will take between 60 and 90 minutes to reach the Kyle from Fort William or Inverness.

Route: The main route begins at centrally located **SLIGACHAN ❶** and takes in the sights of the Trotternish peninsula. Take the A87 to **PORTREE ❷**, leaving town on the A855 towards Staffin. About 5 miles (8km) out of town there is a little waterfall and small parking area on the left. This is a good place to pull off for a view of the **Old Man of Storr ❸**, a rock pinnacle that juts forth from the 2360-ft (719-m) Storr plateau. From far below it's hard to believe it is 160-ft (49-m) tall. Continue north for about 10 miles (16km), enjoying the gorgeous views over the Sound of Raasay, with the islands of Raasay and Rona, to the mainland beyond. Stop off at **Kilt Rock ❹** to see the basalt columns shaped like pleats. From the viewing platform you may also spot dolphins or minke whales out in the sound. Just up the road, the

Left
Kilt Rock

ⓘ Dunvegan Tourist Information Centre
2 Lochside; tel: 0845 22 55 121; e-mail: info@visitscotland.com. Open all year.

🍴 Drink in the Cuillins – literally! Skye's local beers are named after its mountains – Red Cuillin is a light ale, Black Cuillin a dark ale. And there is another handsome brew called The Young Pretender.

Staffin Museum ❺ has a collection of fossils and Stone Age tools found in the area, dating from 6500 BC, and a dinosaur bone and footprint.

A mile (1.6km) beyond Staffin is the left-hand side road to the **QUIRANG** ❻. It is 2 miles (3km) in to the lay-by at the top. This road cuts across the peninsula to Uig through what must be some of the bleakest land in Scotland. It is, however, golden eagle country and even if you're not lucky enough to spot one, you can imagine them swooping down on their prey.

Return to the main road and continue 3 miles (5km) north to Flodigarry, where Flora Macdonald lived during her early married life. Her cottage is now part of a country-house hotel. At the northwest tip of the peninsula is **DUNTULM CASTLE** ❼ and, a couple of miles (3km) south, the museum and monument at **KILMUIR** ❽. On the shores of a lovely bay, **Uig** ❾ (pronounced 'yoo-ig') is a picturesque harbour town, the ferry port for boats to Harris and North Uist in the Outer Hebrides. From here it is 15 miles (24km) back to Portree on the A87.

Detour: To visit **DUNVEGAN CASTLE** ❿ on the west coast, turn right after about 9.5 miles (15km) on the B8036 and right again on the A850. From here it's under 20 miles (32km) to the castle, with views of the Western Isles off to the right. Return to Sligachan on the A863. After about 8 miles (13km), as you approach Struan and Bracadale, look out on your left for **Dun Beag** ⓫, a well-preserved Pictish *broch* with thick walls and several rooms intact.

Also worth exploring

The **Talisker Distillery** at Carbost, near Sligachan, produces Skye's fine peaty malt whisky. **Sleat** (pronounced 'Slate'), the island's southernmost peninsula, has ruined castles, the Clan Donald Centre and the Gaelic college. On the drive in on the A87, about 10 miles (16km) from Kyle of Lochalsh, is **Eilean Donan Castle**, which has been called 'the most photographed castle in Scotland'.

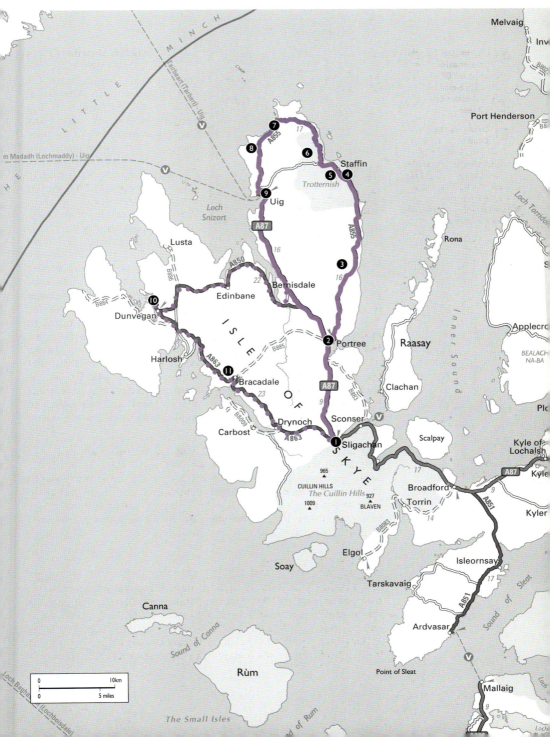

Language

Gaelic is a Celtic language originally brought by settlers from Ireland, although by the 13th century Scottish and Irish Gaelic had become two separate dialects. It was once the language of the Scottish king and court, as well as the majority of the people. After the break-up of the clan system, the use of Gaelic died out, except in the far north and west Highlands and the Western Isles, where it remained the first language. Today it is spoken by more than 69,000 people, and a Gaelic revival is under way, with new initiatives in primary schools and on television, as well as Gaelic organisations such as Comunn na Gidhlig and the Gaelic college, Sabhal Mor Ostaig, on Skye. You will notice bilingual signs for place names in the northwestern Highlands and Islands. And you will probably become tongue-tied when trying to pronounce them. Spoken Gaelic bears little relation to the written word. For example, *bh* and *mh* are pronounced like the English *v*, *sh* and *th* like the English *h*, *ch* as in loch. You will come across Gaelic-based place names time and again, containing words such as *ben* (beinn), a high hill; *glen*, a valley; *strath*, a river valley or low grassland; and *kyle*, an inlet or strait between the coast and an offshore island.

The third language you will hear in Scotland is Scots, which is more than simply an accented version of contemporary English. It is the remnant of a distinct Lowland tongue akin to medieval English. In addition to broad Scots vowels such as *'bool'* (bowl) and *'tak'* (take), you may hear descriptive new words such as *dreich* (dull) and *daundering* (walking slowly).

Index

Acknowledgements

Project management: Cambridge Publishing Management Limited
Project editor: Karen Beaulah
Series design: Fox Design
Cover design: Liz Lyons Design
Layout and map work: Concept 5D/Hilary Austin, Pixel Cartography/Cambridge Publishing Management Limited
Repro and image setting: Z2 Repro/PDQ Digital Media Solutions Ltd/Cambridge Publishing Management Limited.

Thomas Cook wishes to thank the photographers, picture libraries and other organisations for the loan of the photographs reproduced in this book, to whom the copyright belongs:

Donna Dailey (pages 23, 34, 66, 74, 76, 92, 94, 95, 98B, 100, 103, 104A, 106, 108, 109, 110, 113, 114, 116, 118, 119A, 119B, 121, 122, 134A, 134B, 140, 141, 146, 148, 150A, 152, 160, 164A, 166, 169, 170, 172, 174, 176, 177, 179, 182, 184, 186, 188, 191, 192, 202A, 205, 206, 207, 208, 210, 212, 214, 218, 219, 220, 222, 225, 227, 232, 234, 236, 238, 239, 241, 242, 244A, 254A, 254B, 256, 257, 258, 264, 268, 277, 278 and 280); **John Heseltine** (pages 5, 30, 32, 63, 71, 98A, 104B, 120, 124A, 124B, 126, 127, 128, 130, 131, 136, 138, 139, 142, 150B, 154A, 154B, 156, 159, 161, 162, 164B, 202B, 230, 244B, 246, 247, 248, 252, 266, 270, 272 and 275); **Neil Setchfield** (pages 3, 8, 20, 37, 38, 39, 41, 44, 46, 49, 52, 56, 82, 84, 85, 86, 88, 90, 193, 250 and 282); **The Still Moving Picture Co** (pages 64 and 195); **Ethel Davies** (pages 12, 68 and 72); **Historic Scotland** (page 181); **The National Trust for Scotland** (pages 197 and 198); **The Greywalls Hotel** (page 9); **Duff House** (page 180); **Pictures Colour Library** (pages 6 and 61); **World Pictures/Photoshot** (pages 16, 59, 201, 217 and 228); **Edinburgh International Festival/Paul Klonik** (page 51); **Skyscan** (page 64).